D0065345

AFTER THE FALL

AFTER THE FALL

SAVING CAPITALISM

FROM WALL STREET— AND WASHINGTON

NICOLE GELINAS

Encounter Books  New York · London

First American edition published in 2009 by Encounter Books,
an activity of Encounter for Culture and Education, Inc.,
a nonprofit, tax exempt corporation.
Encounter Books website address: www.encounterbooks.com

Manufactured in the United States and printed on
acid-free paper. The paper used in this publication meets
the minimum requirements of ANSI/NISO Z39.48-1992
(R 1997) (*Permanence of Paper*).

FIRST AMERICAN EDITION

LIBRARY OF CONGRESS CATALOGING-IN-PUBLICATION DATA

Gelinas, Nicole, 1975-
After the fall: saving capitalism from Wall Street—
and Washington/by Nicole Gelinas.
p. cm.
Includes bibliographical references and index.
ISBN-13: 978-1-59403-261-5 (hardover: alk. paper)
ISBN-10: 1-59403-261-0 (hardcover: alk. paper) 1. Free enterprise—
United States. 2. Capitalism—United States. 3. Financial crises—
United States—History. I. Title.
HB95.G444 2009
330.973—dc22
2009032187

10 9 8 7 6 5 4 3 2

For my husband

CONTENTS

PREFACE

The only reasons I can think of why firms might underinvest to control risk are due to failures in government: Firms may believe that government will not let them fail under a Too Big to Fail Policy ... or that the bankruptcy code may not impose sufficient penalties for failing.
— Wendy Gramm, former Commodity Futures Trading Commission chairman, September 1993[1]

The authority to decide how to resolve a failing [financial] firm under the special resolution regime should ... be vested in Treasury. ... The regime ... should provide for the ability to stabilize a failing institution ... by providing loans to the firm, purchasing assets from the firm, guaranteeing the liabilities of the firm, or making equity investments in the firm.
— United States Department of the Treasury, June 2009[2]

THE CREDIT CRISIS AND THE RESULTING RECESSION are the work of an invisible hand—not the invisible hand of free markets but of an overwhelming government interference in those markets. Over a quarter of a century, Washington gave the world of finance a terrible privilege: freedom from the fear of failure.

Until the early 1980s, banks, securities firms, and insurers, like all other companies, operated under market discipline. Federal laws prescribed a consistent, predictable way in which financial firms could fail, with investors, including lenders, taking their warranted losses.

Starting in the early eighties, though, the financial industry began to escape these orderly mechanisms. Many banks and securities firms eventually became "too big to fail." They thus gained an invaluable advantage as they competed with other companies and industries for resources: their lenders knew that they did not have to worry about losing their investments. As a result, these market participants no longer transmitted vital signals about the prospects for success or failure.

Financial firms, implicitly subsidized by the government, replaced measured risk-taking with recklessness. Bankers and traders, insulated from the full market consequences of their decisions, created instruments that circumvented reasonable government limits on borrowing and exposure. These innovations further sidestepped requirements for disclosure of information.

Under four successive presidents, from Ronald Reagan to George W. Bush, Washington's response to concerns that regulation had become inadequate to deal with modern finance was to say that the markets could regulate themselves better than the government could.

Paradoxically, though, even as Washington placed such great reliance on self-regulating markets, government policies short-circuited the ability of the markets to do their work. Washington's too-big-to-fail policy increasingly hampered the markets from forcing financial companies to rein in excess. The complex instruments they created gradually heightened the risk to the economy posed by the failure of even a small financial firm.

Government subsidy of financial failure kept the free market from doing its work in other ways, too. Financial firms lent profligately to American consumers. In their unique ability to offer executives and employees multimillion-dollar bonuses, financial companies made it difficult for companies in other industries, like engineering and technology, to compete for talent.

Starting in 2007, the free market had had enough. Fleeing investors and plummeting asset prices exposed the modern financial industry's untenable risks. By 2008, Washington had no choice but to step in and take over virtually all activity within the industry in an effort to keep the economy from spiraling into depression.

Without changes in how Washington approaches Wall Street, the financial industry will continue to operate without the benefit of clear market signals. The inevitable result would be even more economic distortion, because finance is responsible for one of the most important roles in the economy: determining which people and which businesses should have access to investment capital and on what terms.

Robust financial markets do not imperil capitalism but support it. To ensure that financial markets can do their job, lawmakers and regulators must re-create an orderly, consistent way for lenders to failed financial institutions to take losses, reintroducing market discipline. So that the economy can better withstand inevitable financial-company failures, lawmakers and regulators must reasonably regulate financial markets and instruments, using well-tested principles that, as the following pages show, have worked in the past and would work again.

INTRODUCTION

The verdict of the jury in the Insull case came as a surprise to most people. This may be because they had not heard the testimony at the trial, as the jury had.... [Insull] had built up an enormous structure of interlocking securities, which fell with a great crash and ruined thousands of investors. The question was, however, whether in the process anything criminal had been done, and the jury decided that there had not been.

—editorial, *New York Times*, November 26, 1934

This was about the real costs for normal people who suffered because of the machinations in the executive suites at Enron.... Many long-standing employees . . . lost huge chunks of their retirement funds and still face an uncertain old age. We hope the jury's verdict deters other corporate kingpins from breaking the rules.

—editorial, *New York Times*, May 26, 2006

O N JUNE 14, 1935, THE DISGRACED TITAN SAMUEL Insull left court a free but broken man. The former utility executive had won acquittal at three separate fraud trials stemming from the collapse of his Chicago-based electricity giant in 1932, a collapse precipitated by complex, unregulated financial engineering. "He is without money and faces life anew, perhaps to take a job," the *New York Times* observed.[1] He would die three years later in near-poverty in a foreign city.

Insull's acquittals, seen in one light, were bitter failures for the government and the American public. President Franklin Roosevelt himself had identified Insull as a public face of the Great Depression even before taking office, calling him a "reckless promoter" whose "hand is against every man's"[2] in September 1932. Yet the government had compiled and presented thousands of pages of evidence and hours of witness testimony to no avail.

Seventy-one years later, in another case of a fallen energy company, Enron, the government would fare better. On May 25, 2006, two of the firm's former executives also left court broken men—not free to skulk away in ignominy, as Insull had been, but convicted of twenty-five counts of fraud and other crimes. Former Enron CEO Kenneth Lay, the marquee defendant, died weeks later. Jeffrey Skilling, also a former CEO, was soon sentenced to more than twenty-four years. It seemed that the government had succeeded in dispatching the two men who represented another era of corporate misdeeds and, just as important, protected the public by preventing similar wrongdoing in the future. "The jury has spoken and they have sent an unmistakable message to boardrooms across the country that . . . no matter how rich and powerful you are, you have to play by the rules," a prosecutor said.[3]

Yet the two verdicts, separated by nearly three-quarters of a century, paint a misleading picture of government effectiveness in protecting the broader economy from the financial system. The government's success in prosecuting the Enron defendants obscured a larger threat to the economy that the criminal-justice system could not address, while the government's failure in the Insull case was insignificant compared with its achievements in crafting a regulatory framework for the markets that would serve the nation enormously well.

Yes, prosecutors had lost their case against Insull. But by the time the juries had served up their acquittals, Washington had already correctly diagnosed, and the public understood, the larger problem surrounding the company's collapse—not a sudden outbreak of greed and immorality, but the systemic failure of financial capitalism to regulate itself. The judge in the third Insull trial, John C. Knox, put it best: "We must consider the peculiar situation and conditions of 1931–32 when these transactions took place. Many persons who thought they were exercising good judgment then later found they were wrong."[4]

The searing experience of the late 1920s and the Depression that followed showed that the world of finance, if left completely unrestrained, threatens the free market itself. In the twenties, bankers, corporate executives like Insull, and investors expected only more good times—and acted accordingly. They borrowed against every last dollar of expected future profit, and then some, leaving themselves no leeway if those future profits faltered even slightly. In wringing ever more from tomorrow's profits for today, they trusted themselves to design financial structures many magnitudes more complex than straightforward stocks and bonds.

Most potently, banks and investment firms lent freely for the purpose of making bets on stock securities. The lending allowed the fevers of short-term speculation to affect credit creation—that is, the long-term business of borrowing and lending. Borrowing and lending are vital to any healthy economy because some companies always need to borrow, at least modestly, in order to grow. Infusing credit creation with excessive speculation, then, made the entire economy vulnerable to a financial crisis. But bankers, largely free of regulations, didn't understand the risks that they were taking. "Young men thought they could do anything," Albert Gordon, an executive who had helped rescue one Wall Street firm, Kidder Peabody, from the depths of the Great Depression, later said.[5]

When something finally went wrong, starting in 1929, it wasn't only the rarefied financial world that suffered. The bankers had used the public's savings—the hard-earned dollars of regular Americans—as fuel for their financial experiments. People stopped trusting their neighborhood banks, which fell victim to the crisis. Without customer deposits to lend out, surviving banks couldn't make new loans or recoup their losses on the old ones. The infrastructure of money and credit disintegrated.

It took a decade for the economy to recover from the shock that American finance had administered to it. During the 1930s, FDR and his policy wonks inevitably committed policy errors that contributed to the delay. But they also designed regulations to protect financiers from themselves and, more important, to protect the economy from financiers' future mistakes. By 1935, when Insull walked free, the Roosevelt administration had spent two and a half years building the consistent rules that free financial markets need to function effectively and support a free economy.

Because failing banks had helped cripple the economy, policymakers created a mechanism for bad banks to fail in an orderly fashion without imperiling the rest of the economy. Guarantees of small banking deposits through the new Federal Deposit Insurance Corporation (FDIC) assured ordinary citizens that they wouldn't lose their savings when banks did fail. These regulations made it less likely that masses of people would once again suck the economy's lifeblood—money and credit—out of the banks. By saving small depositors and thus the overall system from panic, regulators ensured that bad banks could continue to go out of business, allowing the market to help discipline their risk-taking.

Regulators also forced financial institutions to decide whether they wanted to be in the securities business or the banking business, and thereby separated the relatively sober world of long-term bank lending and borrowing from the often-frenzied world of underwriting and trading stocks and bonds. This separation gave banks some insulation—but not immunity—from the short-term shocks, whether from exuberant optimism or abject pessimism, of future economic cycles.

Washington wisely did not banish risk-taking in the financial world. FDR understood that financial sophistication had helped drive American economic growth after World War I, attracting the world's money to U.S. shores. Instead, policymakers imposed clear, consistent limits on risk-taking in the securities business, which remained freer than the banking business.

New regulations prohibited securities firms and their customers from borrowing excessively to purchase securities, whose values could swing wildly. These restraints on speculative borrowing reduced the risk that debt supported by securities wouldn't be repaid if the value of the securities plummeted, thus straining the financial system. The government also imposed an obligation of full and fair disclosure on the securities industry, requiring companies that wished to raise money by selling stocks or bonds to the public to explain—soberly, clearly, and regularly—the financial, business, and economic risks that the companies and their investors faced. The public could make investments with its eyes open.

Taken together, these regulatory reforms enabled the financial and business worlds to continue to innovate and take risks, so long as those risks didn't endanger the broader economy and so long as the risk-takers disclosed their activities. The system worked well, more or less, for over half a century, helping propel American capital markets to even greater dominance after World War II. The world's investors knew that their wealth was safest in America, in part because of fair regulations.

Starting in the 1980s, the regulatory infrastructure started to decay. In 1984, the government stepped in to rescue a large commercial bank, Continental Illinois, extending protection not just to the bank's insured depositors but also to all its other lenders, including big corporate depositors whose accounts exceeded FDIC limits as well as global bondholders. The event proved a watershed, and it set a now-familiar precedent: "too big to fail." Big, complicated financial institutions outgrew the government's ability to impose the market's verdict on them by shutting them down, since too much was at stake for the economy if they went under. Uninsured lenders to big banks no longer worried that they would lose their investment; the government would intervene if things spiraled out of control. As a result, financial innovations proceeded without the natural checks and balances of market forces. Banks became adept at turning their insulation from disorderly failure into insulation from market discipline.

Innovations in finance, mostly in the world of credit, blurred the thirties-drawn line between banking and the securities industry. Financial firms learned how to turn long-term debt, such as corporate bonds and mortgages, into tradeable securities. In doing so, they made the vital business of credit creation more vulnerable to short-term gyrations between optimism and pessimism.

The financial world also found ways to avoid the government's borrowing limits on speculation. Because Depression-era regulations restrained them from borrowing unreservedly to speculate on stocks, financiers created financial instruments in the derivatives world that escaped the regulations. Often, such innovations also escaped Depression-era disclosure requirements. The public and the media, and even regulators, had a hard time identifying, understanding, and quantifying the changes. Financiers' experiments with making tradeable securities out of long-term debt—from junk bonds at an investment bank, Drexel Burnham Lambert, to mortgage-backed securities at a hedge fund, Askin Capital Management—caused miniature financial explosions that Washington should have seen as warnings but instead regarded as aberrations. Similar eruptions in unregulated derivatives competed, just as vainly, for attention.

In 1998, a mix of the two—unbridled derivatives creation and speculation on long-term credit—created a near disaster. An obscure hedge fund, Long-Term Capital Management, proved that though not a large bank, it, too, was too complex to fail through the normal bankruptcy process that governs nonbank failures. The fund's opaque endeavors, enabled by unregulated borrowing, nearly brought down the financial world and the economy. Three years later, Enron demonstrated how easy it was to use modern innovations to create credit out of nothing but blind trust and proved how eagerly the nation's biggest financial firms had enabled such spurious credit creation. Enron's collapse showed how quickly it could all fall apart when the trust vanished.

The government treated the failures that the increasingly fragile system served up from time to time as discrete matters best addressed with one-off, extraordinary solutions, from weekend financial rescues to criminal prosecutions. Mainstream thinkers said that financial markets didn't need much regulation. Alan Greenspan, who took the helm of the Federal Reserve in 1987, told lawmakers and the public that financial companies, powered by a rational motive not to lose money, could police themselves and one another, using new financial innovations to decrease risk, not increase it. The financial world operated increasingly freely under a long-running illusion that elegant modern theories and technologies made the creation of nearly all manner of credit—lending to corporations and consumers alike—perfectly safe. Yet with each new innovation, financiers left themselves even less room for error, were the tiniest thing to go wrong—just as they had done in the twenties.

Thanks to the illusion of safety, financiers were able to manufacture vast amounts of debt, and they encouraged Americans to become more dependent on borrowing, whether on credit cards or against the value of their homes. In this way, ordinary Americans, too, became more vulnerable to any eventual sharp decline in the availability of credit.

Bankers had accomplished the opposite of what they, and regulators, had thought they were doing. They hadn't created safety out of danger, but danger out of safety, eventually turning the most sober investment that many people make—the purchase of a home—into a risky bet. The financiers made mortgage lending, for many investors, seem risk-free, meaning that money became available for anyone to get a mortgage for any house, regardless of ability to repay the debt. When more money is available to buy something, the price of that item goes up. Once the risks emerged from behind the veneer of safety and the easy credit tightened, the plunge proved more disorienting than the rise.

The inevitable financial catastrophe reminded us of something that we had forgotten. When financial markets are *too* free, they will eventually destroy themselves and damage everything around them. Starting in 2007, the financial world slipped loose from its carefully constructed illusions. One financial institution after another collapsed seemingly overnight.

By 2008, sober-minded people feared that the government, with all its modern knowledge and powers, would not be able to prevent another Depression. To avoid the severe economic disruptions that cascading failures of financial firms would cause, the government, on behalf of taxpayers, effectively took over all risk in finance. Private investors, having so thoroughly miscalculated the risk that they had freely undertaken, no longer wanted any part. Policymakers from both parties, starting in the Bush administration, felt that they had no choice but to use trillions of taxpayer dollars to protect failed firms and their lenders from their tremendous losses. Much of the financial industry now depended on its ability to hold the economy hostage just to stay afloat.

The financial crisis should not have come as a surprise. It is the natural result of two and a half decades of decisions and nondecisions that made the financial regulatory system irrelevant. Nor are creative solutions necessary to prevent another such catastrophe. The same regulatory philosophy that protected the post-Depression economy and created the conditions for prosperity afterward would have prevented the postmillennial financial meltdown. It can work again, if policymakers apply it to the financial system that exists today.

First, no private company in a free-market economy should be too big or too interconnected to other firms to fail. The government must once again create a credible, consistent way in which failed financial companies can go out of business, with lenders to those companies taking losses as well as shareholders, if warranted, without dragging the economy down with them. Second, the government must once again insulate the core economic functions of long-term borrowing and lending from potential short-term excesses. Third, the government must reimpose clear, well-defined limits on activities such as borrowing for speculation. Last, the government must make sure that markets do not become opaque over time as new financial creations escape existing reporting requirements. Financiers must disclose the scope of their innovations to the public and to investors. Creative financial risk-taking then can flourish within these reasonable limits.

Washington must understand—from the facts at the core of the financial crisis—that consistent, predictable regulation of financial firms and markets is a prerequisite for a free-market economy, not a barrier to it. Consider the price that our economy is now paying for our failure to regulate the markets prudently.

Government's extraordinary interventions have given it great power over the financial industry, eclipsing the private sector in one of the most vital functions of a free economy: deciding which people, companies, and projects deserve investment, and on what terms.

This development is a threat to the market economy. The financiers and investors who decide which businesses, new and old, are worthy of investment must make decisions based on their judgments of the risks and rewards involved. They won't judge effectively if they have an implicit understanding that the government will save them from their bad decisions. They certainly cannot do so if they have an eye toward the political concessions that a government guarantor inevitably demands. Washington cannot solve this problem by extricating itself from its direct role as lender, guarantor, and sometimes part-owner of financial firms as the immediate crisis eases. Financial companies and their own lenders will know that, absent credible regulations to the contrary, the government will once again save the industry in the next crisis. Such distortion of market incentives harms the private sector's free assumption of financial and economic risk, which powered the American economy to its industrial and technological heights and has helped hundreds of millions of people around the world escape poverty.

The government's response to the financial crisis has further damaged free markets by altering the global perception that investors in America can expect fair treatment according to a predictable and consistent rule of law. Washington has used its new leverage over the financial sector to intervene arbitrarily in cases like the Chrysler and General Motors bankruptcies, upsetting precedents for treating creditors to bankrupt firms that date back centuries.

The very real damage is done. But the nation must make sure that it does not turn these episodes, too, into precedents, which show the world that we don't trust markets to work the way that they should. At the height of the financial crisis, American leaders' loss of faith in free markets was so troubling that the former prime minister of the once-Communist state of Estonia felt the need to take to the pages of capitalism's organ, the *Wall Street Journal*, to remind readers that the biggest threat to the economy was the perception that markets had failed. "Actually, it is not markets that have failed, but governments, which did not fulfill their role of . . . creating and guaranteeing market rules," Mart Laar wrote.[6] If the nation fails to understand this truth, it may lose its status as a global nexus of the world's wealth, as investors worry that personal contacts and political power matter more than laws and rules.

Ordinary citizens do not share Washington's new distrust of markets. Throughout the financial crisis, they have consistently defended free enterprise. They have opposed bailout after bailout, even bailouts meant to help their next-door neighbors who couldn't afford their mortgages. Many politicians and executives have misinterpreted public anger as anti-rich and anti-capitalism. But the public has grasped—better than sophisticated financiers—what healthy capitalism requires. Americans enjoy seeing success rewarded with great wealth—as long as they aren't forced to subsidize failure.

Americans don't want their government picking winners or losers in the economy. Just the opposite: the public wants the government to do its job of rationally regulating financial markets so that financial markets can then rationally manage the private distribution of capital, funding good businesses that power the economy. The nation finds itself in its current weakened position largely because of a crisis created by unregulated financial capitalism. It's sad that we could have prevented the crisis, but it's also good news—for we know how to prevent the next one.

CHAPTER I

THE RISK OF FREEDOM

I have no cash or securities to put up and I feel sure that my speculative stocks are going higher in the future. If you do not share my enthusiasm I shall be very pleased to sign a temporary waiver on any dividends, profits, etc., that may accrue on my Radio and Woolworth shares as far ahead as you like—25 years if necessary—to meet your requirements. I feel sure that both of these companies will pay immense dividends in the next quarter of the century.
—investment client to broker, summer 1928[1]

AN ENEMY HATH NOT DONE THIS.
—editorial, *New York Times*, November 2, 1933

I N THE 1920S, MANY COMPANIES FOUND AN EASY WAY to make a decent profit on spare cash: invest it in "brokers' loans," through which financial firms lent people money to buy stocks. An investor could borrow $80, buy stocks worth $100, and, when the stock value soared to $200, sell enough to repay the $80 plus interest and have a tidy profit left over. This practice—called borrowing on margin—is dangerous because stocks can go down as well as up, while borrowers must repay the amount borrowed.

While such danger seems clear today, almost everyone back then missed it. To the few naysayers at a 1926 New York State

Bankers' Association conference, the New York Stock Exchange's public-relations man gave this reassurance: "It is a fair statement that the increasing popularity enjoyed by security collateral loans is due to the growing recognition that no safer investment exists. There is not a single instance of a loss suffered by lenders within the memory of those engaged in the handling of this type of loan."[2] The *Wall Street Journal* dismissed the worry that stocks would fall, editorializing that any stock-market collapse would be limited "by the very volume . . . represented on the New York Stock Exchange and by the normal increase in [stock prices] as a result of the economic progress of the country."[3] The paper further noted that lenders themselves adequately controlled borrowing, often requiring 25 percent cash down payments that turned stock lending into "very safe and sane gambling" (although not all firms were this conservative).[4]

Brokers' loans didn't cause the Depression. But they were a symptom of the casual exuberance that did help cause it. The twenties proved that it isn't so much people's willingness to take crazy risks that imperils economies, but our inability (or refusal) to recognize risk where it exists. The gravest peril comes when everyone becomes willing to bet everything on the idea that the future will be just as purportedly riskless as the present—and exponentially more profitable, too.

In the twenties, ever-rising stock prices were the most potent evidence of an exuberant view of the future and of the financial world's reasoning that the increase in asset values didn't represent a risk. Between 1923 and late 1929, the Dow Jones Industrial Average, the best-known measure of stock values, nearly quadrupled.[5] Wall Street insiders, echoing the *Journal*'s argument, said that the stratospheric rise tracked progress in the nation's real economy. A "major cause of securities speculation . . . consists in the very rapid changes occurring in American industry and trade," said E. H. H. Simmons, the New York Stock Exchange chief, in May 1929.[6]

For a while, such optimism had been healthy, and finance had worked the way it was supposed to. The first time the Dow doubled—from 1923 to 1927—the index's increase measured the

profit growth that came with industrial and technological progress and accounted for a reasonable expectation that such profits
would continue to grow. Through risk-taking in pursuit of profits,
the financial world fueled the real economy. Investors used financial resources to create a more productive future. Investors large
and small shared in the gains.

Eventually, though, speculative fever outran what the real
economy could support. From early 1928, it took less than
two years for the Dow nearly to double once again, though the
economy hadn't doubled its prowess in so short a time. Dazzled
investors looked into the future and saw decades upon decades
of unending profit growth—and they included all that future
growth in the stock price. The same went for land and other
investments. Markets' ability to reflect information about future
profits *now* testifies to their efficiency. In a bubble, however,
markets can price systemic distortions into asset prices far too
efficiently.

With no regulations to limit such behavior, investors large
and small borrowed and lent liberally against that confidence.
Such aggressive borrowing signals investor certainty about future
growth, profits, and asset values. Certainty about the future had
helped total debt grow by a rapid 25 percent since 1920, after
decades of slower growth, to nearly twice as high as the value of
everything that the nation could produce in one year, a level that it
wouldn't reach again in boom times until the 1980s.[7] Banks lent
money for everything from land purchases in Florida to corporate
expansion in the nation's industrial centers to municipal projects
in postwar Europe.

People saw no risk. Lenders didn't worry about the extent
of borrowing against stock values, for example, because if they
needed the loan repaid, they knew that the borrowers could sell
their shares instantly on the always-liquid stock market and pay
the money back. The *Wall Street Journal* noted that "the speculation in stocks can be liquidated in a few hours or days with no
damage as concerns the country."[8] The same confidence that any
asset could always fetch a higher price at a painless sale buoyed
other investments.

Decades later, in the mid-2000s, investors would see the same illusion of liquidity in the market for securities made up of bundles of individual mortgages. Just as in the twenties, few remembered that liquidity exists only when there are buyers as well as sellers, and that buyers disappear in a panic. Few asked, then or now: What if asset values were rising only because there was so much easily borrowed money available to push them up? And what would happen to asset prices if the borrowed money supporting them vanished?

In the twenties, without an external force to stop it, the market eventually trapped itself in a speculative circle. Rising asset prices, supported by debt, justified even higher prices, and even more debt. Banks became even more complacent in limiting how much money they would lend against stock. They lent money, for example, to huge "investment pools" whose managers invested the funds in more securities. The banks lending the money often were not independent of these securities-speculation vehicles. At Chase National Bank, the bank's securities affiliate operated half a dozen of these pools, some of which speculated in hundreds of thousands of shares of Chase's own stock.[9] The banks even lent money to their own executives so that they could bet on rising stocks, too—often the stock of their own employers. These activities created a circular risk to the banks and to the economy. If the banks ran into trouble, they would have to pull back their lending to such pools, thus pulling the support out from under their own stock prices and the stock market in general, taking even more losses on the pools and on their other stock investments and pulling back lending even more severely, harming the economy and causing stock prices to fall further.

To understand how confident executives and their bankers were, remember Samuel Insull, chief executive of Chicago's Commonwealth Edison Company, the high-flying utility. Edison was a solid company with strong profits based on breakthroughs that literally powered the economy. Insull was able to use financiers' and the public's expectations of permanent future growth to erect a rickety tower of stock securities on top of bond securities, bond securities on top of stock securities. "Holding" companies borrowed tremendous amounts to control the "operating" companies that actually delivered the power.

Insull's complicated corporate structure was based on a simple premise: it was fine not only to spend all of tomorrow's profits today but to borrow liberally against those future profits, because the next day's profits would be even higher. Insull borrowed so extensively that he "only had to invest slightly more than $50 million to control a $500 million company," wrote John F. Wasik in *The Merchant of Power*; as the mania grew, he needed only $27 million to support the same amount, borrowing nearly $18 for every $1 he had in hand. Profits had to rise stratospherically every year to support expectations of this kind. It would take only a slight weakening of corporate profits for the entire structure to collapse. But the financial world wasn't worried. "Since banks were tripping over themselves to lend him money in the 1920s, he had easy access to capital," Wasik observed.[10]

Companies like Edison did not have to disclose their business practices and the possible threats to their business and financial models clearly and regularly to investors. Firms often put positive spins on the reports they did issue, with optimism untempered even by cursory warnings about the bad things that could happen. In 1915, Edison reported "all of 12 lines" on the state of its financial assets and liabilities, Wasik wrote. In 1931, even as scrutiny had grown in a plummeting market, the company's seven-page annual report "did not mention that [a related company] was purchasing Commonwealth Edison's stock in the open market, the impact of the Depression on the company, the relationship of [parent companies] to Commonwealth Edison nor much significant detail at all about anything. . . . Considering what had happened to the economy . . . , the report is laughable in its lack of detail."[11]

Pre-Depression America trusted the financial market to protect itself from disaster. "Speculation may be able to correct itself a great deal better than it can be controlled by official action," the *Wall Street Journal* opined in mid-October 1929. "If the stock market is left alone, it will liquidate itself in due course and do so safely."[12]

So great was the belief in the financial market's ability to regulate itself that Robert Owen of Oklahoma, a progressive senator who favored more government involvement in many areas of life, couldn't conceive of imposing limits on markets. Regulating brokers' loans and other aspects of the securities market was "a task much too intricate for government and could not be accomplished except by . . . the destruction of individual liberty. The remedy would be worse than the disease," Owen said in April 1929.[13] Even small bank depositors were on their own, with housewives expected to police their own banks for signs of reckless investment and withdraw funds at the first sign of irresponsibility. But nobody seemed to mind. The market had made geniuses out of the 16 million small investors who turned to stocks and corporate bonds after their successful experience in buying war bonds at the government's urging a decade earlier.[14]

The government had only two modest means for discouraging excessive speculation. The first was the young Federal Reserve, the nation's central bank, created little more than a decade earlier. The Fed could help control speculation with one blunt tool: setting the interest rate at which it lent to banks. If the Fed thought that money was too "tight"—that a scarcity of money was squelching economic growth—it could slash the interest rate. If it deemed money too "loose"—when too much money chasing the same amount of goods and services around threatened to increase inflation or to feed speculation—it could raise interest rates, making it more expensive to borrow.

The Fed had to be perfect because other regulations did not exist to cushion the financial markets and the economy from its mistakes. But the central bank had an impossible job. First, it couldn't target speculators by hiking interest rates only for certain lending practices. It had to raise rates for everyone, affecting the entire economy, giving it little room for error in raising rates too high and hurting growth.[15] Second, the Fed was the steward of much of the world's monetary policy, not just America's. Since the end of the World War a decade earlier, the U.S., as an export powerhouse, had amassed huge stores of the world's gold, just as China, an export powerhouse eight decades later, would amass huge stores of the world's dollars.

This global imbalance was just as important in the twenties as it would be eight decades later. Because of the gold standard of the time, governments couldn't create money without backing it in part with the precious metal, so as other nations relinquished their gold to America, they also sacrificed their ability to mint money. If America's central bank made a mistake in setting interest rates on the outsize share of the world's money that it controlled, the mistake would hurt not only the nation's economy but the world's.[16]

The Fed's powers seemed theoretical, anyway, in the face of a far stronger market. In June 1928, the Fed finally raised rates, but the market didn't care. In an article titled "Loss of Credit Control," the *Wall Street Journal* reported that "corporations and private and foreign lenders . . . are finding a way to make their . . . loans through channels outside the banks."[17] The market didn't need the Fed; it could create credit on its own. As asset values continued to rise, lenders felt increasingly comfortable lending money against those assets, creating more credit no matter what the Fed did.

The government's other tool against speculative excess was to prosecute stock fraud—and it's an enduring myth that the government did nothing on this front. More than three years before the crash, President Hoover's Treasury secretary, Andrew Mellon, worried that average Americans were proving no match for the immoral actors plaguing the markets. "Each year," Mellon wrote, "a very appreciable amount of capital is being lost so that it would seem to be the duty of the federal government to provide adequate legal machinery for protecting the public." He suggested that the nation's "Attorney General be authorized to investigate [suspect] securities and . . . issue a summary order forbidding their further sale under heavy penalties."[18]

No legislation came of Mellon's idea, but the government did what it could under common-law provisions. In October 1929 alone, it announced that it had investigated twenty-two securities houses for fraud, closing ten. Penalties were severe: one "bucket-shopper"—slang for stock swindler—got a five-year federal sentence on October 19, just in time to miss the crash.[19] Reviewing one federal antifraud push, the *Wall Street Journal* declared that "with the indictment of 20 persons in the past week or two by the federal grand jury, the drive being conducted . . . on promoters of spurious securities entered its major phase. . . . [I]ts effect has been far-reaching."[20]

State and private efforts to combat fraud were even more aggressive. In 1925, New York State, the stock-fraud capital and a pioneer in prosecuting such crimes, estimated that stock fraud cost victims $500 million annually.[21] The state stepped up its efforts to prosecute hucksters, using its unique power, the 1921 Martin Act, which directed the state attorney general to investigate securities crimes and empowered him to close down bucket shops and other suspicious operations. Other states—California, New Jersey, and Pennsylvania among them—specifically targeted stock-fraud scandals, with front-page prosecutions that put swindlers on notice.[22]

The New York Stock Exchange worried about fraud, too. In 1925, it launched an operation to publicize reports of securities vulnerable to scams. NYSE chief E. H. H. Simmons toured the nation to expose "the bucket-shop keeper and the security swindler" as "a dangerous thief and a menace," calling for business, law enforcement, and newspapers to cooperate.[23] By 1927, Simmons despaired of the efforts' results, saying that "the fraud problem . . . will be one of constantly increasing menace."[24] Despite high-profile investigations, prosecutions, and closures of firms, some quite prominent, the fraudsters just kept coming, often selling worthless securities through the mail to unsuspecting "investors."

Though fraud's human toll was painful, the government's focus on it, however important for justice's sake, was a distraction from the real problem. Often, fraud was a symptom of the lack of skepticism that powered the twenties-era markets, the result of a bubble mentality that asset prices could go nowhere but up.

Prosecutions, while justified, did nothing to address this graver problem and did not lessen the risk of a systemic financial and economic meltdown. The imbalances of the perfectly legal financial world endangered the economy far more than the avarice of criminal swindlers.

The market, lacking an external force to act upon it, finally stopped itself in 1929. Corporate profits faltered, cracking the edifice upon which all that debt teetered. Profits wouldn't rise forever, people now understood, and therefore couldn't support stock prices based on that mistaken assumption. People also noticed, suddenly and belatedly, that the Fed had made borrowing more expensive. Psychology changed quickly. As Sears, Roebuck executive J. M. Barker reminisced half a decade later, "Whenever you have a group of people thinking the same thing at the same time, you have one of the hardest emotional causes in the world to control. . . . If you consider the universality of the speculative mania of the later days of the last boom, you will see how completely the people of this country . . . were under the influence of the mob psychology. . . . When the break came, cupidity turned into unreasoning, emotional, universal fear."[25]

Fear begat fear in the bust, just as certainty had created more certainty in the bubble. As stock investors sold, other investors realized that stock prices could go down further. Those investors sold, too, causing further declines. Investors pulled their money out of the stock "pools," so the stock pools, in turn, sold their stocks, magnifying the losses. The crash immediately affected the economy, as people who had invested their money in the stock market—the most democratic in the world—felt poorer and stopped spending, and companies followed suit.[26]

The falling stock market directly influenced borrowers' ability to repay their debts, and not just their brokers' loans. Companies like Insull's Edison, which depended on rising stocks to raise money from *new* investors to pay its lenders, could no longer do so. Insull's "company structure . . . was a straw house that could not have been sustained during any economic downturn. Its complexity and reliance on consistent streams of income made it precarious, particularly when cash was tight," wrote John Wasik in his Insull biography.[27]

Terrified financial leaders tried to halt the slide. J. P. Morgan executive George Whitney later testified that in late 1929, bankers cobbled together $250 million to support stocks, well aware that money lent against the equities market posed "danger." The bankers created the buying pool "to preserve some order in the whole financial community."[28] What Whitney and his colleagues didn't realize—and what their successors wouldn't realize, either, nearly eight decades later, when they tried a similar tactic with the mortgage-securities market—was that a determined group of financiers was no match for unregulated financial-market forces.

After the crash, many investors lost everything. In the purest sense, that's how capitalism is supposed to work: the promise of great reward carries great risk. Banks, though, should not have been able to lose everything so quickly and in such disorderly fashion. For the economy's sake, banks, because they were the stewards of the nation's money and credit, needed more buffers than did securities firms against the most extreme ups and downs of financial speculation. Bank failures had helped turn a down-turn into a disaster.

The role of banks is to transfer surplus money from people and businesses—lenders—to people and businesses that need such money now but don't have it—borrowers. When people save money in a bank, they lend that money to the bank, in return for interest. The bank, in turn, lends some of that money to its bor-rowers, charging more interest than it pays the depositors—and keeping the rest as profit. In normal times, as the economy natu-rally and steadily expands—the result of both a growing popula-tion and increased productivity, through technological innovation and other improvements—the business of banking must expand, too, to account for an expanding money and credit supply. Further, as the value of assets—from stocks to houses to office buildings—rises steadily (but not wildly) with economic growth and produc-tive use, these assets can support greater borrowing themselves, also helping to expand the money and credit supply, and thus the economy. A contracting money and credit supply, conversely, will shrink the economy.

Without government insurance to shield depositors from bank failure—insurance that didn't exist on a national level in the twenties and early thirties—the financial system can work only if people trust banks. In a panic, as trust collapses, everyone tries to withdraw money at once. Even a healthy bank cannot withstand such panicked withdrawals because the money is not at the bank; the bank has lent most of it to other individuals or businesses, whether directly or through market investments. Since the bank has so little cash on hand, a run will cause it to fail, and most depositors will lose their money.

In the early 1930s, distrust and fear of bank runs crippled the banking system, not only bringing the economy to a halt but reversing economic growth. The government did not have a mechanism to guarantee ordinary people's bank deposits. Nor did the government effectively separate commercial banks, responsible for supposedly safe deposits, from the more speculative securities side of the financial world dealing in stocks and bonds. So when people worried, often with good reason, that their banks had speculated excessively, their only recourse was to withdraw their money. The only market forces available to discipline the bad banks—panicked customers—created a disorder that disrupted the entire system of money and credit throughout the early 1930s.

The government did not initially notice that bank failures were destroying the broader economy. In 1930, examiners declared that the problem of failing banks was contained. A North Carolina bank examiner, commenting in November on one of the state's eight bank failures that year, said that the problem resulted from "a highly inflated plane of real estate values" and was a "purely local" situation.[29] In the first eleven months of 1930, 981 banks failed, a number "unprecedented in the history of this country," the Fed reported[30]—yet in the same month, state bank commissioners still believed that "sound and satisfactory banking conditions" held throughout the country, with failures actually benefiting the banking system by ridding it of weak participants.[31] With such complacency, the problem multiplied. In 1929, bank failures swallowed up less than 0.2 percent of all customers' deposits. By 1931, the figure had risen fivefold, to over 1 percent, and would more than double again, to over 2 percent, in 1933.[32]

The government had two reasons for its inaction. First, banks always failed in the nation's free-market system. Second, many bank failures were small and rural and often went unnoticed on the East Coast. The nation's biggest coastal banks—Chase National Bank, Manhattan Bank, and National City Bank—remained relative pillars of strength. In late 1930, though, two bigger banks, the Bank of United States in New York and the Bankers Trust Company of Philadelphia, collapsed, jarring New York and Washington. New York's fifty-nine-branch Bank of United States had offered depositors certain guarantees if they would invest in the bank's own stock and the stock of an investment trust run by the bank—a particularly egregious example of banks' house-of-cards securities speculation.[33]

Disorderly bank failures cascaded throughout the financial system. As even relatively robust banks feared that they'd be the next to face a run, they sold off noncash assets, like stocks and bonds, so that they'd have money on hand to meet depositor panic. This forced selling drove down the prices of those investments, pushing more banks over the brink, forcing more panicked selling and causing yet more dread. The financial tsunami swamped even "safe" assets, moving from stocks and land to railroad and utility bonds.

The shrinkage in asset values affected even the most conservative bank. J. P. Morgan, then an august, patrician private bank, had deposits of $492 million in 1929. It had invested wisely, with, for example, $165 million in government securities, $59 million in cash, and $79 million in loans against stocks. By 1932, though, economic evaporation had left "Morgans," as it was known, with deposits of just $340 million. It was investing those deposits even more conservatively, with $225 million in government bonds, $34 million in cash, and just $7 million left in stock loans.[34] In 1932, more than three-fourths of the firm's assets were "liquid"—government bonds that were relatively easy to convert into cash, or cash itself. Three years previously, only 46 percent of the firm's assets had been liquid.

Morgans' 30 percent contraction in deposits—which pushed the bank to make fewer investments, in turn, in people and institutions—was well below the national average. Between 1929 and 1932, bank credit in the American economy contracted 40 percent.[35] Without the credit provided by banks, companies could not get funds to expand or hire. They could not turn to the shattered stock or bond markets as a substitute, either. In 1929, corporations issued $8.6 billion in public securities; by 1932, that figure had shrunk to $325 million.[36]

As credit vanished and as consumers stopped spending, the price of everything from steel to movie tickets plummeted along with demand. Falling prices made it even harder and less sensible for borrowers to pay back outstanding loans, since the amount of the loan stayed steady, the value of the asset that the loan had purchased was declining, and the value of cash in the hand, rather than going to repay debts, was increasing.

Falling prices meant lost jobs. The price of goods and services dropped faster than wages did, so employers wanted to cut wages to match the lower prices they were getting for their products. But workers balked at pay cuts and organized against them. Unable to slash pay, employers slashed jobs instead. Unemployed workers cut demand further, pushing prices down more and causing employers to cut still more jobs. Failing companies and unemployed workers had an even harder time repaying their debt, and the cycle of bank losses spun faster. Recession turned to depression.

For nearly eight decades, scholars and critics have debated what caused the Great Depression. Often, they focus on government inaction starting in the early 1930s, when the extent of the economy's woes, they argue, should have become clear, and the government should have responded differently.

Monetarists, who believe that the government's main economic job is to regulate the money supply to keep prices steady, contend that the Depression was the Fed's fault because the

Fed, after being too loose with money in the mid-twenties, did not expand the money supply after bank failures had caused it to contract. As economists Milton Friedman and Anna Jacobson Schwartz posited in their 1963 work, *A Monetary History of the United States, 1867–1960*, the Fed, starting in the early thirties, should have asked the Treasury to print up new money and then lent it generously to the banks so that they would resume lending and borrowing, stimulating a recovery. "Throughout the contraction, the [Fed] had ample powers to cut short the tragic process of monetary deflation and banking collapse," Friedman and Schwartz wrote.[37] "Moreover, the policies required to prevent the decline in the quantity of money and to ease the banking difficulties did not involve radical innovations."[38]

Disciples of John Maynard Keynes, the British economist, insist that it was the government's job to stimulate demand not just by printing money and handing it over to banks, but also through direct spending. The government should have spent more, and more quickly, on public works, which would have created more government jobs, for example. The problem, they say, was that Presidents Hoover and Roosevelt didn't spend enough after people and businesses stopped spending.

Other economists and historians—most recently, Amity Shlaes—observe that the government's continual interference in the economy caused so much uncertainty that businesses and individuals became too scared to start the recovery themselves. FDR tried to impose thousands of micromanaging regulations on businesses ranging from tiny chicken slaughterhouses to big electric utilities. And for years, almost all respected economists have pointed to government blunders—such as protectionist trade barriers and fiscal emphasis on balanced budgets, which required tax hikes that took more money out of people's pockets—as having severely aggravated the crisis.

The lesson of the Depression, though, may be that there is no straightforward policy fix when a burst asset bubble, precipitated by unregulated finance, has created such a huge field of debris. As Lazard Frères partner Albert J. Hettinger, Jr. wrote in the original introduction to Friedman and Schwartz's masterpiece, gently questioning their conclusions, "High-powered money, intelligently administered by a regulatory body, can, as the authors point out, accomplish much. It cannot accomplish the impossible."[39] Policymakers had enormous difficulty steering America and the world out of the Depression partly because they often did the wrong things and should have done other things or instead not done anything—but that was because they were human.

The enormity of the crisis was unknowable to those living through it, just as the scope of today's crisis has been. A full year after the crash, the *New York Times* observed that "the scope and violence of business [contraction] in 1930 unquestionably took the financial community completely by surprise."[40] Five months later, the world's central bankers, still in shock, ruminated at a conference in Switzerland that "estimates regarding the extent and duration of the economic crisis have now proved completely wrong."[41] And even at the end of 1931, the *Times* said that "in the months immediately following that event the mind of Congress was divided between bewilderment and belief in immediate recovery."[42]

A sudden crisis, even one so severe, could not overcome decades of economic orthodoxy as well as natural impulse. Crisis instead caused people to retreat further into orthodoxy. Elected officials and central bankers had a hard time letting go of their notion that gold, not people, governed monetary policy. Globally, respectable nations did not issue currency unless it was backed by gold, and they held to a consistent standard for the amount of gold required for each dollar issued. Fed board members and elected officials worried that if the nation jettisoned historical precedent and printed currency not backed by gold, or if it reduced the amount of gold it required to back each dollar, the rest of the world would lose faith in the economy. Lawmakers, for their part, worried that the world would lose confidence in America if it didn't balance its budget. And as American jobs vaporized, it was natural, if misguided, for politicians to impose trade barriers, trying to protect remaining jobs.

Nor could the actions that the government did take overcome the banks' own instincts in a sharply shrinking economy. In 1931, for example, Hoover unveiled a plan to spend $500 million to "thaw out frozen banking assets." He didn't realize that "frozen" assets weren't the problem (and nearly eight decades later, policymakers would announce similarly wrongheaded plans to "unfreeze" the market for mortgage securities).

The problem was that the assets were worth significantly less than they had been two years earlier. Banks wouldn't lend money even if the government bought these legacy assets because bankers didn't know if the value of any *new* loans would quickly shrink, too, as the economy continued to do. A year later, in 1932, Hoover tried to pump more than $1 billion in government money into struggling banks "to check the further degeneration in prices and values."[43] But a frustrated Atlee Pomerene, in charge of the Reconstruction Finance Corporation, which headed the effort, said that the banks involved were acting like "parasites," as they were "boasting" that they were healthy, yet not lending out money.[44]

Banks didn't lend partly because few clients needed to borrow money in a contracting economy; businesses weren't expanding, and customers were bankrupt. In 1934, the Fed said that banks wouldn't lend until there was "a demand for credit on the part of good borrowers."[45] The bankers concurred, with one executive saying that they were "most anxious to put their idle funds into circulation" and that when a "sound borrower appears, considerable competition ensues for his account."[46] In our current crisis, policymakers have heard similar explanations for banks' refusal to lend.

Most important, though, the unregulated financial world had lost faith in itself. After the market self-destructed, financiers had no idea what anything was *worth*. As stock-exchange chief Richard Whitney told Congress in early 1933, describing how to determine a stock's true value: "I used to think that it meant the worth of the . . . corporation, . . . that they all had a certain intrinsic value. But in these days, you do not know whether anything is worth anything. That might wipe out what was very important in constituting the intrinsic value of a corporation and, therefore, its securities."[47] Valuation of securities was—and still is—how markets communicate information. But after 1929, that language turned to babble.

The inability to value securities—or anything else—presented more than just a mathematical or an economic challenge. It was a catastrophe for the recovery of markets. Financiers and businessmen no longer had any measure to distinguish acceptable from unacceptable risk in their investments—in short, they could not trust their own judgment. Bankers did not know how to be bankers any more. The public, too, had lost faith in its financial and business leaders. "During the boom years, the white-shoe world . . . had been portrayed as a conclave of wise men," economic historian Steve Fraser has written. "Under the new circumstances of economic ruination, the same world was treated as . . . an object not only of censure but of mockery. And there is perhaps nothing more fatal for the life expectancy of an elite than to be viewed as ridiculous."[48]

It's possible that huge infusions of government cash into banks, if made before this psychology set in, would have stopped the crisis. But even if Hoover and his policymakers had recognized the need for such drastic action, politics would have tied their hands. The Reconstruction Finance Corporation's proposal to put money into banks was a political nonstarter, "a dole to the wealthy to be paid for by the poor workers," as one citizen complained.[49] In the end, Hoover had no choice but to direct much of the RFC's money toward direct relief for individuals. Voters viewed Hoover as trying to keep a gilded age glued together by serving the interests of financiers, not the public. Roosevelt would succeed in similar efforts to infuse banks with capital only because by then, it was clear that he was picking up the pieces of a smashed system for the public's sake.

Starting in 2007, the nation's credit infrastructure once again began to disintegrate before our eyes, seemingly uncontrollably. Washington policymakers, economists, and ordinary citizens feared that all the federal government's unprecedented actions to stop the financial crisis from turning into an economic disaster would not work. Americans have experienced some of the fear that their Depression-era ancestors felt.

Back then, policymakers knew that the risk of a future generation facing another financial and economic shock on a similar scale was unacceptable. Their job was to prevent the conditions that could create a future shock, not just by encouraging markets to repair themselves but by protecting the economy long after the markets had done so. To that end, Roosevelt, for all his missteps, spent much of the thirties effectively reducing the chances that an unregulated financial world could destroy itself and the nation's well-being ever again. His reforms, which the next chapter considers, helped create the conditions for a well-regulated financial world to flourish and support the economy.

CHAPTER 2

THE BLESSING
OF THE FREE
MARKETS

[I]f control of our currency were necessary in the beginning of the republic, control of banking is in the same class now.
—Owen Young, General Electric chief, February 4, 1931[1]

[F]inance shall be not a game of magic to mystify, bewilder and mislead the investing public, but a forthright business.
—James M. Landis, SEC chairman, December 4, 1936[2]

L ITTLE MORE THAN A WEEK AFTER TAKING OFFICE, President Roosevelt, in his first radio "fireside chat," told Americans what they already knew. Their banks had failed, and badly. "We had a bad banking situation," the president said. "Some of our bankers had shown themselves either incompetent or dishonest in their handling of the people's funds. They had used the money entrusted to them in speculations and unwise loans."[3]

FDR understood that fixing the banks was the first step in repairing the nation's financial infrastructure. He told listeners something that they didn't know: the government would protect them from bad banks. "Let me make it clear that the banks will take care of all needs," the president said to people who still wanted to withdraw their money. "When the people find that they can get their money . . . the phantom of fear will soon be laid. . . . I can assure you that it is safer to keep your money in a reopened bank than under the mattress." Over the next two years, the president and Congress formalized this new system of permanent deposit insurance for small savers so that banks would never face the kinds of crippling panics that had plagued them over the previous three years.

It's hard to overstate the importance of Roosevelt's action, despite his insistence that it was not "radical." For the first time, the federal government had announced that the core of the country's money and credit system—people's hard-earned small deposits—would be safe from speculation. No longer would big-city wives worry about the safety of their families' dollars should rumors stalk a neighborhood bank, nor would rural farmers grow anxious that a weak state deposit-guarantee program wouldn't be able to withstand a collapse in commodity prices and its impact on multiple banks. The government had decreed that savings would be protected. People understood the significance of this change and quickly began to redeposit their funds, returning to the banks more than half of the money that they had withdrawn within two weeks, according to William L. Silber of New York University.[4]

FDR knew that the answer wasn't to prop up weak banks indefinitely with government money, though. As the president spoke that night in March, in fact, the nation's banks were closed. The president had closed them a week earlier upon his inauguration to protect them from their own terrified customers, but the bank-closure proclamation was a formality. Even before the announcement, "scarcely a bank in the country was open to do business . . . in almost all the states."[5] During the closure, government officials—armed with a congressional mandate that the Hoover administration had helped draw up—cracked open the closed banks' books to see which were strong enough to survive. They quickly reopened the healthiest banks, using federal funds to shore up fragile but viable institutions so that the firms wouldn't be swamped again by panicked customers, and closed down what remained of the worst.

Banking patricians—and even FDR himself—worried that deposit insurance would accomplish the opposite of its intended purpose—they worried that it might encourage banks to take even more risks because depositors, protected by the government, would become complacent and wouldn't discipline imprudent banks by withdrawing their funds. Chase National chairman Winthrop Aldrich called insurance "a premium on bad banking."[6] Bankers also were concerned that insurance would punish good banks because they would have to pay in to the insurance fund, too. American Bankers Association president Francis H. Sisson charged that deposit insurance was "unsound, which will ultimately force its own repeal. . . . [Y]ou simply cannot cover up vice . . . by forcing the good banks to carry the burdens of the weak."[7]

People like Aldrich were right to argue that failed banks, like other businesses, should be allowed to fail, with management and investors suffering for their mistakes. This discipline is a core tenet of free markets. But free markets don't operate in a vacuum. They operate in the real world, with real-world consequences that are sometimes too great for free societies to bear. Aldrich and others were wrong in thinking that small depositors, who needed a reliable place to store their earnings, should suffer as the price for exacting market discipline on banks. They were wrong, too, in believing that massive financial and economic disruption, along with a loss in the confidence that Alexander Hamilton, the nation's first Treasury secretary, had called the "soul of credit," was an acceptable price for average citizens to pay to assure market discipline in the banking industry.

To handle the new job of guaranteeing small customers' confidence in the banking system, the government created the Federal Deposit Insurance Corporation, which would pay for its operations through fees that it collected from banks. As the FDIC evolved, its officials, working with other government regulators, solved the problem of how to shutter bad banks without causing the collateral damage of economic disruption. The FDIC could shut down failed banks in an orderly fashion, often transferring customers' accounts to other banks so that the clients would barely notice the change. The transfers also ensured that valuable economic assets would fall into more competent hands, without hurting small customers in the process.

In return for the benefit that deposit insurance gave banks— they no longer had to worry about small customers, who funded the banks' operations through their deposits, suddenly fleeing— the FDIC also gained the permanent power to regulate and monitor banks, including making regular assessments of their ability to withstand losses, their prospects for future earnings, and the "character" of their management. These regulations joined existing requirements that banks hold a certain level of capital— non-borrowed money from shareholders—as a cushion against losses. Together, these regulations helped ensure—though they never outright guaranteed—that banks would not use the government protection of their depositors as a cover under which to take reckless risks.

The government had struck a delicate compromise to preserve capitalism. Failed banks would still cease to exist, but the economy would not suffer needlessly in the process. Market discipline would continue to operate on banks, but the core system of money and credit won the modicum of public confidence that it needed to function, particularly in times of economic woe. The government would provide a buffer against panic between banks and the public.

True, the fresh government enjoyed some luck in its efforts. Nearly four years of the Depression ensured that the worst banks had already failed before the FDIC even started its work. Moreover, big banks like Chase and National City still remained relatively strong. The government did not face the dilemma of a huge, failed bank that was entwined in the world's financial system, as were the big East Coast banks even back then.

Financial experts quickly came to understand the importance of orderly bank failures. "The cleansing of the American banking structure of 'the parasites of occasional incompetency and dishonesty' in the last year and a half has put it in the strongest position of safety and good management," Eugene H. Stevens, chairman

of the board of the Federal Reserve Bank of Chicago, told dele-
gates of the American Bankers Association in 1934.[8] A year later,
many former opponents, including the association, had changed
their minds and embraced banking insurance.

The government decided, too, that because banks were so
important to the nation's economy, they needed extra protection
from themselves. In what later became known as the Glass-Steagall Act, the president and Congress agreed that banks should
be separated from securities firms. Securities firms, in the business of floating stocks and bonds and investing their own capital in such securities, were too vulnerable to short-term market
fluctuations for banks' purposes. Banks like National City had to
decide, by the mid-thirties, whether they wanted to be commercial deposit-takers and loan-makers or securities-underwriting
and investment firms. Never again could a bank use its securities
affiliate, supported indirectly by customers' deposits, to speculate
on its own stock, creating a dangerous feedback loop through
which destruction in confidence in the stock market could cause
a destruction of confidence in the bank and in its deposits.

The government offered no FDIC-style protections to the now-
separate securities firms, also called investment banks. Lenders
to such firms, unlike insured depositors at commercial banks,
knew that their investments carried more risk—but they had
more sophistication to assess that risk. The government determined that securities firms, if insolvent, could fail through the
normal bankruptcy process without harming the nation's money
and credit supplies.

A banking system better insulated from the stock and bond
markets created the conditions for a securities industry that could
continue to take big risks in those markets, because securities
speculation could no longer bring down banks. After convincing
Americans that their money was safe in banks, FDR faced a harder
and more complex task in encouraging Americans to reenter the
securities markets, though. By contrast with small bank deposits,
the hazard of possible losses is the entire point of securities markets; investors expect a higher reward for taking a higher perceived

risk. The most efficient way to destroy the American securities market for good, then, would have been to introduce certainty.

But in the thirties, investors were too demoralized to attempt such calculations of risk and reward. They saw the market as a rigged game or, worse, as a game that seemed not to make any sense at all. Such perceptions emerged from the long months of hearings that started in Washington in January 1933, when a Senate committee appointed Ferdinand Pecora, a former New York assistant district attorney, to head the investigation into the financial and economic crash.

Just as is the case today, it was hard for lawmakers, the press, and even financial insiders to know where to start in figuring out what had gone wrong. The Pecora hearings revealed that the banks and securities firms had kept "favored lists" of celebrities, politicians, and other friends, who enjoyed the privilege of buying stock early from underwriters and "flipping" them to the public at much higher prices. Firms manipulated markets at the public's expense: underwriters of one securities house, for example, would ask traders at other houses, as well as managers of investment pools, to make artificial trades to maintain a certain price, creating the impression of outsize demand. Banks and brokers did not disclose conflicts; National City, for example, bundled up bad loans as bonds and sold them to unsuspecting customers of its securities arm.[9] Underwriters there had also taken a cut of a bond meant for New York's Port Authority and given the money to an agency director, charging it to "syndication expenses" and then promptly losing the record.[10] Banks also freely lent money to their own officers and employees for the purposes of speculation.

Tales of how marquee corporations had trapped themselves in intricate financial structures frightened the public. After Samuel Insull's Chicago behemoth collapsed, Owen Young, chief of General Electric, tried to help figure out the failed company's finances. He couldn't. "I think Samuel Insull was very largely the victim of the complicated structure that he created," Young told Congress. "He . . . was unable to comprehend all the ramifications of that complicated structure. . . . I remember the feeling of helplessness

that came over me when I began . . . to examine the structure."
Nobody could figure out what Insull's companies were worth.[11]

As it learned how much Wall Street firms had borrowed to
speculate, the public found it difficult to comprehend the risks
involved. In one investment pool, the reputable securities firm
Dillon Read had controlled $90 million in investments with just
$5.1 million in actual capital. This "leverage"—nearly $17 in borrowed money for every $1 in hand—"was terrific," an observer
noted.[12] Another stock pool had required no cash at all to raise $33
million in borrowing for stocks because "the purchase price was
paid as the stock was sold to the public." One financier, Blair &
Co.'s Arthur Cutten, admitted that toward the end of the bubble
years, his firm "didn't have to manipulate the market" because "it
was a perpendicular market—always going up."[13]

Some prominent bankers revealed that they had lost fortunes.
"I put all that I had back into this institution, and for its stability,"
City Bank's chief, Charles Mitchell, told Congress. "If . . . anybody that you know has suffered a loss in gross that I have in
City Bank stock, then you know somebody that I do not." Such
revelations weren't comforting. They made plain that the bankers
hadn't understood the risks that they had taken for themselves
and the public.

One immutable truth seeped through the murk: twenties-
era Wall Street had nothing to stop it but its own judgment. The
American public wondered how the men entrusted with the
fate of the economy could have let this disaster happen. Pecora,
observing that Wall Street had had no idea that "this thing was
inflated beyond all reason," asked how the public could "rely on
the judgment of the big financial crowd in these matters at all."
He won an exhausted concession from City Bank's Mitchell.
"There are so many factors over which the men in finance have
no control and really have comparatively little knowledge, that it
is just as impossible for them to predict a definite future as it is
for anybody else," Mitchell replied. "We are human, we are filled
with error, and it does not matter how good our intention may be,
we are going to make mistakes."[14]

FDR and appointees like James Landis, the Harvard professor who helped design new market regulations, knew that they needed to help Americans regain trust in markets. The number of shares traded on the stock exchange in 1932 was just a third of what it had been three years earlier, mirroring and perpetuating the Depression.[15] Yet policymakers couldn't rebuild the financial system by whipping up outrage and throwing people into prison. The problem wasn't that individuals failed through poor judgment or criminal intent; it was that these inevitable human failures resulted in systemic economic catastrophe. The job of the president and his technocrats was to create a framework for risk-taking that focused on prevention: consistent principles and rules to protect the markets and the economy from human folly *before* it could cause cataclysmic damage.

Roosevelt's approach to repairing the securities industry was boldly American. He offered no guarantees that bubbles wouldn't recur or that future fortunes wouldn't be made and lost. Instead, he assumed that enterprising Americans would naturally want, and need, to take market risk again as long as they had access to one invaluable tool: accurate information.

The Securities Act of 1933, which FDR signed into law just two and a half months after taking office, helped change the perception that Wall Street and corporate America possessed a monopoly on the valuable commodity of fact. The law provided the tools with which even small investors could seek knowledge. Before issuing securities to the public, companies would now have to file a registration statement with the government, disclosing objective, dry facts about the company's business, finances, and management, the reason for the financing need, and any "material" information that executives and underwriters thought potential investors would want to know. Corporations were required to make this registration statement available to the public, as well. A year later, Congress strengthened the disclosure requirements by requiring companies that sold securities to the public to issue regular, audited reports on their activities and financial results, and required company executives and big stockholders to disclose their holdings publicly. Congress also required stock exchanges to register with regulators and to create consistent ways to monitor and report on their own activities.

Disclosure was a powerful tool, and exposing a risk was sometimes the same as cutting a risk. As Garland Ferguson, commissioner of the Federal Trade Commission (FTC), which initially oversaw the securities law, noted, exposing the mind-numbing complexity of some securities would sometimes be enough to discourage companies from creating them—thus lessening the need for hard restrictions. "Top-heavy and intricate corporate structures, with confused layers of various different types of securities, require many words to tell the story, if, indeed, it can be told," he said, predicting that the revelation of byzantine corporate structures would warn investors away from such "Chinese puzzles." Dry facts served as a defense against credulity that a particular stock or market could do nothing but go up and up. The law contained the "simplest requirement of common honesty . . . which consists of telling all the truth and not merely the savory part of it."[16]

The administration's new securities regulators, first at the FTC and a year later at the newly created Securities and Exchange Commission (SEC), repeatedly explained to investors that the new law did not absolve them of their own responsibility in taking measured risks. It intensified that responsibility. The commission "in no sense approves a security," FTC securities division chief Baldwin Bane cautioned in September 1933.[17] William Douglas, the SEC's third commissioner, put it more strongly a few years later, saying in 1937 that "we can demand full disclosure of the facts, we can insist upon a market free of manipulation, we can fight fraud, but we cannot provide sound business judgment, nor can we save a fool from his folly."[18]

The government didn't need to create an environment of close, constant supervision of companies. The market, now armed with consistent, comparable information about companies issuing securities, offered new opportunities for the private sector to do this job. "I should like to emphasize the importance of statistics," said the SEC's director of research to a statistical analysts' group

in New York in 1935. "The information now available, when properly studied, should enable us to advance a long way in shedding
light on our corporate life and making the financial process less
wasteful, more balanced, more responsible, and more orderly. As
you know, one of the cornerstones of the 1933 and the 1934 acts
is disclosure. By improving and increasing the fund of statistical
knowledge available to the investor, we are progressing toward a
fairer financial process."[19] It's no coincidence that between 1934
and 1940, legendary investment analysts Benjamin Graham and
David Dodd, the Warren Buffetts of their day, perfected their
classic treatise, *Security Analysis*,[20] which encouraged consideration of business, financial, and managerial fundamentals as the
basis for assessing stock values. These principles endure today.

Roosevelt and his regulators believed that, while disclosure
was vital so that the public could assess risks, stronger tools,
including outright bans on certain practices, would be necessary
in some cases. FDR and Congress thus strengthened protections
against fraud, creating both civil and criminal penalties to enforce
the new securities laws as well as banning manipulative activities
like releasing false information to markets and making artificial
stock trades.

More subtly, the president imposed gentle stabilizers on
market forces, letting financial markets flourish within these
broad limits. In the Securities Exchange Act of 1934, the government removed the financial industry's discretion over lending to
customers for the purpose of purchasing securities—the brokers'
loan business. The new law gave the Federal Reserve the power
to set margin requirements—the percentage of cash required to
purchase a security. Ever since, stock purchasers have generally
had to put up fully half of the price of stock securities in cash,
dampening speculation and its effect on the economy. This law
worked well after the tech bubble burst starting in 2000. While
investors lost money, most did not *owe* money because they had
not been able to borrow against the full, inflated value of their
securities at the height of the mania. Lawmakers also gave the
SEC the authority to regulate "short" sales. Short-sellers borrow a
stock from an owner and sell it, betting that the price of the stock

will go down, at which point they will repurchase it for the lower price on the open market and return it to the stock lenders. The new regulation, called the "uptick rule," prevented short-sellers from driving a stock down to zero. It required that short speculators wait for a stock to rise slightly in the market before making a bet that it would fall again.

Each regulation served as an automatic check on financial markets. The first kept them from soaring too high with borrowed money in times of exuberance. The second kept them from plummeting too low in times of despair. Both rules partially insulated the economy as a whole from short-term excess and panic, but neither prevented financial markets from transmitting their important signals about expectations for the future through securities prices.

Through its new regulations on banking and securities, the government showed that it knew that it couldn't depend on the Federal Reserve to regulate the entire financial system via monetary policy. Instead, independent regulatory forces, like limits on borrowing for stock, would tamp down the speculative fever expanding a bubble even if monetary policy unintentionally encouraged it. Though many government regulators—the Fed, for example—wielded considerable discretion in the limits they set on the economy, some rules, at least, would be more immune from human discretion. Such a balance was important because regulators as well as bankers can get caught up in a bubble psychology. FDR and Congress had lessened the severity of a problem about which the *Wall Street Journal* had complained in 1931: "[I]t would, no doubt, be very nice if we could so arrange things that credit could be siphoned into industry and commerce and withheld from stock speculation, [but] . . . credit, once brought into existence, is a natural fluid which cannot be kept from flowing into the nearest channel available."[21]

The point of the new rules and regulations was not to punish the securities industry, so important to the nation's prosperity, but to rebuild it. In the early thirties, FDR's new financial regulators crisscrossed the country to make the case for the new laws, soothing the industry as well as its investors. Even as the president told the public that the old way of doing business was over and done with, his securities policymakers were telling the scared businessmen and financiers that the president's actions weren't capricious, radical, or prohibitive.

Of the new securities-registration law, regulators explained that it had not come out of nowhere. "Many of its features . . . have been drawn from the English Companies Act, which represents the culmination of almost a hundred years of struggling with this problem abroad" as well as from state securities laws at home, FDR's bureaucrats soothed the business world. In late 1933, the FTC's Bane repeated what was becoming a talking point—that the law was not "startling radicalism." Bane also informed an audience of state securities regulators that "nothing in the Securities Act . . . prevents the most speculative type of security being offered for sale."[22]

The image of securities regulators traveling the country to explain to skeptical businessmen, financiers, and state officials that the law did not outlaw risky finance and, in fact, encouraged Americans to reenter the market makes it easy to dismiss the old legend that Roosevelt named Joseph P. Kennedy, the former stock-pool speculator, as his first SEC chairman because Kennedy had the experience to root out the crooks. It's just as likely that Roosevelt named Kennedy to the post to convince the remaining speculators and risk-takers—so integral to a functioning economy—that the president welcomed the survival of such business. As Kennedy told the National Press Club and a radio audience in 1934, "We . . . do not regard ourselves as coroners sitting on the corpse of financial enterprise. . . . [W]e are not working on the theory that all the men and all the women connected with finance . . . are to be regarded as guilty of some undefined crime. . . . No honest man . . . need fear the regulations that have been set up" with no "vindictiveness" of intent.[23]

Nonetheless, even in its chastened Depression state, Wall Street often reacted violently to these new requirements and regulations. "The financial liabilities imposed upon practically every person connected with the creation and distribution of new issues

are proving to be serious obstacles in the way of important and necessary financing by reputable concerns," declared the Chamber of
Commerce after the 1933 act's passage.[24] As securities issuance fell
in the late summer and early autumn, compared with increases in
new securities creation in both Britain and Canada, critics were
quick to say that the new rules were killing finance.[25]

The financial and business community's reaction was natural.
Just a few years earlier, the idea of such permanent government
interference in their private spheres would have been unthinkable. Well into the thirties, New York Stock Exchange chief Richard
Whitney insisted that any regulation of a private club such as the
stock exchange amounted to the government's "taking over the
securities exchanges" and that it would be futile, anyway, since
nothing "will ever happen to prevent booms and panic."[26] Recalci-
trant financiers grumbled that market forces ably punished bum-
blers and that existing laws were enough to police the criminals
who harmed the financial markets and the economy. The crowded
criminal-court dockets sometimes seemed to make their point:
everyone, from Bank of United States executives to Insull to the
New York State banking regulator (for not foreseeing the Bank of
United States collapse), seemed to be on trial.

It took years for the White House to convince the business
and financial worlds that the new rules and regulations were permanent and wouldn't be quietly lifted once the crisis was over. It
also took years for investment houses and corporate issuers to
figure out how courts would interpret the new laws and for investors to figure out how to digest the reams of new information presented to them. Complaints about the fact-heavy annual reports
abounded. One *New York Times* reader complained: "There are
two ways of deceiving the public—one is to tell them too little and
the other is to tell them so much that they cannot separate the
wheat from the chaff. It strikes me that Mr. Roosevelt's Securities
Act, if it produces prospectuses like this, is going to be primarily
useful to the paper trade."[27]

But such adjustment was unavoidable after the financial
disaster that the nation had experienced. As Representative
Henry Steagall, chairman of the House Banking and Currency

Committee, said in 1933, "it has taken 50 years to develop the great financial system of the US, which is now prostrate and in ruins. We cannot rebuild it in a day or a week. We can only do it step by step."[28] Indeed, long after the Depression, Americans remained skeptical of finance and investment. The financial industry, so mighty in the twenties, shrank so that it once again became a tool of business, rather than the other way around. It was only in the eighties that finance would regain its twenties-era heights as a share of the American economy.[29]

Yet over time, the new laws and rules governing banking and markets succeeded. At their core were conservative principles. Bad banks could fail and bad ideas could die, allowing markets to discipline the financial world without unduly harming the economy. People and companies, armed with basic facts available to everyone, could take risks in pursuit of profit and would suffer losses if their expectations were wrong. Automatic financial stabilizers—like limits on borrowing to buy stock—helped check irrational exuberance.

Employing these elementary principles, FDR and Congress helped make it possible for free markets and vital speculation to reconstruct themselves from the rubble. American finance gained as a share of the global financial industry, as prudent regulations helped propel American capital markets to their position as the most trusted in the world. Depression-era regulations, because they encouraged free markets rather than smothered them, served the country well for more than half a century.

CHAPTER 3

TOO BIG TO FAIL

It is inconceivable that any major bank would walk away from any subsidiary of its holding company. If your name is on the door, all of your capital funds are going to be behind it in the real world. Lawyers can say you have separation, but the marketplace is persuasive, and it would not see it that way.
—Walter Wriston, Citicorp chief executive, October 29, 1981[1]

These big banks have the ultimate anticompetitive government subsidy. They are too big to fail, and regardless how mismanaged they may become, the buck will stop with the taxpayer.
—Kenneth A. Guenther, executive vice president, Independent Bankers Association of America, *New York Times*, August 5, 1987

INTERNATIONAL NEWSWIRES STARTED TO SPREAD THE rumors on the Tuesday before Mother's Day, 1984. *The nation's eighth-largest bank, Chicago-based Continental Illinois, was in distress. It was about to submit to a Japanese takeover. Its holding company was exploring bankruptcy.* By Thursday, Continental's stock price had collapsed. Depositors whose accounts exceeded the FDIC's $100,000 insurance ceiling withdrew their money, compelling usually discreet regulators to announce publicly that Continental would be able to meet its obligations. The depositors, along with other short-term lenders to the bank, ignored the statement.

The next weekend, the Federal Reserve arranged for sixteen of the nation's biggest banks to pump $4.5 billion into the faltering institution, hoping to restore confidence. The plan failed.

By late spring, the government took a step that business reporters and editorial boards billed as unprecedented. The Federal Reserve and the FDIC, in their "race to save Continental and thereby sustain confidence in the nation's banking system,"[2] pledged that no uninsured large depositor would lose money should the bank fail. And the government went even further: the other lenders to the bank, including bondholders, wouldn't lose a penny, either.

The government figured that this ratcheting up of support, along with the support that the Federal Reserve offered through its ability to lend to commercial banks, would calm the panic. A week later, though, the credit markets remained "paranoid," in one analyst's worlds. Rumors swirled that the rescued bank, trying to sell its bad loans, had received a sole bid of only 23 cents on the dollar.[3] Regulators started to worry that the nation's *fourth*-largest bank, Manufacturers Hanover, could suffer a similar confidence collapse. "People are scared of banks," said one dealer in bank certificates of deposit. Another two months of slow-motion turmoil ensued, as the half-alive Continental continued to lose billions of dollars in deposits and shed assets at fire-sale prices.[4]

As spring turned to summer, the government finally went all the way. To avoid "a major financial crisis,"[5] it nationalized the hobbled bank outright, with the FDIC taking 80 percent ownership as well as responsibility for bad loans in exchange for nonvoting shares. The adventure eventually cost the FDIC $1.6 billion before administrators returned Continental to the private sector seven years later. BankAmerica later bought what was left of the institution.[6]

The era of "too big to fail" thus began. Five decades after the FDIC helped to create a new foundation for free markets by allowing bad banks to fail, imposing necessary market discipline on the financial world without endangering the nation's core workings of money and credit, the government's extraordinary 1984 rescue of Continental Illinois initiated a reversal that would endanger this principle. Continental's failure also marked another aspect of regulatory breakdown: the economy's banking and credit infrastructure was making itself increasingly dependent upon the vicissitudes of short-term speculation.

Continental's meltdown should have been instructive. Continental was a financial innovator and, as it turned out, also the willing victim of a fellow financial pioneer, Oklahoma-based Penn Square, which failed two years before Continental did. (Penn's uninsured depositors and other lenders, including bondholders, took their losses.) Penn Square collapsed in large part because of an innovative business model that enabled it to indulge a "deal-making appetite [that] exceeded its capital capacity."[7] Penn Square held deposits of only $500 million, meaning that under the traditional banking model, it could make loans and investments of slightly less than $500 million after fulfilling regulatory requirements. But the bank decided that it wouldn't let its small deposit base constrain it.

Rather than earning long-term profits from long-term lending by keeping loans on its books for years, supported by its deposit base, Penn created short-term profits from long-term lending. The bank used its modest deposit base as a temporary way station for $2 billion in risky loans, mostly to the energy industry. It sold these loans off to other banks as it made them so that it could make still more loans, continuing to handle only the administrative tasks—collecting interest payments and forwarding them on to the new owners of the loans—for the old loans it sold. Penn based its model on volume, not on the good credit of borrowers. It had little incentive to investigate thoroughly its borrowers' creditworthiness as it rushed to make as many loans as possible—loans that immediately became somebody else's problem.

Penn collapsed when the oil industry foundered. It hadn't sold all its bad loans to other banks; neither would the financial firms underwriting and selling risky mortgages under a similar model two decades later. But before it fell, Penn infected other banks with its loan sales. The loans "weren't well secured, and they lacked good documentation, which is the detail on collateral and the reasons for approving the loans," said one news report—

an eerie prelude to what observers would say, two decades later, of the hundreds of billions of dollars in mortgage loans made and sold to outside investors.[8] Continental was one of Penn's best customers.

Continental might have survived; other banks had bad loans on their books back then, too. But Continental made an even more serious error in how it funded its investments. Banks, as seen in Chapter 1, borrow from depositors and then lend the money out; shareholders earn the difference between the profits a bank earns in its lending and the interest payments it pays on its borrowing, minus operating costs. Depositors in the modern age can be local residents who save a few thousand dollars for years, covered by the FDIC, or global corporations that park their money in a bank for just a few days and exceed the FDIC's insurance limits. Banks raise money from other lenders, too, including bondholders, whose investments don't enjoy any FDIC insurance. Bonds can range from debt that matures only after thirty years to "commercial paper" that matures every night.

But banks cannot fund all their investments with debt. Because of the important role that banking plays in the economy, regulations require that they set aside high-quality, non-borrowed "capital"—historically, 8 percent of their investments. A bank's capital serves as a cushion; if the value of the bank's investments falls, the capital absorbs losses and enables the firm to make its debt payments. Capital is not a fail-safe: severe losses can overwhelm capital, plunging the bank into insolvency.

Continental's big mistake was in the mix of borrowing it did to buy and hold its risky loans. It took in more money than most banks did from "volatile, uninsured commercial deposits from big companies and financial institutions."[9] Continental's reliance on these short-term "hot money" markets was fateful because the speculative loans that the company had bought from Penn Square should have made securing long-term funding an even more important goal.

By depending heavily on short-term, uninsured depositors as a key source of borrowing, Continental made itself particularly vulnerable to a drop in confidence that could leave the bank without money just when it needed it most. The bank's short-term lenders could pull their money out of the institution instantly if they perceived new risk. Without a constant flow of money coming in to fund its investments, Continental would have to sell those investments quickly, possibly at a steep loss.[10] A bank that depends more on longer-term bonds or on insured deposits, by contrast, has more room to earn its way out of a slump, because long-term bondholders can't demand immediate repayment, and insured depositors don't worry too much about what a bank does with their money. Continental relied on such short-term uninsured deposits anyway, because the growing demand for them on investors' part made this source of money cheap and easy.

Continental's short-term global depositors quickly showed that they wouldn't stick around to see the bank through any trouble. The depositors' panic caused problems not just for the bank but for the entire financial industry, because fear of Continental's books quickly became worldwide fear of *all* American banks' books. Many other banks, too, had started to rely on uninsured short-term deposits for their funding, though not to the same extent as Continental did. The danger was that global lenders would not differentiate among banks, pulling their money uniformly from the American banking system and roiling world markets as banks had to sell off their assets.

The actions that Washington took were a response to a new type of crisis that posed a new risk to the economy, which had for so long enjoyed consistent government protections against the old-fashioned variety of runs on the bank. As William Ogden, whom the government tapped to run Continental, said: "A modern run on a bank"—with the same cascading panic to other banks and the same ensuing economic damage that such runs caused five decades earlier—"doesn't show up in lines at the teller windows, but in an increasing erosion of its capacity to purchase large blocks of funds" in global markets.[11]

The Fed, the FDIC, and the Comptroller of the Currency, a major bank regulator, considered the risk of doing nothing to be too great. Federal Reserve chairman Paul Volcker said that the decision was necessary to avoid the risk that other banks wouldn't be able to fund their operations as their own uninsured depositors fled. C. Todd Conover, the comptroller, said that the government may have averted "a national, if not an international, financial crisis" that would have ensued if banks, with their own funders nursing both losses and fears, had fallen like dominoes and caused global credit to disappear.[12] The press agreed, running stories alerting readers to the "growing danger of what the failure of even a single huge international bank, and certainly of a few such banks at the same time, would mean for the stability of the domestic and international economy."[13]

The rescue startled the business world after a decade of deregulation throughout the economy. "The decision . . . appears to prove once again," after a government bailout of Chrysler five years earlier, "that Washington has accepted far-reaching responsibility not only for the success of the economy, but also for individual enterprises—if they are big enough."[14]

The break from normal practice that the bailout represented divided the Reagan administration. Donald Regan, the Treasury secretary, found the intervention troubling: "We believe it is bad public policy, would be seen to be unfair . . . , and represents an unauthorized and unlegislated expansion of federal guarantees in contravention of executive branch policy," he wrote to his colleagues.[15] But the White House, by offering its quiet support despite Regan's objections, agreed implicitly with the regulators' compelling argument that the only other choice was to "risk worldwide financial havoc."

As the *Wall Street Journal* reported at the time, "even within an administration committed to extricating government from the financial machinery, there wasn't much of a debate. . . . Contemplating the failure of a large, money-center bank is 'thinking the unthinkable,' says a White House official who staunchly supports free-market principles on most issues."[16] President Reagan himself said little about it, noting through a spokesperson that he did not consider it a bailout because "not one red cent's coming out of taxpayers' pockets," as the FDIC would use the fees that banks paid to it to fund the bailout.[17] Volcker told Congress that the decision was not a precedent. "We have a very strong safety net, a very strong apparatus . . . to deal with these problems when they unexpectedly occur," he said.[18]

But it quickly became clear that fifty years of policy was dead. Two months after the rescue, Conover told Congress that none of the nation's top eleven banks would be allowed to fail, "the first time a government official acknowledged that such a policy existed."[19] Executives at smaller banks were apoplectic, quickly recognizing the ramifications of what had happened. They understood that they would now have to compete with bigger banks that could find funding on easier terms, by virtue of the new, implicit government guarantee of their lenders. Jokes flourished about investors not wanting to put money into the nation's twelfth-largest bank—the first unprotected one on the list. "How often and to what extent can the government, and in turn the taxpayers, prop up institutions that are neither the nation's best or brightest? Does being too big to fail also imply being too big to be independent of the government? It's a sobering thought," the Independent Bankers Association commented.[20]

Whether regulators were correct in thinking that the financial system couldn't survive Continental's collapse is unknowable. We cannot know to what extent lenders would have pulled their money out of healthier banks in response to a shocking bank failure. In their actions, though, regulators and elected officials showed that they believed that the FDIC's system for winding down failed banks and enforcing lenders' losses had become inadequate for a new reality. In saving the financial world and the economy from Continental, government officials felt that they had no choice but to insulate Continental's lenders from market forces. In the absence of credible evidence to the contrary, financial firms would assume that the government would act similarly in the future.

After the immediate dangers abated, elected officials and regulators did not address this problem that they had created. Instead, they struggled halfheartedly and unsuccessfully to come up with a solution. In 1991, Congress prohibited the FDIC from protecting uninsured depositors if doing so would increase the insurer's losses. But an exemption allowed for cases of "systemic risk," and the government did little to undermine the notion that it would rescue the biggest banks in times of acute distress—and gave banks an incentive to become big enough to pose systemic risk. Throughout the savings-and-loan crisis of the late eighties and early nineties, Washington saved uninsured depositors and other lenders to big banks where it saw a risk to the broader system, while letting uninsured depositors and other lenders to smaller banks languish. In the summer of 1991, Fed chairman Alan Greenspan—just a few years removed from saying, as a private-sector economist, that he wasn't "a great fan of deposit insurance"[21]—informed lawmakers that "there may be some banks, at some particular times, whose collapse and liquidation would be excessively disruptive."[22]

The Continental bailout, along with the later savings-and-loan crisis, chastened the financial world—for a while. "Many banks [are] re-examining their risks with other banks" and reducing their own dependence on volatile short-term deposits, the *Wall Street Journal* reported.[23] But the long-term implications of the government's Continental guarantee eclipsed bankers' memory of the fears that they had suffered before the government had stepped in.

Gradually, lenders to the biggest banks understood that their money was not at risk. The banks thus won insulation from market discipline that only uninsured lenders could provide, making more harrowing tests of the government's nascent "too-big-to-fail" policy inevitable. Banks grew bigger—and further eroded regulators' ability to protect the economy from their mis-haps, eventually testing the Reagan administration's assertion that "not one red cent" would come from taxpayers as a result of the precedent that was set. As time passed, financial historian Ron Chernow wrote that "the government has had more than six years since [Continental] to reintroduce the concept of depositor risk in large institutions. . . . [N]ow . . . the regulators have become hostage to the system."[24]

Lawmakers and regulators had emerged with a belief that would define the next two and a half decades of finance. They felt confident in the government's ability to contain financial-industry crises. In 1991, after regulators successfully rescued the economy from the Bank of New England's meltdown, for example, they believed, and the media agreed, "that the modern-day bank run is containable. . . . The safety net of federal insurance and regulation does appear to hold."[25]

By the time Continental had made itself too big to fail, other banks were already following suit. They did so in part because of natural market forces, as they sought to compete in a changing world that no longer saw banks as a necessary haven from the more turbulent securities world. But because the government had stepped in to protect Continental Illinois, banks acted not only in response to market forces but also to take advantage of their new, implicit government support.

Encouraged by their own government and market forces, securities firms, walled off from banks thanks to the Glass-Steagall Act that Congress had implemented during the Depression, posed a new market challenge to the banks. As an alternative to bank savings accounts, securities firms began to offer higher-paying "money-market" accounts to small customers. Fund managers invested the customers' money in seemingly safe government bonds and high-quality, short-term corporate debt, including commercial paper issued by banks. Those money markets, just as with the uninsured bank deposits upon which Continental had relied, paid more in interest partly because the FDIC didn't guarantee them. Banks faced competition from securities firms on another front, as a rising stock market encouraged people to pull money out of banks and invest in mutual funds made up of individual stocks. The middle class had new investing options that it hadn't previously enjoyed.

To meet these competitive threats, banks kept growing. With 1982 legislation friendly to acquisitions, healthy banks often purchased distressed banks in the savings-and-loan crisis. They took advantage, similarly, of friendlier rules and regulatory decisions that governed interstate banking on both the federal and state levels, allowing them to enter into more mergers that crossed state borders. Size, scale, and the promise of bigger profits spurred banks to invest heavily in technology, ushering in the age of the ATM. Gone were the days when the bank closed at 3:00 and opened only for a half-day on Fridays.

As banks grew, they lobbied Congress and regulators to let them compete with the securities industry, which was already competing with them. In the early eighties, banks won the right to compete with money-market funds by paying depositors the going market rate of interest rather than paying government-decreed below-market rates that put them at a disadvantage against their less regulated counterparts.[26]

One young Democratic congressman, New York's Charles Schumer of the House Banking Committee, thought that the Continental bailout would put a stop to this expansionist trend. "If the government believes that some institutions are so important that it must step in to guarantee all deposits, is it wise for us to further destabilize the system by allowing banks to enter the securities, insurance, and real estate businesses?" Schumer asked. "Depositors would not pause to distinguish between parents and affiliates" if a securities affiliate of an insured bank suffered a crisis. "The larger the institution, the more threatening the risk of collapse, and the higher the cost of a federal bailout. Banks should continue to serve a distinctly different function . . . , offering the public a low-risk place to hold savings."[27] A year later, Schumer suggested increasing bank capital, arguing that "given the more hazardous atmosphere that financial institutions have been forced to operate in, and the greater risks they are taking, a higher level of capital is needed."[28]

But the trend of breaking down the Depression-era separation of the banking and securities businesses only accelerated; market forces and a new implicit government guarantee that amounted to a subsidy were more powerful than a few stray frets. In 1984, regulators gave Chemical Bank permission to underwrite corporate bonds—an activity prohibited fifty years earlier.[29] Three years later, executives from J. P. Morgan, Citicorp, and Bankers Trust petitioned the Fed to let the bank sell municipal bonds, commercial paper, and bonds backed by credit-card debt and mortgage debt, with Morgan head Dennis Weatherstone arguing that the banks were at a competitive disadvantage.

Fed chairman Paul Volcker expressed objections. At a hearing on the proposal, Volcker pointed out that the head of Citicorp's predecessor firm, National City, had written way back in 1934 that "I personally believe the bank should be free from any connections . . . which might be taken by the public to indicate a relation with any investment banking house." Said Volcker of the change of heart since then, Citicorp's attitude was " 'we don't have to worry a bit,' but I guess I worry a little bit." The Fed allowed the change; Volcker, soon to be replaced by Alan Greenspan, was one of two dissenters.[30] The Supreme Court later upheld the Fed's authority to make these allowances. Old-fashioned banks were well on their way to persuading the Fed to allow them to increase the profit limit that they could reap from the corporate underwriting of stocks, too, from 10 to 25 percent of their already-growing securities business.

By 1999, when Congress officially repealed much of the Glass-Steagall Act, the Depression-era regulations separating banking from securities had become largely a formality. They had become irrelevant by 1997, when Bankers Trust, a commercial bank, purchased brokerage house Alex Brown, "shattering the wall long dividing banks from brokers."[31] The differences between securities firms and commercial banks were becoming harder and harder to see.

By itself, the banks' embrace of the more volatile securities business, of which their executives had little institutional knowledge, would have added risk to their business models and to the taxpayers who implicitly backed the banks, even if everything else had stayed the same. The headline atop a 1984 *Wall Street Journal* analysis of the banks' forays into the securities business said it all: "Investment Banking Proves a Tough Field for Commercial Banks—They Lack Ties to Investors, Can't Hold Top Talent, but Have Size, Money."[32] Banks had shown, over and over again, that they were not always good judges of their own enterprises. In addition to Continental Illinois and big savings-and-loan failures, Citicorp, in 1992, had weakened itself so thoroughly with real-estate loans that its leaders felt forced to respond publicly to presidential candidate Ross Perot's assertion that it was insolvent.[33] Now they were entering a business in which small securities firms routinely took ill-judged paths and failed, declaring bankruptcy.

But everything else did not stay the same. Banks' new securities ventures changed the nature of risk within the securities industry itself. Big banks enjoyed a big, blunt advantage over old-fashioned securities firms. They could attract financing for a lower cost because of perceived lower risk, partly thanks to the government's implicit guarantee of their bondholders, uninsured depositors, and other lenders. Big banks, then, introduced implicitly government-subsidized competition into the volatile securities industry.

These developments occurred just as the securities business itself was becoming riskier. Seventies-era regulatory changes abolished the fixed commissions that customers paid to investment firms to buy and sell stock, cutting firms' profits. The popularity of cheaper mutual funds, too, cut these profits, because big mutual-fund managers had more power to negotiate commission prices that they paid to the securities firms for stock trades than did small customers. And as securities firms faced global competition, often from European and Asian financial giants that had their own forms of government support, the fees that the securities firms earned through activities like floating stock and bond issues for companies fell, too. One measure of securities firms' performance—companies' return on equity and thus their returns to shareholders—declined steadily over the decade or so starting in 1980, from 50 percent to 20 percent.[34]

Wall Street found it more difficult to earn profits through offering advice, through sales, and through underwriting—activities that didn't require securities firms to take too much risk. To make up for this profit erosion, firms increasingly exposed their own capital to risk to earn new profits, rather than offering advice and services to others. Firms used shareholder money, enhanced by short-term, borrowed funds, to make multibillion-dollar bets on their own accounts on seemingly everything: the direction of interest rates in Malaysia, the price of electric power in California, the value of banks in China. Each firm struggled to distinguish itself from its rivals by offering customized products, creating ever more exotic financial instruments that fluctuated, sometimes wildly, depending on a wide range of factors from interest rates to the credit quality of corporations. Such creative innovations often helped business and the economy, but they introduced new volatility and vulnerability, too.

In raising money for such activities, securities firms didn't enjoy an implicit government guarantee of their funding, as the banks did. Alan Greenspan made this distinction clear, telling Congress in 1990 that "the authorities would almost certainly refuse to rescue even the largest securities firms from the brink of collapse" because, the chairman said, "it's not good for discipline."[35] That year, Drexel Burnham Lambert, a prominent securities firm, declared bankruptcy under the usual corporate process after its short-term lenders pulled their funds. But after the Federal Reserve brought interest rates under control in the early eighties, and with the dollar serving as the expanding global economy's currency of choice, it wasn't hard for Wall Street to attract the world's capital to fund its risks.

To raise money to compete with government-supported banks more easily, securities firms injected another risk into the financial system. Many became publicly traded firms rather than private partnerships, with Dean Witter issuing stock in 1972, Morgan Stanley following suit in 1986, and Goldman Sachs converting in 1999.

This change in firm structure changed traders and investment bankers' incentives. Wall Streeters, like everyone else, will take more risks with someone else's money than with their own. Back when investment banks were private partnerships, each partner's capital was permanently at risk; moreover, each partner often had unlimited liability even beyond what he owned for any losses that ensued from reckless bets. Partners, then, policed one another, with older partners counseling younger ones against flirting with dangerous open-ended losses.

When investment firms became publicly traded firms, the former partners—now "managing directors"—no longer had open-ended liability; shareholders, not partners, took losses. Instead, managing directors earned annual bonuses based on each year's profitability—and once a director had earned his bonus, it was his, even if the activity behind the bonus caused huge losses the *next* year. Now employees bet someone else's money for individual gain and suffered little downside if those bets didn't pan out, rather than risk their own money and their colleagues' and run the real risk of debilitating personal losses.

As securities firms took bigger risks, the government-guaranteed banks matched them and raised them, using their cheaper money to compete in the same activities. Each side's risk-taking spurred the other side's activities. As early as 1993, the nation's six biggest commercial banks, employing "vast trading desks . . . of computer screens," earned more than 40 percent of their profits from trading, "the most profitable business banks have," the *New York Times* reported.[36] "Investors may wonder whether the banks simply had a good day at the track," the *Wall Street Journal* observed.[37]

The risks of the changing financial model quickly became apparent. In 1994, Bankers Trust and Citicorp each lost $150 million trading for their own accounts, while Standard and Poor's, the bond-rating agency, warned the same year that J. P. Morgan could lose its AAA rating because of such trading, adding that the firm's mathematical models could underestimate exposure to losses.[38] Stockholders perceived the higher peril because they, unlike the firms' lenders, couldn't count on a Continental-style bailout in a crisis. So they demanded that banks generate even higher returns with the lenders' cheap money, spurring the banks to make even more aggressive trades and deals.

Wise hands warned of impending trouble. Citicorp chief executive Walter Wriston noted in 1981, at the beginning of this era, that investors wouldn't distinguish between a bank and the bank's securities affiliate in a crisis, potentially putting FDIC money (and taxpayer money to back up the FDIC if necessary) behind securities ventures. Wriston was no foe of financial deregulation, but he was clear-eyed and honest about the challenge it posed. Henry Kaufman, managing director of Salomon Brothers and a prominent economic and market researcher, warned in the mid-eighties that short-term trading by financial institutions that relied on short-term financing "undermines the system." He soon resigned his management position in protest.[39] Later, he worried that too-big-to-fail banks could "confer too much power on a corporate and financial elite, with close ties to the government," as the *New York Times* described his words.[40]

When they did worry, government officials were more concerned about the here and now, including the threat to American finance posed by global competition. Charles Schumer, who had warned so eloquently of the risk of speculative banks in the eighties, became one of the biggest champions of financial deregulation a decade later. Schumer, now a senator, said of the repeal of Depression-era regulations: "If we don't pass this bill, we could find London or Frankfurt or . . . Shanghai becoming the financial capital of the world."[41] This threat was real, as financial institutions such as Germany's WestLB and Switzerland's UBS came to New York to compete with American finance on its own turf.

Another force was at work, too. The financial industry, which found itself prostrate for so long after the Depression, started to regain its power relative to the rest of the economy. Between the early 1980s and the early 1990s, the financial sector's pretax profits as a percentage of the nation's income more than doubled,[42] while the share of corporate financial services, as a percentage of gross domestic product, rose 30 percent.[43] These changes reflected much more than government support: financial innovation made American capital markets preeminent in an industrializing world that had more wealth to invest.

Bigger banks making bigger profits had more clout in Washington, making it more politically difficult and personally disadvantageous for the few clear-eyed regulators and elected officials to challenge them. Continental Illinois' meltdown provided a window into this problem. When congressional investigators asked regulators why they hadn't reined in the bank's obvious risk-taking, Federal Reserve Board governor Charles Partee answered forthrightly: "To impose prudential restraints is meddlesome and it restricts profits. If the banking system is expanding rapidly, if they can show they're making good money by the new business, for us to try to be too tough with them . . . is just not going to be acceptable."[44]

The financial world's newfound power in the nation's capital wasn't just about money, though the lobbying cash and campaign contributions helped. Its appeal was psychological and cultural. High-flying East Coast financial firms seemed glamorous. Movies like *Wall Street* and *Working Girl* showed a new generation that finance was cool. In 1989, Michael Lewis published his exposé of modern Wall Street's excesses, *Liar's Poker*, meaning it as a cautionary morality tale—but he found, he later said, that college students used it as a "how-to manual."[45] Nobody wanted to be the fuddy-duddy at the party, stuck in the past while everyone else moved ahead.

CHAPTER 4

HOLLOWED OUT

Securities are liquid and tradable, while most loans are not.... [U]p to now, credit securitization has been done largely with loans with little risk, such as government-guaranteed residential mortgages.... But it's quite possible that within a decade, most all borrowing will be done in a securitized form.
—*Wall Street Journal*, October 20, 1986[1]

For many, [mortgage securities] have been the worst of both worlds.
—*Wall Street Journal*, October 3, 1994[2]

HEADLINES FROM SUMMER 1986 WOULD SEEM familiar to readers who have followed the financial crisis more than two decades later. "Panicked selling" overwhelmed Wall Street. The trading strategies that financial institutions had employed to "protect their huge holdings of mortgage-backed securities plunged them deeper into the red rather than keeping them afloat," the *New York Times* reported. The securities, held by pension funds and other big investors, weren't behaving the way the investors expected. Venerable firms like Goldman Sachs were "believed to have lost hundreds of millions of dollars," as investors sold their holdings "as fast as they could, often back to the Wall Street firms they had been bought from." One trader lamented that "you take your worst-case scenario, and it came true." "It was devastating for some people," said Robert Andres, head of Merrill Lynch's mortgage business. Lewis Ranieri, who had helped create the concept of mortgage-backed debt securities at the Salomon Brothers bond house, said that "we learned a very expensive lesson: that we're not as smart as we thought we were."[3]

Starting in the eighties, even as market and government forces transformed the financial industry's structure, the same forces transformed one of the industry's main businesses: credit creation. Credit gradually escaped the regulatory constraints that protected the economy from uncontrolled debt growth or contraction. It could do so because financiers increasingly turned all long-term debt into tradeable securities, often as fodder for short-term bets. The government encouraged this practice, believing that it reduced risk to banks and to the economy, though it did the opposite.

This great innovation in "securitization"—the packaging of long-term loans and other streams of future cash flows into securities—began with home mortgages. A crude form of securitizing mortgages had been around since the seventies, when financiers devised it to make money helping the government advance its social goal of encouraging homeownership.

Since the Great Depression, the government had supported a financial conveyor belt of sorts that increased the capital available for Americans to buy homes. Commercial bankers and other lenders made mortgages to homeowners, but instead of keeping the mortgages on their books, they sold them off to the now-infamous Fannie Mae and Freddie Mac, giving the banks more funds with which to make more mortgages. Fannie and Freddie were private-sector companies with their own shareholders, but their predecessor firm, the Federal National Mortgage Association, created by FDR, was a government agency with the express goal of supporting homeownership.

In the first securitizations, Fannie and Freddie retained investment bankers to sell some of the mortgage debt they had bought from the banks. The investors who purchased the debt received a guarantee that Fannie or Freddie would reimburse them if any

of the underlying mortgages defaulted. Because Fannie's predecessor firm was a government entity, the markets assumed continued government support behind the companies' mortgage
guarantees, and buyers believed that investing in debt backed by
Fannie or Freddie was similar to investing in government Treasury bonds.

The new system became an efficient conduit, with commercial bankers and other lenders making mortgages to homeowners,
and investment bankers taking those mortgages, bundling them
together, and then selling the securities. To sell the Fannie- and
Freddie-guaranteed mortgages to investors, financiers would take
a few thousand mortgages and put them into a trust. The trust, in
turn, received all the principal and interest payments from homeowners. It sold debt securities to investors and, as it received
the payments from homeowners, passed those payments on to
the securities holders. In this way, the financiers achieved economies of scale that would not have been possible if they had had to
match each individual mortgage with an individual lender.

But until the early eighties, it was difficult to market these
mortgage securities to investors. As financial historian Charles
Morris has written, the instruments fell into an awkward "middle"
netherworld of risk that "never completely delighted" potential
buyers. They paid a bit more in interest than Treasury bonds
because they didn't carry an explicit government guarantee, but
they still paid too little to "stir the pulses" of investors who wanted
higher returns.[4]

In the eighties, bond-securities firms worked with Fannie and
Freddie to address this problem. The bond firms, notably Salomon
Brothers and First Boston, took a novel approach using financial
engineering to make some of the mortgage-backed securities
riskier, so that they paid a higher interest rate to attract aggressive investors, and some of the securities less risky, in return for
a lower interest rate to attract investors who wanted safety. In
the original mortgage securities, by contrast, all investors shared
equally in the possibility that something would go wrong with
the underlying loans that made up each mortgage-securities pool,
and all investors had consequently earned the same interest rate.

The chief risk that the Wall Street wizards tinkered with wasn't that mortgage borrowers would default. It was hard to see how mortgage securities could pose any such credit peril to their investors. In addition to the Fannie or Freddie guarantee, home buyers generally put down 20 percent of a house's value in cash, in accordance with strict rules followed by the two agencies as well as conservative regulatory practices governing bank lending. Through this down-payment requirement, Fannie and Freddie reduced their own risk in two ways. First, a homeowner who put down several thousand dollars in cash was likely to do everything possible to keep paying his mortgage, even in stressful times. Second, if a homeowner couldn't pay his mortgage, the guarantors had a big cushion that allowed them to sell the house without losing any money, since they had lent a maximum of 80 percent against the value of the house, allowing the house to decline in value by 20 percent at resale before they would suffer losses.

Investors worried much more about the risk of "prepayment." If interest rates fell suddenly, homeowners would scramble to refinance their mortgages, getting new loans at the lower interest rate and paying back the old ones. Mortgage-securities investors would find their money repaid *too* quickly. They'd be stuck with cash at a time when lower interest rates gave them few opportunities to invest at the rate they had expected to earn over a particular time period. Investors also ran the risk of interest rates rising too rapidly, in which case nobody would refinance their mortgages, and the investors would have no cash available to take advantage of the many better investment opportunities elsewhere.

Interest rates had to remain within a limited range, then, for the securities to become popular. In the second generation of mortgage securities, in the early eighties, the bond houses figured out a way to accomplish this task by structuring some of the securities to insulate them from what happened with interest rates in the real world. They stopped slicing the combined mortgage pools into identical pieces so that all investors shared equal risk, and started slicing and dicing different "tranches"—French for "slices"—out of each combined mortgage pool. Henceforth, some investors would take slices with bigger prepayment risk and others would take slices with a smaller chance of prepayment, as calculated by formulas that took into account past interest-rate and consumer behavior as well as mathematical predictions of future such trends.

The financial engineers did not erase any uncertainty surrounding interest rates in the mortgage pool; people would still refinance their mortgages and pay their old debt back too quickly if interest rates fell, and do the opposite if the rates rose. Instead, financiers rearranged the pools so that investors could buy slices that satisfied their different appetites for uncertainty. Investors who bought the riskier slices took most of the prepayment risk in the pool in exchange for a higher return. That is, if interest rates fell and everyone rushed to refinance his mortgage, the investors who bought these tranches got their money back first, as they had agreed. They would be stuck with their money back at a time when it was harder to find attractive investments. Because these investors agreed to shoulder the disproportionate risk of being repaid too quickly, other investors in the same mortgage pool didn't have to shoulder that risk. These more conservative investors, protected from prepayments because their slice of risk was now lower, earned a lower return.

Salomon and other firms found buyers aplenty for the new securities. Between 1983 and 1986, outstanding mortgage-backed securities doubled to $600 billion. Moreover, financial wizardry created more than one market. Mom-and-pop investors liked the safer tranches, which provided a comfortably modest return from the underlying mortgages over the long term without the worries of prepayment or default. But Wall Street traders liked the riskier securities. Because the securities' value depended on interest rates, traders could buy and sell them on a short-term basis to bet on the direction of interest rates for day-to-day profits, rather than holding them over a period of years for the regular payments.

In 1986, though, the models designed to engineer the prepayment risk proved flawed. In response to an unexpected decline in interest rates, people rushed to refinance their mortgages, accelerating prepayments faster than Wall Street expected. A mini-panic ensued. Though it quickly calmed down, market participants, it seemed, had learned their lesson: the securities were sensitive to extreme volatility in difficult market conditions—just when investors needed them to work as advertised. Said Merrill Lynch bond chief Andres: "This will probably make people more disciplined and more reflective." Salomon's Ranieri concurred. "People realize after this that securitization is not a panacea," he said. "We'll be more careful."[5]

Some observers weren't so sure, though. "[B]uyers of securitized instruments are . . . other [financial] institutions," the *Wall Street Journal* noted in September 1986. "Should any of the instruments turn sour, the problems of these institutional holders could affect their ability to meet commitments to other institutions, setting off a chain reaction of problems." SEC chairman John Shad told the paper that while securitization had "enormous benefits, . . . there's a lot of risk in people not understanding what they're investing in."[6]

Indeed, a few months' turmoil faded from memory against the glow of tremendous profits. In 1994, when the mortgage-securities market had grown to nearly $1 trillion, events showed that nobody had learned the lesson of eight years earlier. That year, the Federal Reserve raised interest rates—for the first time in five years—and the prepayment assumptions proved wrong, just as they had before. This time, however, the blowup was deeper and wider. "The bloodbath in mortgage derivatives is claiming new casualties as investors and dealers continue to rush for the exits, feeding a vicious cycle of falling prices and evaporating demand," the *Journal* reported in April. One hedge fund couldn't find a single buyer willing to put a price on its securities, so panicked investors didn't know the extent of the losses.[7] "Several mutual funds . . . hold so many hard-to-value [mortgage securities] that their pricing service has found it difficult to value these portfolios."

Another hedge fund, Askin, went bankrupt, and its losses spread fear through financial markets. Askin's liquidation led to losses "for several big firms that lent money to the funds, including Lehman Brothers Inc. and Bear Stearns Co."[8] It was five months before the press reported a glimmer of hope. In October, prices finally found their floor. "But buyers still are skittish, and it's easy to see why," the *Journal* reported.[9]

The market managed to right itself for reasons that are crucial to understand. Bankers and traders had taken specific actions that protected the market, actions that they would neglect to take years later, precipitating the current credit crisis. First, financiers back then had built in some room for error in structuring the securities, so that the investors who had bought the tranches that contained the lesser amount of risk enjoyed ample protection; the securities wavered, but they held. By contrast, Askin went bankrupt because it had freely loaded up on the riskier securities. Most investors who used the securities to speculate on interest rates gave themselves room for error, too. Though they borrowed, they didn't borrow excessively and thus leave unpaid debt between every exploded assumption. Askin did borrow excessively and wound up bankrupt. Fund manager David Askin, in hindsight, thought his fund had borrowed too much. "If I had to do it all over again, I would have used less leverage," he said.[10] But Askin's debt level—for every $1 of its own actual cash, $2.50 borrowed—would seem laughably modest for the big banks that themselves were starting to make similar trades.

Second, where financiers had experimented, they had continued to do so largely with the interest-rate risk and prepayment risk of the mortgages, not the credit risk, or the risk that borrowers wouldn't repay the loans. This distinction is important because it meant that financial miscalculations largely stayed within the financial world. The bankers, for example, had not approved mortgages for people who couldn't afford them, as they would a decade later under an illusion that they could engineer away such risk for many investors through their financial structures. Buyers of the safer mortgage securities in 1994 weren't worried that bankers had disastrously miscalculated the risk that people could make good on the loans. So credit remained available, even as the financial world worried about how better to structure that credit into more robust securities.

Policymakers and regulators should have learned a lesson from both 1986 and 1994. While the system ultimately held together in each case, Wall Street's use of the securities had done unexpected damage and roiled the markets to an extent that showed that the models were more fragile and vulnerable to unexpected forces than their creators had thought. Moreover, the short-term lenders who provided firms with the money to speculate on the models were fickle and acutely sensitive to any perceived change in risk. Askin's short-term lenders gave the fund no time to recoup its losses, for example. Askin and a few funds like it had to dump their securities to pay back demanding lenders; the sales forced further price declines and sparked further sales. What would happen to the investment banks and commercial banks that increasingly traded in the same complex securities if, someday, a similar cycle—falling prices begetting forced sales begetting falling prices—wouldn't stop itself? Could banks be sure that their uninsured depositors and other short-term lenders wouldn't flee, too, as Continental's had, drying up credit in general?

Even as the innovative structures designed to limit mortgage-backed securities' interest-rate risk proved brittle in a crisis, financiers began using similar innovations to experiment with credit risk, too. Here, markets provided a lesson that policymakers and regulators ignored: systemic experiments with credit could cause big short-term swings in credit availability, which, in turn, could affect the economy.

Prior to the eighties, corporate borrowing was difficult and expensive for all but blue-chip companies. Then, Michael Milken, a bond trader for the Drexel Burnham Lambert investment house, created from scratch a market that spun risky loans made to risky borrowers into familiar securities that Wall Street bought and sold. His new "junk bonds" brought an epiphany to Wall Street: Milken explained that the higher interest rates that less worthy companies would pay their lenders "more than compensated for their original risk," as the *Wall Street Journal* put it.[11] Milken learned this lesson from Princeton professor W. Braddock Hickman, who found in the 1950s that "a low-grade bond portfolio, if very large, well diversified and held over a long period of time, was a higher-yielding investment than a high-grade portfolio," even after accounting for defaults.[12]

Milken's innovation transformed markets and the economy itself. Junk bonds provided the money that fueled the corporate raiders who purchased controlling stakes in companies, shaking up many sclerotic management teams and boards of directors and helping spark the restructuring that corporate America badly needed in that era of fierce foreign competition. Junk bonds also gave visionary entrepreneurs, such as CNN founder Ted Turner, much-needed cash. Idea merchants now had a new, direct source of funding from investors who were comfortable with the higher risk of each investment, freeing them from dependence on banks, whose sometimes unimaginative executives often valued connections over merits.

But this useful innovation lacked necessary regulatory checks, and junk bonds eventually became a self-perpetuating speculative mania. As investors reaped huge profits from easy takeovers, lenders saw less risk, so they lowered their required return demands. Easy money pushed stock values up as well as bond values, not because the stocks were intrinsically worthier, but because everyone hoped to benefit from the next takeover of a publicly traded company. In 1985, investment sage Felix Rohatyn, who had become famous a decade earlier for helping to bail out debt-ridden New York City, fretted that a booming market fueled by debt obscured the risks of the debt. "There'd be no junk bonds . . . if institutions weren't often willing to ignore substandard credit ratings in exchange for higher yields" without asking "why they were getting higher yields . . . if [junk bonds] were really as safe as Treasury bills," Rohatyn warned.[13] In other words, investors took on risk that they didn't understand.

Regulators acted. In December 1985, Federal Reserve chairman Paul Volcker applied tried-and-true Depression-era rules to the evolving marketplace. The Fed voted, 3–2, to apply 1934 margin requirements—which restricted borrowing for securities purchases—to the hostile-takeover market. Henceforth, companies created to execute corporate takeovers could borrow only half the money that they would need to buy the targeted company's stock. The Fed reasoned that just as brokers had limits on how much they could lend for stocks, junk-bond investors must have limits, too.[14] Volcker's move ignited a firestorm. Reagan administration officials and the president himself opposed the measure, and the financial industry reacted with outrage.

The Fed's sensible action showed leadership, however—and showed, too, how regulatory discretion can interact with hard-and-fast rules in a way that benefits the economy and the broader society. The laws and principles to check credit-fueled specula-tion in the stock market already existed. Someone had only to rec-ognize the need to apply them to a new form of speculation. If Volcker had not acted, this speculation could have done intense damage to the economy before it burned itself out.

Nevertheless, when the junk-bond market did crash in 1990, the collapse offered important lessons. First, market participants found it impossible to value the bonds in a plummeting market, contradicting one of the bonds' selling points: instant valuation. During the bust, investors trying to learn what their junk-bond investments were worth found that the price quotations they read in the papers "aren't wholly reliable." The depth and breadth of the market, controlled by a few investment firms, had been an illusion. Mass sales induced by worry over prices depressed prices further. "It's a death spiral," one research analyst told the *Journal*.[15] Milken's own firm, on its way to bankruptcy, "ended up keeping many junk bonds it had wanted to sell" for a lack of buyers, even after bundling the bonds into securities to make them more marketable.[16]

Second, investors who purchased junk bonds for short-term trading purposes weren't interested in waiting around to find out if Professor Hickman's key finding—that low-grade securities performed well over time—was true. "I don't care if a bond is in default or not," one trader said. "I care about how it is trading."[17]

The third lesson was that cheap debt created in order to feed a trading business could vaporize just as suddenly as it had appeared. Companies that borrowed heavily in a time of easy money had a hard time meeting their obligations when they found the credit tap turned off. "The debt crisis at many companies is the impending bill for junk-bond financing in the mid-to-late 1980s that carried deferred or low-interest payments," the *Journal* noted,[18] with "the big debts . . . narrow[ing] managers' margin for error."[19] Said Craig McCaw of McCaw Cellular Communications, which had relied on the market: "Two years ago, you had all these different sources of funds. If you take out a huge part [of the credit supply] and you cripple the rest of the lenders, it's not good for the country."[20] Speculation born of financial innovation, in this case, had an impact on the real economy.

But after Volcker's 1987 departure, the government failed to grasp that as financiers changed the business of credit, regulations were becoming inadequate to protect the economy from excessive credit speculation. Instead, Washington and New York focused on something sexier: bad behavior. Milken became famous across America not because of the implications of his financial ideas but because the government charged him with lurid crimes, from insider trading to mail fraud. He eventually pleaded guilty to some charges.

Securities markets need criminal sanction for lawbreakers, but the government missed the real story. As interest-rate observer James Grant wrote, Milken's innocence or guilt was beside the point when it came to protecting the economy from systemic risk. The real problem was "the relaxation of lending standards in almost every corner of the American economy." Grant continued:

> *Just as the corporate bond market has been opened to speculative-grade corporations, so has the . . . mortgage market to the speculative-grade home buyer. No less important than the growth in the volume of debt over the past several years has been the steady decline in its quality. . . . Mr. Milken was a pioneer of this movement, and his success is emblematic. He began his career in the early 1970s as a generation of Depression-burned leaders ended theirs. . . . Just as it enhanced Mr. Milken's investment results, so did [debt] expand gross national product. Climbing up on the ladder of debt, people*

bought more cars and more securities than they could have afforded. . . . [W]ith the indictment of Mr. Milken and the non-indictment of so many loss-making lenders, we have created a costly irony. . . . We will not have another Great Depression . . . but we will have something.[21]

Even as junk bonds proved that credit experimentation in the securities world could deeply affect the real economy for good and for ill, financiers realized that they could use their mortgage-tranching model to experiment with credit risk, too. They found that through the slicing and dicing of the risk behind debt, they could transform long-term loans into tradeable securities well beyond home lending, finding investors who wanted to take more risk and investors who wanted to take less on a particular pool of loans.

Financiers tweaked the securitization model using what they had learned in distributing prepayment risk to different investors. On a pool of loans, the bankers created a tranche of securities whose investors (in return for a higher interest rate) agreed to take all the risk if losses on all of the loans stayed below, say, 20 percent. The risk that these investors assumed meant that other investors, who bought the safer, or "senior," tranches, would be protected unless the magnitude of defaults in the entire loan pool exceeded that level. Some investors were so protected that their tranche was rated AAA—as safe as a U.S. Treasury bond, even without a Fannie or Freddie guarantee.

The ratings agencies Fitch, Moody's, and Standard & Poor's, which worked with financiers to help design the tranches, used a concept called a "loss-coverage ratio" to explain to potential buyers of the AAA-rated tranches how well protected these investors would be. The higher the loss-coverage ratio, the safer the securities. Consider a scenario in which analysts at the ratings agencies expected a pool of loans to suffer losses of 10 percent. Under the contract that governed the slicing of the pool into different tranches of securities that would take different risks, investors in the AAA-rated tranche would suffer only if losses in the *entire* pool reached 30 percent. Purchasers of the AAA-rated tranche thus enjoyed a very comfortable loss-coverage ratio of three—thirty divided by ten. But if the outlook for the loan pool changed suddenly, and expected losses rose to 15 percent, the loss-coverage ratio for the AAA-rated securities would decline to just two—thirty divided by fifteen.

This change in expectations would make a big difference because a ratio of two would not be enough to retain the sterling AAA rating.[22] Over the years, though, financiers became comfortable with years of data showing predictable losses for all kinds of loans, so they worried less that actual losses would vary much from their estimates. Financiers eventually could create a "safe" AAA tranche out of any pool of loans, no matter how risky, as long as the bankers could find investors for the lower-rated tranches willing to shoulder the burden of expected losses.

At first, this model had limited relevance for mortgage securities because of their negligible credit peril. But it was useful for another form of home-loan debt that became popular in the nineties: home-equity loans, which allowed homeowners to withdraw money that they had already invested in their homes so that they could spend it. Before securitization seemed to reduce the risk, the financial world considered such loans dangerous because people traditionally would not pull money out of their homes unless they were truly desperate.

By the late eighties, this market remained tiny, with only $28 billion in asset-backed debt not related to mortgages outstanding. But it was growing.[23] The new model was useful in increasing the size of the market for everything from credit-card loans and auto loans to commercial real-estate mortgages. The sterling ratings on the top tranche of the securities was the key to unlocking a whole new class of buyers—institutions such as pension funds, money-market funds, and European and Asian banks that operated under regulatory mandates as well as their own internal rules permitting them to purchase only the highest-rated investments. With these big buyers jumping into the market, consumer borrowing costs shrank.

Wall Street firms kept some of the securities for themselves, too—often the lower-rated tranches. In 1986, the *Wall Street*

Journal noted that investment banks, in purchasing such instruments for trading purposes, "are assuming direct credit risks just as banks do."[24] It seemed irrelevant at the time—but it meant that people's ability to get a mortgage or a credit card depended increasingly on a Wall Street firm's appetite for risky short-term trading rather than on a commercial bank's ability to make a long-term loan on its own books.

The financial world and its regulators saw safety in securitization, especially for the commercial banks that increasingly embraced the practice. Executives and regulators alike assumed that by turning loans into securities and selling them, banks would no longer be stuck with loans gone bad, which prohibited them from making new loans in past recessions. In the early nineties, in fact, the government encouraged struggling S&Ls to securitize their loans and sell them off. It even issued its own securitized loans, made up of commercial real-estate debt, to sell off some of the bad loans that it owned after so many banks had failed. Often, the government agreed to shoulder the biggest risk of future defaults.[25]

Moreover, securitization seemed like a remedy for banks' increasing reliance on hot money—that short-term financing through uninsured deposits and, increasingly, through the global money markets. This dependence had persisted despite Continental Illinois' 1984 downfall. Since banks' funding sources were now often short-term and liquid, it made sense that the loans the banks made should be liquid and tradeable, too, even though the securities themselves were still long-term debt. Banks could "cut funding needs by packaging loans and selling them to institutional investors," the *Journal* noted.[26] By making tradeable securities out of long-term loans like mortgages and car debt and selling those securities to outside investors, banks freed themselves from the worry that they'd be stuck holding a long-term loan when funding dried up.

Commercial banks adopted securitization as their new business model. Just as Penn Square had done, but on a much greater scale, they sold securitized loans to outside investors for a fee,

rather than booking slow profits from mortgages they held on
their own books for years. Banks' "margins on [consumer] loans
were razor-thin," until they found that almost any loan, whether
a thirty-year mortgage or a credit-card bill, "could be packaged
as securities and resold to big institutional investors," the *Times*
reported in 1990.[27]

Through securitization, banks could make more loans while
holding less capital on their own books to absorb any losses. Capital can be expensive to banks, which must compensate the investors who provide it for the higher risk they take. To avoid having
to hold more capital as they created more loans, some commercial banks, notably Citicorp, created their own outside investment
funds through which big investors, such as pension funds, insurance companies, and money-market funds, could buy securitized
debt—"structured investment vehicles" and other "off-balance-
sheet vehicles." Because the banks did not officially guarantee
the special funding vehicles off their books, they did not have to
put their own capital behind them—freeing up that capital for yet
more loans. Investment banks, too, could do this job just as well
as commercial banks could, with firms like Morgan Stanley purchasing loans from mortgage brokers to securitize and sell off.

Some financiers worried about securitization's unbridled
growth. In 1985, a Morgan Stanley executive, John Zacamy, cautioned that "there is not a lot of history to how these instruments
perform in different types of markets."[28] Others worried about
financial firms' liability, both legal and reputation-wise, if something did go wrong with the securities. For instance, big firms
such as Citicorp increasingly used securitization to find buyers
for their customers' credit-card debt. A few observers raised the
concern that if too many credit-card borrowers defaulted on the
securities in a credit-card trust, the investors in the securities
might expect the original card issuer, the bank, to make up for the
losses, even though, legally, the card issuer would have no such
obligation. Such an expectation could encourage complacency
on the part of investors, who might not consider the underlying
risk of the securities but instead look to the safety of the bank's
name.[29]

Just as with Penn Square, volume, rather than the underlying credit quality of borrowers, generated the profits in this business. Financiers lost sight of the fact that they hadn't erased risk but only rearranged it. No matter how bad the credit risk, financial innovation could engineer it by identifying it and transferring it to the investor explicitly willing to shoulder it in return for the higher interest rate. In 1996, a Long Island shopping-center developer who couldn't get bank financing because local banks were reluctant to lend in an uncertain business climate turned to securitization instead, telling the *New York Times* that "Wall Street has replaced the banks."[30] The developer was imprecise. In fact, the commercial banks and investment banks had together become middlemen for outside investors, replacing the commercial banks that had once been long-term lenders and thus would have been more skeptical of speculative projects.

In the mid-nineties, investors, through their purchases of the securities that the investment banks and commercial banks devised, started funding mortgages to home borrowers with poor credit histories, without the income needed to support required mortgage payments, or with historically small down payments. The firms simply levied a higher interest rate to offset the higher theoretical risk, and then passed those profits on to the investors in the riskier tranches, confident that they had structured the danger away for investors in the higher-rated securities.

Investors were so confident in Wall Street's risk modeling that they put money in such securities even when some of them represented loans that didn't carry the usual guarantee from Fannie or Freddie. In fact, the originators of such mortgages used the Fannie and Freddie computer systems expressly to identify borrowers who *didn't* qualify for such guarantees, paying a fee to the agencies for the privilege. As Jonathan Hornblass, editor of the *Home Equity News* trade publication, told the *New York Times* in 1997: "The growth of the securitization market has meant that lenders sell their loans, in essence, to investors, and get funding at a cheaper rate. . . . In the past, if a loan was rejected by Fannie Mae or Freddie Mac, that was it." This eventually infamous business— "subprime" lending to sketchy borrowers—quintupled between

1992 and 1996, to $37 billion as a share of the mortgage-backed securities market, well before Fannie and Freddie themselves invested heavily in this arena beginning in the mid-nineties.[31]

Banks often did keep securitized debt on their own books. They sometimes could do so with less capital behind each dollar loaned when compared with their traditional lending, largely because of an idea that made its way into financial regulations starting in the eighties. This concept emerged in the decade-long negotiations that led to the worldwide financial agreement called the Basel Capital Accord (referred to as "Basel"), enacted in 1988 and named for the city in Switzerland where the negotiations were decided. The world's central bankers convened in Basel because they were worried that without global coordination of regulation, bigger, more sophisticated, financial firms posed a new risk to the world's economies; they also worried that some countries, such as Japan, required too little capital from their international banks, lowering global standards. Basel is not global regulation; rather, national regulators enforce its principles.

Basel negotiators worked at first under a broad principle that because some investments were obviously less risky than others, they required smaller capital reserves behind them. Banks did not have to hold any capital against government securities, for example. At first, Basel considered a requirement that banks hold a full 8 percent capital behind all consumer loans, including mortgages, reflecting their risk. West Germany, though, lobbied to cut the capital requirement for mortgages in half to encourage investment in homes. Unsuccessfully, the Federal Reserve argued that "requiring lower capital levels for mortgages would create an artificial incentive for banks to enter more mortgage lending."[32]

As Basel evolved over the years, it both reflected and encouraged an increasingly more sophisticated philosophy, embraced by American regulators, that the financial world could competently and constantly assess its own risk. Securitization and other forms of financial engineering helped financiers and regulators grow comfortable that financial firms could scientifically assess and mitigate the risk of borrowing and lending through quantitative models. Alan Greenspan summed up the general attitude when he said in 1996: "[T]o continue to be effective, government's regulatory role must increasingly assure that effective risk management systems are in place in the private sector. As financial systems become more complex, detailed rules and standards have become both burdensome and ineffective."[33]

Eventually, Basel and its domestic interpreters allowed banks holding certain AAA-rated securities to avoid significant reserve requirements for those securities because the investments were so intricately engineered as to make losses seem less and less possible. The Federal Reserve and the Comptroller of the Currency decided in the late nineties, for instance, that J. P. Morgan needed just one-fifth of the usual reserves against select tranches. Whereas Askin, the hedge fund bankrupted by the 1994 mortgage crisis, had supported $2.50 in borrowing with $1 in capital to absorb losses, banks, in some cases, now could support $61.50 in borrowed money with the same capital. Though J. P. Morgan financiers had pioneered the deals and asked for the regulators' ruling, "when they were doing these deals for other banks, the question of reserve capital became more important—the others were mainly interested in cutting their reserve requirements," the *Financial Times*'s Gillian Tett reported. The room for error was small. On one of J. P. Morgan's loan pools, losses had to reach just 7 percent before the AAA tranche would suffer, too.[34]

By the mid-2000s, as regulations and market forces pushed them to borrow more and keep less capital, commercial banks in the U.S. had borrowed $35 for every $1 they had in hand. The few stand-alone investment banks left, not subject to the same regulatory standards as commercial banks and their parent companies like Citigroup, Citicorp's successor company, had borrowed $50 for every $1 in hand, 60 percent above the average between the eighties and the early 2000s, an average that itself had steadily grown.[35]

Regulators and policymakers acted partly with a good motive in mind; they did not want to penalize banks that lent prudently and thus earned smaller returns for the same amount of capital than did banks taking bigger risks and earning bigger returns. But the policymakers and regulators erred gravely. They believed that the banks' models had reduced risk to such an extent that prudent, uniform limits on borrowing—limits that would have been achieved with consistent reserve requirements—had become obsolete. Quantified and tamed, it seemed, risk needed little room for error. The regulators neglected to wonder what would happen if the banks' models and the ratings agencies that endorsed them were mistaken. Twenties-era bankers had thought that brokers' loans were perfectly safe, too. Prudent limits are most essential when conventional wisdom about perceived safety is systemically and catastrophically wrong.

Financiers' transformation of all manner of long-term loans into instantly tradeable securities dovetailed with the era's other trend, discussed in Chapter 3: big commercial banks like Citi increasingly earned their profits through trading and speculation, just as the investment banks already did, as global competition shrank the profits on their traditional businesses. The big banks' cheap funding sources made it easier for them to amplify by volume, with borrowed money, the otherwise tiny profits that came with such trading. Securitized debt was a ready vehicle for that speculation.

Accounting rules, though, still assumed a business model in which banks held mortgages for years and in which it didn't matter what the value of a mortgage was from one day to the next. Almost accidentally, the government stumbled upon a much more sensible way to measure banks' new business model—one that measured a world in which financial institutions acted not with long-term goals in mind but in pursuit of short-term profits. Regulators, as they determined how better to measure a changing financial world, had another opportunity to consider the risks that these changes posed to the economy.

After the savings-and-loan scandals, regulators recognized the shortcomings of existing accounting rules and grew concerned that banks could hide bad construction loans and other investments by reporting them at their original values without acknowledging permanent losses. They also worried that banks made their positions look artificially healthy by cherry-picking the best investments to sell, making it seem like other, similar investments still on the banks' books were worth equivalent amounts.[36]

After years of debate, federal regulators settled on a system to address this problem. Starting in 1994, financial institutions could continue to report the loans they had made and most of their other investments at their original values only if their intent, from the beginning, was to hold on to those loans and investments until they naturally matured, thus insulating the banks from day-to-day market fluctuations in the values of these loans and other investments. For the securities that financial institutions held to make profits through trading, including mortgage-backed securities, though, the institutions would have to value them, each quarter, at the price that an outsider would pay for them, with the increase or decrease to be totaled into reported profits. Regulators created a kind of middle category, too, of securities "available for sale" but not actively traded, requiring reporting of current values but not asking the banks to include fluctuations in current values in earnings.[37]

Financial institutions at first fought these changes. Citicorp veteran Walter Wriston said that this system, called "mark to market," would cause "chaos," noting that for many investments "a quoted market . . . is not a reliable guide to value. The situation gets worse when there is no market" in a crisis.[38] Federal Reserve chairman Alan Greenspan questioned the wisdom of forcing commercial banks to mark their loans to current value because the banks will not be "out of business tomorrow. . . . Commercial banking is the practice by which you make illiquid loans. . . . The basic process is not to get paid back immediately or to sell the loan."[39]

Wriston and Greenspan were right, in that the new system would have been inappropriate to measure the banking system that had once existed. For his part, Wriston was poignantly correct when he said that liquid securities could turn dangerously illiquid in a crisis, creating a catastrophic negative feedback loop. But it was the banks that created this risk, by believing that the securities in which they increasingly dealt *could* be continually bought or sold in a crisis. The new accounting did not create this peril but only measured it. For Greenspan's part, the Fed chairman had failed to see that a bank *would* have to sell a security, loan, or other investment at its current value if the bank's short-term funding for that loan evaporated. He also failed to understand that banking had changed: it was no longer that business of long-term lending. It had made itself much more vulnerable to day-to-day price changes in the securities markets.

As a result, credit supplies themselves—so vital to a functioning economy—became much more vulnerable to market fluctuations. Banks and investment firms had to rely on constant investor confidence in the value of their instantly tradeable securities. If confidence faltered in the banks' modeling of such securities, the prices of the securities would fall, and the investors who generally bought such securities would flee. The banks would have no one to whom to sell the securities they held, and the banks' uninsured depositors and other short-term lenders, with their own confidence in the banks' investments falling as the investments so quickly reflected market sentiment, would flee, too, drying up credit. It wouldn't matter that many banks, such as Citicorp and Bank of America, continued to classify some mortgage loans, along with other loans that they kept on their own books rather than packaging into securities, as long-term holdings. The banks still had to revalue securities that contained similar loans, as they reported their earnings. Investors would take those valuations and use them to estimate values for the banks' other assets, too.

Even as bankers and regulators made credit and the economy more vulnerable to a panic, they increased the likelihood of such a panic in another way. Under the traditional model, a bank that had made bad loans could work out some of those loans with the borrower to minimize or avoid losses. If they thought that a compromise would result in less of a loss or even a profit, bankers could give a home buyer or a corporation more time to pay or cut the amount owed. When financiers had sliced and diced loans into different pieces and sold bits off to one another and to other investors, however, it was much harder—almost impossible—to get all the investors in the loan-backed securities to agree to restructure a loan gone bad. Further, some investors had little incentive to cooperate in the early stages of a downturn; an investor in a AAA tranche had no reason to negotiate until he was certain that losses would exceed the level of protection that investors in lower-rated tranches provided. Investors in those lower-rated securities, with dim hopes for loss reduction, would have a new incentive to sell their securities quickly in a falling market to cut their losses, exacerbating pessimism and curtailing credit.

Greenspan's Fed showed in another way that it didn't understand how the volatility of a business model based on short-term trading posed new risks to banks. The Fed said in 1994 that it would not consider the volatility of particular securities holdings as it set capital requirements for banks, even though Greenspan, in 1990 testimony, had tentatively suggested that regulators require additional capital of financial institutions "with assets like high-yield, high-risk 'junk bonds' that might be illiquid or subject to big price swings."[40] Without regulatory action rather than words, the banks didn't set extra money aside to cover sudden losses in the event of rapid swings in the value of the tradeable securities that they had created from long-term loans.[41]

The problem with the new accounting system wasn't that it was inappropriate to measure banks' activities; the problem was that it was acutely relevant in a world where the nation's core credit markets were becoming vessels for pure speculation in pursuit of trading profits. It was far too relevant, too, in a world where financial institutions, as they became hollow warehouses of speculative credit dependent on a ceaseless supply of short-term financing, could go out of business overnight if that financing dried up.

Since the current credit crisis started, Washington, the media, and academia have revived the debate over whether the government was wrong to repeal Glass-Steagall in 1999, allowing commercial banks and securities banks formally to commingle. Repealing Glass-Steagall, though, was inevitable. The law's Depression-era wall between old-fashioned banking and the securities business seemed outdated and constrictive.

The Great Depression was history, and Wall Street did not seem to pose such a threat to the economy that the economy needed staid banks as a buffer; in fact, Wall Street seemed only a boon to the economy, with consumption powered by the debt it structured. Breaking down barriers to Wall Street's growth would only "strengthen the economy and help consumers, communities and businesses across America," President Clinton said.[42] Further, European banks combined securities and long-term lending and seemed adequately regulated.

Financiers and government officials missed a different, potent lesson in formalizing Glass-Steagall's irrelevance. As investment banks' short-term speculation and commercial banks' long-term lending businesses increasingly converged through securitization, it became impossible to distinguish between commercial banks that needed tight regulation as the stewards of the nation's core credit supply and investment banks that merited looser regulations as providers and conduits of speculative capital.

The answer shouldn't have been largely to allow the looser regulations that governed investment banks to reign, as the Clinton administration and Congress ultimately did, reflecting bipartisan agreement that had cemented itself for more than a decade. It should have been instead to wonder if a financial world in which so much of the economy's credit depended on short-term speculation needed new regulations to tame this new potential peril to the nation's health.

As the government repealed Glass-Steagall, the investors who bought securities created by Wall Street financiers and their commercial-bank counterparts had already begun to provide much of the nation's consumer and business credit. By 2000, the mortgage-securities market had grown to nearly $3.6 trillion, up 43 percent in less than five years. The securities market backed by loans other than mortgages had grown to $1 trillion, more than double its 1996 level. From next to nothing, these markets came to represent one-third of household and business debt outstanding.[43]

A "run on the bank" now would be a catastrophe. Because credit increasingly depended on the willingness of global investors to purchase highly structured securities from commercial and investment banks acting as middlemen, there would *be* no physical bank to protect from panic—only a vanishing mass of global debt-securities buyers who turned instantly into sellers.

In 1993, six years before Glass-Steagall's repeal, *Time* described this new world succinctly. "What would happen to the U.S. economy if all its commercial banks suddenly closed their doors?" the magazine asked. "Throughout most of American history, the answer would have been a disaster. . . . But . . . the startling answer is that a shutdown by banks might be far from cataclysmic. . . . Who really needs banks these days? Hardly anyone, it turns out."[44]

The unasked question was: What if this uncontrolled, parallel-credit-creation universe suddenly vanished, leaving nothing behind but hollowed-out financial giants that no longer knew how to be banks?

CHAPTER 5

A RISK-FREE WORLD

As risk management becomes ever more precise and customized, the amount of risk that we all have to bear will be greatly reduced, lowering the need for financial capital.
—Charles Sanford, Bankers Trust CEO, from a 1993 speech,
"Financial Markets in 2020"[1]

Regulatory risk measurement schemes . . . are simpler and much less accurate than banks' risk measurement models.
—Alan Greenspan, speaking before the Futures Industry
Association, 1999

IN THE SPRING OF 1994, CONSUMER-PRODUCTS GIANT Procter & Gamble and greeting-card maker Gibson Greetings rocked the world in disclosing that they had lost, respectively, more than $100 million and nearly $21 million on bad interest-rate bets through financial contracts arranged by Bankers Trust, one of the country's oldest and best-regarded banks. Assured by their bankers, the companies had believed that through these financial instruments, called "derivatives," they were protecting themselves against fluctuating interest rates. But when rates shot up suddenly, in the same event that roiled the mortgage-securities market, this "protection" became a sudden disaster.

Since the Depression, the government had encouraged nimble financial innovation within broad but well-defined limits. The rules gently constrained borrowing for speculative purposes and required banks and corporations to disclose to investors the risks behind their innovations. The rules clearly distinguished between what kinds of financial risks required disclosure alone (so that investors could use their own discretion) and what kinds needed hard-and-fast limits to keep them from infecting the broader economy (including margin requirements to limit borrowing to buy stocks). Starting in the late eighties, though, derivatives, another potent financial innovation, began to erode well-defined borrowing limits as well as disclosure requirements. This erosion further weakened the regulatory structure that protected the economy from the excesses of unbridled financial speculation.

Derivatives get their name because their values derive from changes in the value of markets or of other securities. They've been around for centuries, particularly in the form of contracts based on the future price of energy and agricultural products, but they took off as purely financial products in the nineties. Some derive their worth from the changing value of stocks, others from the changing value of interest rates or currency-exchange rates. If an investor believes, say, that global interest rates will go lower over the next two years, he can make an agreement with another investor who believes that the opposite will happen. This agreement—a derivatives contract—will require the second investor to pay the first if interest rates move in the direction that the first investor expects, and vice versa.

Derivatives are useful to markets and the economy in two ways. First, businesses can use them as protection against extreme price fluctuations in the commodities that they need to make their products. A California factory, for example, must buy tremendous amounts of electricity but wants to limit its exposure to fluctuating power prices. To "hedge" this risk, the company can enter into an agreement through which another party will pay it if the price of power rises beyond a certain level, canceling out the higher prices that it otherwise would have to pay. If power prices fall instead, the company must pay its counterparty, but it likely will have the money to do so because it is paying less for its own power supplies.

Second, derivatives make markets more efficient by introducing valuable price information. Speculators, who don't use their trades to hedge costs but instead to pursue profits, help perform this role. Speculators rely on derivatives to make money on predictions—from whether the European Central Bank will raise interest rates to whether Venezuela will default on its debt. Derivatives, in transmitting these predictions to the market, help observers understand what people think the future will look like. Speculators also serve as trading partners for hedgers, providing more liquidity to these markets.

Derivatives, though, can be far riskier than stocks and bonds. A stock investor's losses are limited to the amount of money he paid for the stock. If an investor pays $50 for a stock and it drops to zero, he has lost $50. Even if he has borrowed $25 to purchase the stock—the limit under Depression-era margin regulations— he owes only that $25; the amount does not rise.

With derivatives, it's a different story. If a derivatives trader bets that interest rates will fall, but they rise instead, the trader could end up owing far more than he had expected, as in the Procter & Gamble and Gibson Greetings cases. Through some derivatives contracts—a contract to pay if the price of a stock goes up, for example—participants can take on open-ended risk. Further, even the winner on a derivatives contract shoulders a risk: the risk that the counterparty on the transaction won't be able to make good on the deal. In that sense, derivatives' buyers are creditors, similar to lenders; they must assess other parties' ability to make good on a contract. It is not just derivatives participants who expose themselves to such risk. Financial institutions, in addition to taking derivatives risks themselves, lend clients the money to do so—clients who might not be able to pay them back, either.

Regulators and markets long ago addressed the risks posed by derivatives in commodities and other standard areas, employing Depression-era principles enforced largely by the Commodity Futures Trading Commission (CFTC). Derivatives based on

everyday commodities like oil and on common financial variables like interest rates trade on the Chicago Board of Trade and
other regulated exchanges. These "traded" derivatives—futures,
options, and swaps—are subject to margin requirements to limit
borrowing as well as reporting requirements. The requirements
don't prevent big or sudden losses, but they do ensure that participants can't risk tremendous losses without putting down any cash
at all, nudging them to think twice before they act.

The exchanges, too, play an important role in reducing systemic risk. Exchanges complete their customers' trades through
clearinghouses, which ensure that no participant—say, a big bank
or hedge fund—amasses a tremendous exposure that it could not
honor in a crisis and that jeopardizes the entire financial system.
When an investor enters into a financial-instrument contract, the
clearinghouse, not another financial institution, pledges to make
good on the contract if necessary over its life. The clearinghouse,
in turn, reduces its own exposure by finding another investor
who wants to take the opposite position on the trade. Each side
of the exposure cancels the other side out. In this manner, a big
investor's catastrophic losses don't severely damage other financial institutions, weakening the system. The exchanges also provide pricing and volume data to investors and regulators, who can
search for odd trends and manipulation, respectively.

But starting in the nineties, investment banks, commercial
banks, and hedge funds started to create customized derivatives
that escaped these requirements. They did so partly to meet customer demand, partly to avoid the regulations, and partly to earn
a higher profit by trying to distinguish themselves from competitors. These "over-the-counter" derivatives were private contracts.
They did not trade on exchanges, and they were not subject to
the margin requirements meant to protect the market and the
economy from excessive borrowing; the big financial institutions
that dominated these markets had full discretion on how much,
if at all, to limit risk.

It was this combination—taking huge risks for comparatively
tiny amounts of money down, based on the advice of respected
bankers—that caused the huge losses at Procter & Gamble and

Gibson Greetings, losses "that investors may never have imagined."[2] In the investigations that ensued, executives at Procter & Gamble and at Gibson claimed that they were ignorant of the risks involved in the financial products that Bankers Trust had brought to them.

After such high-profile blowups, regulation seemed inevitable. Throughout the mid-1990s, Congress held hearings, regulators wrote papers, and five separate bills reached lawmakers for consideration. But not much happened. Policymakers' and regulators' lack of action, at first glance, was puzzling, especially because as the over-the-counter derivatives market, after the initial blowups, continued to grow, media scrutiny grew, too.

Fortune's Carol Loomis used the opportunity that the 1994 blowups presented to explain that the graver risk was to the economy, not to individual companies or investors. "Most chillingly, derivatives hold the possibility of systemic risk — the danger that these contracts might . . . cause some localized or particularized trouble in the financial markets to spread uncontrollably. An imaginable scenario is some deep crisis at a major dealer that would cause it to default on its contracts and be the instigator of a chain reaction bringing down other institutions and sending paroxysms of fear through [the] financial market. . . . Inevitably, that would put deposit-insurance funds, and the taxpayers behind them, at risk," she wrote.[3] The *New York Times*, after running several articles detailing the risks of derivatives, cited the high-profile blowups as well as other instances of market turmoil— including reports of hedge funds that suddenly had to fork over huge amounts of cash to their brokers as derivatives trades turned bad—as "good reason for Congress and federal regulators to scrutinize [derivatives'] use by banks so that [they] will not threaten unwitting taxpayers."[4] Fed chairman Alan Greenspan agreed with this assessment, saying in 1995 that "terrific technology" had pushed the potential for fast losses "up very significantly."[5]

The failure to act was strange, too, because as over-the-counter derivatives grew and as banks began manufacturing identical products in ever-increasing volumes, the financial instruments increasingly resembled not private, unique contracts between two parties but tradeable securities. In fact, old-fashioned trading houses like the Chicago Mercantile Exchange complained that they were losing business to competitors not bound by margin and reporting requirements.[6]

The Federal Reserve could have regulated these instruments, just as Volcker did with the junk-bond markets the previous decade in applying borrowing limits for stock purchases to the corporate-takeover market. The Fed, for example, could have suggested that the CFTC oversee these unregulated markets, just as it did regulated derivatives markets. If any concerns arose about its or the CFTC's authority to take these actions, the Fed had the credibility to ask Congress and the president for it.

But politicians and regulators saw no need for a systemic fix, blaming unfortunate incidents on individual misjudgment and misbehavior, not on slow regulatory breakdown. Investigations "turned up more signs of old-fashioned moral decrepitude and management negligence than of the need for green-eye-shade supervision," the *Wall Street Journal* editorialized.[7] Bankers Trust eventually settled fraud charges and civil lawsuits related to Procter & Gamble and Gibson, paying out hundreds of millions of dollars; the bank pleaded guilty to three felonies on a tangentially related matter. The reasoning seemed clear: Bankers Trust had sold bad derivatives under false pretenses, and it deserved retroactive civil and criminal punishment. Certainly, civil and criminal redress to wronged investors is integral to markets. But just as in the twenties, government officials failed to see that the fraudsters were a symptom of a potent systemic risk.

Further, regulators tended to believe that derivatives' supposed victims, including the greeting-card maker, had lost so much money so suddenly because of a lack of sophistication. It followed, then, that more sophisticated investors could handle the complex risks posed by complex derivatives perfectly fine. And who was more sophisticated than a big bank? "You don't put an average pilot in an F-15 fighter," Harvard professor Andrew Perold said.[8]

Charles Sanford, Bankers Trust's chief, had best expressed the banks' confidence in their own risk management. *Time* described a 1993 speech in which Sanford summarized his view: "By allowing institutions to manage their finances more carefully, derivatives offered the possibility of locking in greater rewards at lower risks. Suddenly, what seemed to be the first immutable law of finance—you can't get a bigger reward without a bigger risk—was up for grabs."[9] The inconvenient fact that this risk management, designed by Bankers Trust's top financiers, proved illusory at Procter & Gamble, and the even more inconvenient fact that Bankers Trust soon had to sell itself to Germany's Deutsche Bank because its "sophisticated models to manage risk-taking had failed to perform effectively,"[10] did not interfere with this reasoning.

Regulators, too, voiced confidence in financial firms' risk-management models. Despite the ensuing blowup, regulators and lawmakers seemed to agree with what Wendy Gramm wrote in 1993, shortly after she left the Commodity Futures Trading Commission, where, as chairman for five years, she had helped exempt some over-the-counter derivatives from regulation. Criticism of derivatives "is simply a variation on the old refrain that derivatives are so complex and risky that they might bring the whole financial system tumbling down," Gramm wrote. "As in the past, listening to these critics risks damaging a vibrant and valuable sector of the U.S. financial market. . . . [D]erivatives were developed to manage the risks that already exist in the business world. . . . Internal control systems are evolving to accommodate the increased activity." Gramm further pointed out that the system could withstand derivatives blowups, with the 1990 bankruptcy of the investment firm Drexel Burnham Lambert and the 1991 failure of the Bank of New England examples of "derivatives portfolios . . . transferred or liquidated successfully."[11]

The Fed and other banking regulators agreed. Alan Greenspan concluded that financial institutions themselves were so adept at measuring derivatives risk that their use of the instruments actually reduced the risk that the institutions posed to shareholders and to the economy. "Derivatives should allow banks to better manage risk and so should help to insulate . . . from financial and real shocks," Greenspan said.[12] The Comptroller of the Currency, Eugene Ludwig, noted that the financial system needed "a no-surprises risk-management policy made concrete in systems and controls" and that the task would be straightforward, as many banks "already have systems in place to perform . . . analysis" of unexpected correlations among arcane financial instruments that could produce big losses. "Banks need to put together systems that will allow them to uncover those new risk combinations—in other words, to expect the unexpected," Ludwig said.[13]

The government, through its treatment of the derivatives market, was moving further away from clear, well-quantified limits on financial institutions' risks, just as it was doing with its treatment of securitization, as discussed in Chapter 4. Greenspan told Congress shortly after the 1994 derivatives explosions that "the trouble with legislation is that it is very likely in this type of market to become rapidly obsolete, and could very readily become counterproductive to the required flexibility that we need."[14] "There is nothing involved in federal regulation . . . which makes it superior to market regulation," he observed the same year.[15] Instead of imposing new limits, the government and the financial world would work together to monitor risk-taking, using theoretical models that purported to measure risk in place of concrete limits that constrained it, just as they were doing when it came to setting the rules on how much capital banks had to hold to protect against losses on securitized loans.

Financial firms rolled out more sophisticated financial models to reassure themselves and the government. In the mid-nineties, they started using a measurement called "value at risk" to measure how much money they were likely to lose on any one day.[16] Regulators, encouraged by Basel, embraced value at risk, even though its creators clearly said that it would not work all the time—only 95 or 99 percent of the time. Nobody wondered what would happen during the other 1 to 5 percent.

Financial firms also deployed ever more sophisticated technology to model something called "correlation" risk, which measured the likelihood that whenever one financial instrument rose in value, another would go down, thus making the risk of investing in two securities together lower than it would be to hold just one of the securities. But experienced bankers and traders—

and commonsensical people—had known for decades that during a crisis, correlations often "go to one"—that is, investments rise and fall together.

Though this knowledge was freely available, the only regulatory action the government did take was to require banks to disclose some of the internal measurements of their own risk that these models revealed, and to make more disclosures to Main Street customers about the risks they were incurring. One of the voluntary measures to which the banks agreed was to submit their mathematical models detailing the risks of derivatives to outside auditors.[17]

Regulators had made a catastrophic error. They confused what kind of financial risk-taking could be addressed with disclosure and what kind of behavior needed strict limits. Back in the thirties, Roosevelt had made this distinction clear, when he and Congress agreed that commercial banks couldn't address their risks simply by disclosing them to depositors but should be prevented from taking part in some activities altogether. Because derivatives threatened markets with unpredictable losses, they warranted not only more disclosure but limits, too, including margin requirements.

Regulators' confidence in banks' ability to finesse their own risk encouraged and reflected a fierce financial-deregulatory ethos that reigned on Capitol Hill. As Senator Phil Gramm, powerful chairman of the Senate Banking Committee, said in 1995, "Obviously, you want financial regulation—and every other kind of regulation—right up to the point where the benefits you're getting equal the cost. America clearly wants less regulation."[18] Gramm understood well that deregulation had benefited regular people in industries like airlines and interstate trucking, through more competition and lower costs. But financial regulation was different.

Even as derivatives posed a new possibility for unlimited borrowing, the climate was such that Congress held hearings to consider eliminating Depression-era margin requirements for big investors' stock purchases and letting brokers cut back on the disclosures they were required to make to potential securities customers.[19] While these efforts failed, they showed how few public officials saw any threat in unregulated derivatives.

By 2000, Congress, President Clinton, and the Federal Reserve had banded together to head off the one regulator determined to impose limits on over-the-counter derivatives: the Commodity Futures Trading Commission, under Commissioner Brooksley Born. As the CFTC moved to regulate over-the-counter derivatives, Congress expressly banned it from doing so in the Commodity Futures Modernization Act, and the president signed the bill. Lawmakers ignored Born's 1998 testimony that these unregulated financial markets posed "unknown risks to the U.S. economy and to financial stability around the world" because of their "lack of transparency" as well as "unlimited borrowing . . . like the unlimited borrowing on securities that contributed to the Great Depression."[20] By 2000, global over-the-counter derivatives markets—concentrated in New York and London—had grown from negligible barely a decade earlier to $95 trillion.[21]

It was the market itself, not the government, that took steps to reduce the risks in some common derivatives markets. Gradually, the most common kinds of interest-rate trades and the like moved to central clearinghouses that reduced risk by matching sellers with buyers to cancel out exposures, as central trading houses met customers' demand for the cheaper prices that standardized contracts offered. But the custom derivatives market and its potential for higher profit margins grew too fast for this gradual movement to reduce the overall danger to the broader market. Further, the financial world was impatient in waiting for regulators to approve new products for trading on exchanges, and instead traded innovative instruments off exchanges—away from regulatory reach.

Perversely, while everyone thought that banks were better able than toothpaste companies to handle derivatives, a financial institution's mistakes with derivatives would have an infinitely more disruptive impact on the financial system than Procter & Gamble's ever could. A financial institution that used an unregulated derivative to spin $1 into a loss of $50, for example, would be unable to do much lending. A financial institution that lent money to a client who incurred such losses and couldn't pay it back faced the same risk. Several such banks making such mistakes at the same time would pose a severe, systemic threat to the economy.

As derivatives evolved, this risk became doubly potent. In the late nineties, financiers started using derivatives to try to engineer away credit risk rather than variables like interest-rate risk, just as they were doing in the securitization markets. Because derivatives' behavior was unpredictable and often involved the potential for open-ended losses, banks and investment firms introduced more unpredictability—and the potential for extreme volatility—into the economy's vital credit markets.

The concept of financial firms' use of derivatives to protect themselves and their clients from credit risk was straightforward. Say that a bank owned a General Motors bond and, though it liked the interest rate, it worried that GM could go bust and the bond would lose much of its value. Before the late nineties, the bank had to sell the bond to assuage its worry. Starting in the late nineties, though, the bank could buy a "credit-default swap," a type of derivative that would enable it to collect at least a percentage of its loss in the event of a default within a certain time frame from the institution or person who sold the bank the swap. The seller in turn assumed that the price he received for the derivative amply compensated him for the risk. The financial industry could proceed in this way because its participants thought that their data-modeling techniques could "price" any risk accurately and determine each institution's and investor's capacity to bear it. Banks didn't buy credit derivatives for simple loans on a case-by-case basis. They went on to couple the supposed protection credit derivatives offered with the protection that securitization provided, and they did it in bulk. In 1998, for example, as the *Financial Times*'s Gillian Tett has reported, J. P. Morgan, a pioneer in this area, had on its books nearly $10 billion in securities made from loans to corporations. The securities were the "safer" tranches of the loan pools. Because investors in the less safe tranches had agreed to bear much of the risk of the default, the probability of losses seemed negligible. Ratings analysts thought that fewer than 1 percent of borrowers in one such loan pool would default annually, at most, leaving senior investors well protected.

But, first in response to nervous regulators, and later, as regulators relaxed, to assuage its own worries, J. P. Morgan found an institution to protect against even the small remaining risk of loss: the insurance giant AIG, which earned just two-tenths of a penny for every dollar that it guaranteed (over the next few years, the price rose fivefold, but it was still small).[22] "J. P. Morgan has bought a form of credit insurance, which it had helped pioneer, against many loans so that if borrowers default the bank will receive a payment from the insurer," the *Wall Street Journal* reported in 2000.[23]

Credit derivatives are not insurance, though. The buyer of credit protection doesn't have to own the underlying bond. An insurance purchaser, by contrast, must own an interest in the asset that he is insuring. Credit derivatives are similar to financial instruments through which investors take in an interest in the future price of oil. An investor can hedge his future purchases of oil for his business by locking in what seems like a lower price today, or he can speculate with no such interest in the underlying asset.

AIG did not make these commitments through its regulated insurance subsidiaries, even though it relied on its reputation as an insurer to market them. If it had designed them as insurance, it would have had to put some capital behind the promises, as insurers must do with all regulated insurance products. Instead, it provided the protection through a credit-default swap and handled them through a "financial products" group, based in London, that dealt with such unregulated instruments. Because these derivatives contracts were free from margin requirements that constrained their regulated brethren, AIG could agree to make billions of dollars in potential future payouts in the event of losses from securities defaults for a token (if any) cash commitment, though it would owe cash instantly if something went wrong. With no cash required initially, nothing forced AIG to consider the risk involved; the money it made seemed free.

Competing with AIG, companies called bond insurers, who previously ran a staid business of guaranteeing the performance of still-straightforward municipal securities for a fee, started using the same unregulated credit-default swaps to offer guarantees against losses on securitized credit as well. Bond insurers, such as MBIA and Ambac, capitalized on investors' desire, often driven by regulatory mandates, for securities that carried AAA ratings. In effect, the bond insurers rented out their own AAA ratings to mortgage-backed and other securities without such ratings, using their own sterling credit to guarantee, through credit derivatives, the securities' performance in the event of default.

In reality, there was no free lunch. In using credit-default swaps from AIG or MBIA, investors in securitized debt, including big banks, structured away one seemingly remote risk—the chance that good loans would default in bulk—in return for another. This was counterparty risk—the possibility that the institution taking the responsibility to pay up would not be able to withstand the exposures that it had amassed. MBIA and Ambac often pitched their business by telling potential clients that it was inconceivable that they would lose their own AAA ratings—thus endangering the ratings of the securities they guaranteed—unless financial Armageddon struck. But financial Armageddon was when the clients would most need that protection, a fact that nobody seemed to consider at the time.

Banks were aware of the potential for failure, though, at least when it came to small counterparties. When a bank bought a credit derivative from a small financial institution, for example, it often turned around and bought protection against the possibility of *that* institution going bankrupt. But the banks were only making things more complicated for themselves. They did not have the staff to deal with the mind-numbing complexity of thousands of contracts, many of which were supposed to cancel one another out in a crisis. At Bear Stearns, for example, volume at the firm's credit-default derivatives desks was up 800 percent between 2003 and 2005, while employment on those desks, to monitor all that new risk, was up just 30 percent.

In 2005, the New York Fed expressed alarm at evidence that the unregulated derivatives market was so lax that financial institutions didn't even know who might owe them money and vice versa—never mind starting to cut back the exposure. Traders made deals with one another over the phone for hundreds of millions of dollars' worth of potential obligations, noting each deal and throwing it onto a pile that sat on a desk for weeks. Traders also transferred their firms' obligations to other companies, with the original trading partner unaware that a different company, perhaps a weaker company, was now responsible for the contract. The Fed prodded financial firms quickly to send their records to the Depository Trust and Clearing Corporation, an industry-owned company that handles record-keeping for financial institutions' contracts.[24]

Without public reporting requirements, though, as strand after strand of derivatives contracts entwined into an opaque mass, it became harder for outsiders to discern the risk. The credit-default-swap business was so obscure that the Bank for International Settlements—the central bank of the world's central banks—kept no data on it until 2005. As *Financial Times* editor Lionel Barber said, through the perspective of the current financial crisis, "[T]he credit derivatives story . . . took place in a . . . market with little disclosure and very little day-to-day news. Inevitably, the temptation was . . . to run with the stories that are much less opaque such as public company earnings."[25]

Almost no one noticed that with every credit-default-swap agreement, the financial institution on each side of the transaction—the one that would owe money, and the one expecting to be paid—wove a thread of potential failure deep into the financial system. The collapse of any big firm, or even a small firm that had woven enough threads, could cause market forces to yank on so many strands so harshly that the entire system would unravel. With each slender new thread that they wove, bankers and traders ensured that someday, the government would have no choice but to step in and prevent the market from destroying itself. Too big to fail was becoming too intricate to fail.

Credit-default derivatives introduced another element of opacity into markets. When a company is in distress, its lenders often work together to change the terms of the firm's debt and minimize losses, just as banks once did with their borrowers. If the company declares bankruptcy, lenders go before a judge to determine repayment. A lender that has bought protection against losses through a credit-default derivative, however, has little reason to work with the other lenders to help the company repay its debts. Lenders, judges, and executives at distressed companies had no way of knowing which lenders had scant self-interest in minimizing the total losses that the market must bear.

Derivatives, along with securitization and the transformation of banks, eroded the limits meant to insulate credit markets from short-term excess. Regulators failed to use their ample discretion under Depression-era laws and principles—or their clout with lawmakers—to ensure that derivatives-fueled speculation did not fatally infect the economy. The government's too-big-to-fail policy, discussed in Chapter 3, removed an important component—market discipline—from the financial world just as increasingly inadequate regulations made such discipline even more necessary.

In the absence of prudent rules, the era's defining elements came together to create an immense force whose power had one object: credit creation. As financial institutions increasingly earned their profits through buying and selling securities, they needed fodder for this trading. Securitized debt, which provided that fodder, also made credit seem less risky for investors who bought the safer tranches. Unregulated credit derivatives went further: the protection that such derivatives provided made much securitized debt seem nearly riskless. This illusion helped push America's debt levels up nearly 75 percent between 1980 and 2000 relative to gross domestic product, surpassing peaks reached before the Great Depression and increasing at the fastest rate in American history.

It also followed that, since borrowing and lending were ostensibly so safe, the banks and investment firms could borrow more for themselves, too. By adding lenders' money to their own, they could magnify the profits they earned from trading the securities they created. They then had more money to create even more credit for the economy. Yet they decreased their own margins for error: if something happened to the value of their securities, they would have to pay that borrowed money back, quickly—and this reversal would suck credit straight out of an economy that increasingly depended on it.

Meanwhile, that old 1920s rule still lurked. Economies are in greatest peril not when investors willfully take crazy financial risks but when no one seems to perceive risk and the need to insulate the economy from it.

CHAPTER 6

THE LAST
MILEPOSTS

[I]f Long-Term Capital was simply a casualty of a once-a-century financial storm, the crisis may well deserve to become a footnote to history.
—"Lessons of a Long, Hot Summer," *New York Times*,
December 6, 1998

Wall Street is scrambling to distinguish between the kind of off-balance-sheet financing used by Enron Corp. and that employed in the giant securitization market. It is an important distinction, professionals say, because securitization plays a little-recognized but important role in supporting consumer spending and the broader economy. These transactions have "enabled American consumers to spend to the extent they do."
—"Investors Defend Securitization, Some Entities Tainted by Enron,"
Wall Street Journal, March 18, 2002

N FEBRUARY 1995, THE DIRECTOR OF THE BANK OF England, Britain's central bank, rushed back to London from a French vacation to figure out how a twenty-eight-year-old trader a third of the way around the world had brought down Barings, one of Britain's most storied investment banks, leaving more than two centuries of history in ruins. The trader, Nicholas Leeson, lost so much money—more than $1 billion, it turned out—on derivatives that Barings's chairman suspected deliberate criminal sabotage.

The truth was more startling. Leeson, who worked in Singapore, lost the money by using derivatives to bet that stocks and currencies would move in one direction; instead, they moved in the other.[1] Despite the British government's best efforts to arrange private rescue financing, Barings declared bankruptcy. Administrators soon sold it to a Dutch bank.

In hindsight, the most significant aspect of the Barings failure is what didn't happen. The British government didn't arrange taxpayer money to keep Barings out of bankruptcy. "The Bank of England decided there is no risk of contagion, no systemic risk to the banking industry," Robert Solomon, a former Federal Reserve economist, said.[2] The Bank of England itself made another point: "The Bank of England cannot put itself in the position of signing a blank check," one of its officials told the *New York Times*.[3] "Barings' tombstone now will stand as a warning to bankers everywhere," one observer intoned.[4] Barings was not too big to fail, just as five years earlier, Drexel Burnham Lambert, Michael Milken's investment firm, had not been too big for bankruptcy. And while global markets looked on anxiously in both cases, they didn't collapse.

Just three years after Barings failed, though, the financial world had transformed itself so thoroughly that the American authorities thought that they could not allow a small Connecticut hedge fund—Long-Term Capital Management—to fail through normal bankruptcy, lest it cause catastrophe for markets and the economy. The government's predicament with Long-Term Capital showed that unregulated derivatives had by then threaded themselves to such an extent through the financial system that the "systemic risk" that *Fortune*'s Loomis had warned of in 1994 was no longer a possibility but a reality. If confidence in one big derivatives player such as Long-Term Capital faltered, the distrust would travel through the system, possibly bringing down firm after firm and sharply curtailing credit in the economy. Long-Term Capital offered the strongest signal yet that regulations to protect the economy from excessive borrowing and speculation had badly eroded. It was also a signal that policymakers and regulators could not rely solely on market discipline to rein in risk-taking in the absence of prudent regulation.

Long-Term Capital managed investments for wealthy clients from around the world. Its strategy, which Nobel-Prize-winning theoreticians helped design, was to use derivatives to bet that some securities and financial markets would behave in a certain way, while others would behave in another way. In summer 1998, after four years of good profits, the firm badly miscalculated. Long-Term hadn't expected that the world's lenders would grow anxious over the amount of credit they had extended globally, including to fast-developing nations in Asia and Latin America. Whereas financial firms had competed to lend money to just about anyone a few months earlier, they now stopped cold. Nor did Long-Term foresee that Russia would threaten to default on its domestic debt—and then actually do so. For Wall Streeters, the default was almost unthinkable. They'd learned, through experiences in Mexico and elsewhere, to depend on the U.S. government to bail out indebted countries, but this time, the government didn't act. This time, as international turmoil surprised markets, securities moved in a direction different from what Long-Term expected. Massive losses ensued.

Like Continental Illinois nearly fifteen years earlier, Long-Term had exercised its American right to take risks—and fail. But lax regulations turned Long-Term's right to make mistakes with its own and its lenders' money into a potential global financial disaster. Long-Term had made $125 billion in investments, even though its own shareholders had given it only $2.3 billion. It borrowed the rest—$53 for every $1 it had in hand.[5] But that wasn't all. Through derivatives, Long-Term had magnified its potential obligations to its trading counterparties to a scarcely conceivable $1.25 *trillion*.[6] "Long-Term Capital's total exposure . . . was about 40 times that of Barings and it did not have much more capital than Barings" had had three years earlier.[7] There would be no way for the hedge fund to pay its debts should anything go wrong, and now it had.

The hedge fund could borrow so much because it was an indirect beneficiary of the government's too-big-to-fail policy. The source of Long-Term's credit was none other than the big banks, both commercial and investment. Lenders to the commercial banks knew that the government implicitly protected them and thus didn't worry much about what the banks were doing with their money, including extending so much credit to a four-year-old hedge fund. The investment banks had to keep up as competition intensified and profit margins shrank, so they poured money into Long-Term, too.

To amass such exposures on a slender capital base, Long-Term took advantage of a second regulatory weakness. It made its bets on global stocks' direction not through buying and selling the stock securities themselves—which would have required hefty cash-margin payments under the Depression-era limits on borrowing—but by buying and selling unregulated derivatives that "mimicked the behavior of stocks."[8] Because these derivatives did not trade on exchanges or clearinghouses, Long-Term was subject only to its lending banks' discretion when it came to borrowing against the instruments. As one of the world's biggest derivatives customers, Long-Term possessed enough market power to persuade banks and securities firms that traded in derivatives to be generous with their discretion. Contrary to usual practice, the financial companies did not demand small cash payments from Long-Term as capital cushions against potential losses.[9]

In carrying out this strategy, and in the impact of the strategy's implosion on global markets, Long-Term distinguished itself from Barings. The British investment bank's soured derivatives traded on a central Singapore exchange, where regulators and managers could quarantine them and wind them down.[10] Barings's losses bankrupted it, but the rest of the system, after a few initial shudders, emerged intact. Because the exchange was Barings's counterparty, financial markets could avoid the worry that hundreds of millions of dollars in losses lurked at other firms.

Long-Term, by contrast, represented a huge risk to the financial world—a much greater risk than Continental Illinois had—and an incalculable one. Nobody knew which of the world's banks, brokerage firms, and other hedge funds might be left owing or might be owed billions of dollars if Long-Term declared bankruptcy. This knowledge hole was another aspect of the regulatory vacuum. Where Long-Term traded derivatives on exchanges, information about those trades reached regulators. "Pursuant to . . . requirements that large traders' positions . . . be reported on a daily basis," CFTC chief Brooksley Born later told Congress, Long-Term Capital's "positions on U.S. Futures Exchange have been reported. . . . Moreover, LTCM has been promptly and fully paying margin on its futures positions." But regulators had no idea of the positions that the company had amassed in the unregulated over-the-counter markets through which it made many of its bets because "no reporting of that information is routinely required."[11]

As news of Long-Term's losses reached the markets, fear struck other financial firms. A Merrill Lynch analyst assured investors that Lehman Brothers, a lender to the hedge fund, was "far from insolvent; . . . the firm appeared to be having no trouble financing itself in the commercial-paper market."[12] UBS, the Swiss bank, lost $700 million. Other financial firms saw their market values plummet as investors worried about the unknown.[13]

This opacity wasn't Long-Term's only systemic threat to the financial system. Long-Term's enabling banks, from Lehman to Citigroup, had lent the firm money on a short-term, often overnight, basis. The collateral behind that debt was Long-Term's various investments in derivatives, bonds, and the like. Under the agreements that Long-Term signed with its banks, in the event of a default, these lenders could cut off their funds, seize the collateral behind existing loans, and dump that collateral into global markets immediately to recoup their cash. As had happened with Continental Illinois nearly a decade and a half earlier, it became clear that lenders would not wait for Long-Term's losses to reverse themselves and see if the struggling firm repaired itself. As soon as one firm moved to stop lending to the firm, the others would, too: they would not want to be trapped as the firm's final lenders.

If Long-Term's lenders turned off the spigot and pushed the firm into default, the world's banks, hedge funds, and other investment firms likely would seize and sell hundreds of billions of dollars in securities and other financial instruments into the market—all at once. Such forced selling would drive down the price of every-thing from junk bonds to mortgage securities instantaneously, causing problems for other firms that had borrowed against sim-ilar collateral. One bank executive told the *Wall Street Journal* that "given the leading positions of the firms and their relationships with Long-Term"—everyone from Chase to Bear Stearns—"if any single firm decided to cut and run, then the value of everyone's collateral would . . . deteriorate."[14] According to Roger Lowenstein, who wrote a book about the firm, "[i]f Long-Term defaulted, all of the banks in the room would be left holding one side of a contract for which the other side no longer existed. . . . [T]hey would be exposed to tremendous—and untenable—risks."[15]

The Federal Reserve's overarching fear was a sustained credit crunch, according to William McDonough, the New York Fed president. Long-Term had been a key credit creator, an example of how "companies rely increasingly on financial markets, not banks, to provide their credit needs," the *Wall Street Journal* reported.[16] In fact, when Long-Term's founders started the firm four years earlier, they described it as not a hedge fund but "a state-of-the-art *financial* intermediary that provided capital to markets just as banks did." Just as banks earn their profits by borrowing from depositors, bondholders, and other lenders at low interest rates and then lending that money out at higher rates, Long-Term would similarly " 'borrow' by selling one group of bonds and lend by purchasing another" group of bonds.[17] The firm also consid-ered itself "an insurer of financial risk" a few years before AIG became the dominant player in this market.[18]

With its small capital base, Long-Term fashioned itself into an unregulated steward of the nation's key credit supplies. The chaos that the firm's disordered failure could spread into the world's credit markets presented a chilling predicament for regulators. The economy had become dependent on increasingly complex debt securities and derivatives for its credit supplies, even as these securities were vulnerable to speculative excesses. And as banks increasingly favored trading over long-term lending, the economy, too, depended on investors—including Long-Term and its lenders—to provide credit by buying and selling long-term securities with borrowed money in pursuit of short-term profits.

Long-Term, then, could not fail, the government determined. So in September 1998, under the New York Fed's supervision, the banks and securities firms that had given the hedge fund enough money to lead the entire financial world to the precipice brought it back. The firms infused $3.6 billion into Long-Term and took 90 percent ownership in return, wiping out the fund's private stockholders and minding its managers as they slowly wound their investments down.[19]

Scarcely a half-decade after Alan Greenspan said that he couldn't see the U.S. government bailing out a securities firm, the Federal Reserve had engineered the bailout of an anonymous suburban hedge fund. The government tried to obfuscate this new precedent, noting that no government money went into the rescue package. "I wouldn't call it a bailout," Treasury secretary Robert Rubin, a former Goldman Sachs cochairman, told Washington journalists, skirting questions about whether the government should regulate hedge funds in saying only that "there are issues many people have raised."[20] But Greenspan's statements after the failure made clear, without saying so explicitly, that the Fed would have put taxpayer money in if the banks had refused. "With markets currently volatile and investors skittish," the rescue "seemed entirely appropriate as a matter of public policy," Greenspan said, adding that "it has become evident time and again that when events become too complex and move too rapidly . . . human beings become demonstrably less able to cope."[21]

The danger to the broader economy did not pass immediately after the government and the banks saved Long-Term's lenders. The investors who provided so much credit to the economy remained skittish about purchasing securities that now seemed riskier, even as the Fed cut interest rates to entice them back. "About 70 to 80 percent of the credit that goes to households, companies and institutions . . . isn't funneled through the banks these days, but through other avenues, primarily the capital markets," the *Wall Street Journal* explained six weeks after the bailout.

"And even banks rely more on securities markets as a source of funds. . . . [S]ince banks aren't the primary source of the problem, pumping more money into them won't necessarily help. But the Fed hopes that by lowering rates, it can calm investors and eliminate some of their aversion to risk."[22] Markets continued their stall.

The press misinterpreted one aspect of the story, however. The conventional narrative was that Long-Term Capital Management had been blind to risk, its Nobel-winning mathematicians too immersed in their formulas to notice that they were racing off a cliff. But Long-Term *had* realized the risks inherent in its strategy. As Lowenstein wrote, one of Long-Term's chief architects had read up on the 1994 failure of the Askin hedge fund and understood that Long-Term could face a similar situation, with its lenders cutting it off suddenly in a crisis and not giving it a chance to recover. This worry was a "persistent concern" but one left unresolved because there was no real solution.

In the end, Long-Term could observe itself but couldn't control itself. It needed an external check. But Wall Street's biggest banks, which had helped Long-Term structure its complex derivatives and lent and lent to the firm until they could lend no more, couldn't play that role. The banks had been ignorant—or willfully oblivious—to the risks that they had exacerbated. Merrill Lynch and Bear Stearns executives had even put their own deferred-compensation money into the hedge fund.

The government now seemed ready to do something. Even Greenspan seemed shaken. He contrasted the experience in trying to shore up financial markets after Long-Term's collapse with the savings-and-loan crisis a decade earlier. Back then, it was banks run by people—not largely anonymous short-term markets—that balked at new lending in the face of big losses.[23] Back then, at least he knew whom to talk to in trying to persuade markets to increase lending.

But despite regulators' painful object lesson that unregulated financial instruments posed a new clear and present danger to the economy, the government did worse than nothing. In 2000, even as the banks were still winding down Long-Term Capital's mess, Congress passed its Commodity Futures Modernization Act, prohibiting regulations on the most opaque derivatives and explicitly keeping them away from commodity regulators' jurisdiction.

These actions may seem unfathomable. But Washington had stumbled onto the same lesson that it learned after rescuing Continental Illinois: it was bigger and stronger than the financial markets. When necessary, Washington, in cooperation with the world's big commercial and investment banks, could will those markets out of a panic.

Greenspan had forgotten, or ignored, something that he had said after the government had bailed out Chrysler two decades earlier: that he feared the bailout's success more than its failure, since success would pave the way for more bailouts.[24] The Fed didn't see a need to persuade lawmakers and other regulators to re-create an orderly, consistent method of failure for financial firms to fail and for their lenders to take their losses, such as the one the FDIC had once provided for commercial banks and the bankruptcy code had once provided for other financial firms. Nor did the government see a need to protect credit markets from excessive speculation. It could clean up after the fact, and it ignored the obvious reality: bailouts encouraged more risky behavior, and thus more bailouts, in the future.

McDonough's fear of a "credit crunch" pointed up another, political motive for Congress's failure to enact new regulations. By the mid-nineties, Americans were growing accustomed to a world in which they could borrow at will, on cheap terms, for any conceivable purpose. No one wanted to be responsible, of course, for an acute recession or depression precipitated by a sudden credit cutoff, which Long-Term's bankruptcy, absent a bailout, could have triggered. But neither did anyone want to be responsible for slowing credit growth more gradually by adequately regulating credit's creators, financial institutions, and their instruments of creation—securitization and derivatives. Bailouts of financial firms in the business of creating debt only encouraged those firms to market yet more debt to Americans, exacerbating the problem.

Fourteen years after Continental Illinois shook markets, the bailout trend had reached its natural conclusion. Market discipline of the financial system provided by lenders to financial institutions was gone. Perversely, it continued to exist for hedge funds themselves. Shareholders in Long-Term Capital Management, after all, lost everything, and in the decade to come, it would turn out that unregulated hedge funds would act more conservatively than their regulated brethren.

But *lenders* to those hedge funds—the big commercial and investment banks alike—were protected. In turn, the lenders to those big commercial and investment banks knew that they had no reason to concern themselves with what the big banks did with their money. Lenders' critical role in disciplining the financial system—by refusing to extend credit to overly risky institutions— had been surrendered. The *Wall Street Journal* rightly warned that "you get a market so skewed by the expectations of bailouts that vital signals about genuine risk no longer get through. Eventually, the danger turns into one of systemic collapse."[25]

Long-Term Capital Management also showed that sophisticated models built by the world's smartest people, backed up by the financial industry's discretion, could not replace clear and simple limits on certain risks prescribed by laws and rules and enforced by average people. The banks and securities firms had not used their brilliance to take advantage of the dumb, as regulators had insisted in earlier derivatives implosions. They had taken advantage of themselves and, in a panic, abdicated responsibility to navigate their way out of the crisis so thoroughly that government regulators felt forced to step in.

Shortly after Long-Term imploded, derivatives that provided credit-default protection against financial institutions took off. Why? As the credit-risk director of Bankgesellschaft Berlin, a German bank, said weeks after the bailout, people who saw how reckless the banks were "want to reduce [their] exposure . . . to the banks."[26] This risk reduction, though, was part of a closed circle. If the banks failed, who would pay the bill for such protection?

The responsibility for risk, parceled out and distributed through the financial system so that each individual piece seemed minuscule, now led right back to Washington, D.C.

Long-Term Capital Management was the second-to-last milepost on the road to the current financial and economic crisis, the penultimate chance for policymakers and regulators to see that, for the sake of the free-market economy, financial markets need protection from themselves. Enron was the final opportunity.

Enron wasn't so much an energy-trading company as it was a financial company and, indeed, a distillation of the modern financial industry. It was a business built on the idea that financial engineering could transform any long-term asset into a security, instantly priceable and tradeable. That security, in turn, could serve as handy collateral for short-term debt. When confidence in Enron's ability to perform this alchemy vanished, Enron vanished, too.

Confidence, indeed, was Enron's only asset. "Even though nothing major appears to be wrong at Enron Corp., investor confidence in the world's largest energy trader remains shaky," the *Houston Chronicle* reported in August 2001.[27] The high-flying company's stock price had been cut by more than half in just months. Strangely, though, Enron observers weren't interested in the ongoing health of the company's actual businesses. Instead, they kept returning to one mysterious factor: investor faith. This logic seems circular: when a company is well established and not in need of start-up cash, as Enron was, investor confidence comes *because* the company is doing well and should keep doing well in the future. Investor confidence should be the effect, not the cause, of a company's success.

Six weeks after the *Chronicle* article, Enron reported a massive loss and a massive devaluation of some of its expensive global assets. And six weeks after that, Enron was bankrupt. It was the biggest insolvency in American history (until then). Both of the men who had led the company in its final two years, Kenneth Lay and Jeffrey Skilling, described the implosion as a "classic run on the bank," with the company's short-term lenders withdrawing their money in the firm's last weeks, leaving no money to conduct business.[28]

The press, prosecutors, and Congress derided this defense. On the eve of the criminal trial for Lay and Skilling, a local business columnist noted that "companies as big as Enron don't fail by a fluke. If Enron had its foundation in truth, no 'run on the bank' could have destroyed it. The market's lack of confidence merely reflected the larger ruse."[29] The conventional wisdom—and the criminal repercussions—echoed the Barings chief's first instinct about his firm's derivatives-induced blowup in 1995: someone must have done it on purpose.

But Lay and Skilling were on to something, because Enron had made itself just as vulnerable to a "run" as a 1920s bank. In the nineties, Enron, like the rest of the financial world, began to use modern financial innovation—securitization, derivatives, and the like—to reduce risk while attracting capital to expand its business. But for the three years leading to its demise, it became immersed in ever more complex finance, wrapping itself tightly in layer after layer of securitization, derivatives, and obscure maneuvering of funds held off its books. It lost sight of the fact that finance is a tool that supports a successful business and is not a substitute for it.

In its financial strategies, Enron led the financial industry, just as Enron's failure would precede that of the industry. The firm thrived on mark-to-market accounting, the system that Citicorp's Wriston had warned about but that appropriately measured the modern financial system, as seen in Chapter 4. That is, if Enron signed a contract to provide a customer with gas for twenty years, it would not report the gas payments each month as they came in. It would report all the profits from the contract now, based on its estimates of future gas prices, interest rates, and other variables.[30] Enron fully embraced this accounting method as a profit machine in the early nineties, before the banks did.

Enron's business model was analogous to the financial industry's new business model. It made short-term profits out of long-term assets, the same way that the banks, instead of keeping loans on their books and earning profits from those loans over the years, were increasingly combining loans into tradeable securities and booking the profits now. Both businesses depended on volume, not quality.

In its reliance on a business model measured by mark-to-market accounting, Enron, just like the commercial and investment banks, assumed that all its assets were as easy to value at any time as were perfectly liquid securities, like stock. But many of Enron's assets weren't so easy to value—they were one of a kind, like a power plant in India or a speculative broadband venture. So Enron based its values not on market prices—since there was no market—but on its own models and predictions. Enron's assets were worth what Enron said they were worth, as long as the market believed it. Similarly, banks' increasingly complex securitization instruments were worth what the banks said they were worth, based on their own intricate models, for as long as the markets had confidence in the banks' ability to model and value them.

Enron's financial strategy left it intensely vulnerable to the slightest mistake. When it booked in advance thirty years' worth of future profits from, say, a power plant in Brazil, anything from an increase in interest rates to a local economic downturn to a spike in gas prices could mean sudden, cascading losses. By contrast, under the old-fashioned system of earning long-term profits from long-term assets, Enron could absorb such losses over a number of years as the contract matured, if the losses even materialized as expected. The financial strategy also left it vulnerable to fraud. Because Enron's asset values derived not from independent third-party assessments, as stock securities do through public sale every day, but through internal judgments, it was easy for executives and the workers who wanted to please them to twist those judgments consistently in their favor.

In what should have been a warning for the financial world, Enron's disastrous mistake was in taking its own views of the future—all those mark-to-market profits—and using them as collateral to support massive amounts of precariously structured debt. "Enron borrowed from the future until there was nothing left to borrow," one executive told journalists Bethany McLean and Peter Elkind, who wrote a book on the Enron scandal.[31]

The company did so through its aggressive embrace of the banks' business model and use of two now-familiar financial innovations: securitization and derivatives. As seen in Chapter 4, banks sold their securitized loans into "structured investment vehicles" and other funds off their own books so that they could free up capital to make more loans. The special vehicles' investors, including pension funds and insurance companies, were repaid from the income that the securities in the trust generated. Enron spun assets like power plants into similar special trusts. The trusts then borrowed money to be repaid with the assets' future income. The trust would use that borrowed money to pay Enron for the assets, giving Enron needed cash to make more investments.

Enron, like the banks and, for that matter, like Samuel Insull's Commonwealth Edison in the twenties, used tiny slivers of equity to support mountains of debt within these trusts. Enron supplemented these slivers of equity with guarantees. Often, it told lenders to the trusts that if the assets in the trusts couldn't repay their debt, the company itself would step in. To hedge this risk, Enron used unregulated derivatives that it had created itself. The derivatives' value would supposedly rise if the value of the assets in the trusts sank, with the moves canceling each other out.

For a while, Enron created a virtuous circle. Through a delusion that financial engineering could structure away all risk, it created credit. As it created more credit, the value of its assets rose, because more money could support them. Enron took higher profits from those assets, and created more credit.

Ultimately, though, all these complex structured-finance creations led back to one source—Enron stock. "Enron was hedging risk with itself," McLean and Elkind wrote. "So many of Enron's questionable transactions . . . [were] rooted in the fundamental belief that Enron stock would never fall."[32] If the stock fell, then the firm would have to pay up on many of those guarantees. Of course, if Enron's stock were falling, that would be the very time that it couldn't pay up.

Oddly enough, all this intricate complexity made outsiders *more* confident in Enron's ability to manage risk. The company, just like the big financial firms, seemed to be pulling it off. Just as regulators trusted banks with their own financial models to assess the risks posed by derivatives—since the models' complexity seemed like evidence that they must be good—everyone trusted Enron to assess the risk posed by its own activities.

The architect behind these financial structures was chief financial officer Andrew Fastow. After college, Fastow's first job had been at Continental Illinois, right *after* the government had taken over the bank. Because regulators had no orderly fashion in which to let Continental fail, the markets had no way of killing off the bank's bad ideas. At Continental, Fastow had joined a team that continued to experiment with securitization, including securitizing junk-bond debt.[33] It's fascinating to speculate about what Fastow learned there. Did he realize that Continental's status as a complex financial institution had made it too big to fail? Did he assume that Enron, as it pumped more debt, and more complex debt, into the financial system to support itself, would enjoy the same government protection?

At Enron, Fastow's deals were "so bewildering that few people can understand them even now," said forensic analysts of the failed company[34]—an eerie echo of what General Electric chief Owen Young said about "the feeling of helplessness" that came over him in trying to pull apart Samuel Insull's bizarre utility creation seven decades earlier.

In the end, the byzantine maze of debt that Enron created for itself gave it only two exits: failure or fraud. In the business world, mistakes happen; ventures fail. Enron had no option to take the slightest misstep, though. At his criminal trial, Skilling said that his only mistake at Enron, besides trusting Fastow, who had stolen money under cover of complexity, was in "not selling overvalued assets sooner."[35] But Enron could not have sold its overvalued assets without taking a big loss on those assets. And it could not take a big loss on those assets without puncturing the only thing holding up all that debt: short-term confidence in the company.

The government let Enron fail, unlike what it did with Continental Illinois and Long-Term Capital Management. The messy nature of Enron's bankruptcy, though, should have served as a warning to regulators about the potency of systemic financial risk. After Enron failed, investors lost confidence in the energy-trading industry. Enron's competitors, which had followed the same business model and used many of the same accounting practices to measure that model's successes and failures, had to reestimate asset values and restate earnings and saw their stocks fall by half. Earnings delays and restatements roiled markets, with credit lines revoked and executives departing. Similarly contagious events in the financial sector, rather than in the energy sector, could be catastrophic.[36]

Enron's failure contained itself, though, for reasons that also should have been instructive. The energy industry traded its most common contracts on regulated markets that protected it from one company's spectacular failure. The customized derivatives markets in which Enron dealt were small and contained, relative to broader financial markets. Further, the energy industry didn't perceive itself as too big to fail, and it had institutional knowledge of how volatile commodities markets can be. So where regulations fell short, in unregulated derivatives markets, the industry often took modest steps to protect against failure, including margin requirements on customized trades.

Enron did not benefit from a constituency in Washington to warn that the firm's failure would present an unacceptable risk, thus convincing policymakers that they should not take the chance. As Enron teetered in autumn 2001, the Bush administration's Treasury Department called Wall Street analysts to ask what the government should do. The answer? Let it go. Wall Street was angry at Enron, angry that the firm had duped it with its fancy models and valuations with nothing behind them but—at best— hope. Bank executives, too, felt no kinship with the firm. And nobody on Wall Street worried that after Enron, his firm would be next—as they did seven years later, when Wall Street counseled Washington to rescue Bear Stearns's lenders.

Most crucially, Enron's failure wasn't catastrophic for the financial system because the tens of billions of dollars in credit that Enron had conjured out of nothing had not supported anything but . . . Enron. Enron was a bubble of one. When Enron securitized assets, the money went to *it*; the securitization did not create billions of dollars in credit in the broader economy for homeowners, credit-card holders, and corporations that vanished almost as suddenly and mysteriously as they had appeared.

If only policymakers and regulators had connected Long-Term Capital Management and Enron. Could the financial world, using the same inadequately regulated derivatives and securitization techniques, create a massive credit bubble that wouldn't confine itself to just one company? The question wasn't academic. "Some of the world's leading banks and brokerage firms provided Enron with crucial help in creating the intricate financial structures that fueled Enron's impressive rise," the *Wall Street Journal* reported after the firm's collapse.[37]

Enron's financial enablers had not found the company's behavior strange at all. Citigroup, JPMorgan Chase, and others had eagerly taken Enron's assets and funded them with guarantees backed only by Enron's own stock. Bear Stearns had helped Enron sell "credit-sensitive notes" with interest rates that would go from 9.5 percent to 14 percent if ratings analysts downgraded Enron's debt—when the firm would be least likely to have the resources to pay the higher rate, the same risk that financiers courted when they used credit derivatives to buy protection against securities losses from firms like MBIA.[38] One letter writer to the *Wall Street Journal* wondered about the banks' risk management, noting that "structured finance is complicated indeed, but that is all the more reason for those responsible for a transaction to analyze the source of the cash flow that will ultimately repay the loan. That is banking 101."[39]

Observers noted similarities between Enron and other financial giants besides the banks. With Enron's failure in mind, the *Wall Street Journal* took a hard look at the insurance giant AIG. AIG was a "complex company" in a "complex industry," the paper reported, detailing the insurer's opaque accounting, off-balance-sheet ventures, and vulnerability to sudden disclosures.[40] A similar comparison in the *Times* in 2005, three years later, came close. But it ultimately concluded that "as companies go, Enron was all smoke and mirrors, AIG is substance."[41]

The most salient question for policymakers and regulators should have been whether Enron's failure was a sign that the financial industry's profit model of borrowing heavily to trade long-term debt securities for short-term profit was growing untenable. Enron took this approach to the extreme, until the very language of the markets that the company created ceased to make sense: Enron, by creating so much debt, temporarily had more money to distort the values of its assets. Enron had made it seem that assets were worth much more than they really were, and, in a panic, outsiders saw Enron's assets as worth much *less* than they really were. But financial firms, too, through their earnings from short-term securities trading, were booking expected profits from thirty years' worth of mortgage payments today. If investors' perception of expected losses on the mortgages changed suddenly, pushing the value of the securities down, the financial firms would have to take thirty years' worth of expected losses today, too, even if those loss expectations later turned out to be too pessimistic.

But such searching questions remained unasked and unanswered. In 2002, regulators suggested some new limits on the accounting rules that allowed firms to take immediate profits from short-term trading of long-term financial instruments in the energy industry. David Sidwell, chief financial officer of JPMorgan Chase's investment bank, worried that regulators could apply such restrictions to other financial instruments, an "unreasonable" move, "given the investment-banking industry's years of experience with . . . methodologies" to value complex securities.[42] The financial industry was content to go on booking volatile profits based on short-term swings in the value of long-term assets, just as Enron had, even though those assets, often in the form of unregulated financial securities that did not trade on any exchange, were difficult to value consistently and were vulnerable to sudden drops in confidence.

Nor did anyone wonder whether Enron's technique of creating debt off its books through special trusts could replicate itself elsewhere in the financial world, with far more disastrous results for the economy. Rather, financiers and their representatives explained how *their* off-balance-sheet vehicles were superior to Enron's. "True securitization is about transferring risk to others," said lawyer David Eisenberg of Simpson Thacher & Bartlett, a securitization groundbreaker, in explaining the distinction. "Enron only appeared to be doing that, when in reality they were retaining the risk themselves."[43]

No policymaker or regulator asked whether the banks really could use securitization and special funds off their own books to transfer risk, seemingly to nobody, as they appeared to be doing. True, Enron guaranteed much of the debt that sat off its books, albeit murkily, while the banks didn't. But the banks' names stood behind their own similar trusts. Forgotten was the warning from Citicorp's Walter Wriston twenty years earlier: investors would not parse subtle distinctions among banks' legal entities in a crisis. Banks, then, could find themselves in the same position as Enron: unable to make good on their implicit guarantees when the markets were demanding payment.

After Enron, regulators severely restricted companies from setting up special funding vehicles for securitization—all companies but financial firms. The government continued to believe that the banks and investment firms were the only parties that could assess and assume such sophisticated risks. With financial firms, regulators continued to operate under the general assumption that they had held five years before Enron's collapse. In 1996, when accounting regulators pressed for more disclosure, Jason Kravitt, a Mayer Brown lawyer and securitization innovator, said that such disclosure would be unwieldy because "we would have a very strange accounting standard that was focused on the outcome that is a 1-in-a-100 chance."[44] The proffered statistic was false comfort. If one mortgage-backed security failed, they all would fail because they all depended on the same models built by the same banks.

The regulators had another reason for their inaction: they were afraid that restricting securitization would restrict credit creation. A few years before Enron's failure, in 1997, the Federal Reserve and two bank regulators, the Comptroller of the Currency and the Office of Thrift Supervision, began to consider requiring banks to hold bigger capital cushions (non-borrowed money) against their securitization holdings, protecting them better against losses. Executives from Capital One, Bank One, and MBNA visited the Fed in 2000, "lecturing about the size and importance of the securitization market" and warning that new restrictions on securitization could slow credit creation, "hurting consumers, minorities, and small businesses."[45]

The Fed, even in the wake of Enron's failure, watered down the requirements. Officials did not worry that they should gradually rein in credit's tremendous growth. Nor did they worry that in the absence of reasonable regulations, the securitization market in general, as it had in Enron's case, would prove so vulnerable to external events that it would one day shut itself down—cutting off the flow of credit abruptly rather than gradually.

In missing lessons and opportunity, the government had a useful distraction to help it: bad behavior, just as with stock frauds in the twenties, Michael Milken in the eighties, and Bankers Trust's derivatives blowups in the nineties. After Enron fell, the government successfully prosecuted Skilling, Lay, and dozens of others. Enron's collapse was a useful morality play: the Enron saga sprang from a willful criminal conspiracy of the individuals who peopled greedy corporate America, not from the far more immutable fallibility of financial markets. The outrage directed toward Skilling and Lay was so potent that few people were interested in looking at the subtler aspects of Enron—even though the details offered invaluable information.

The government's only regulatory fix in Enron's wake was the passage of the Sarbanes-Oxley Act of 2002, which imposed bigger criminal penalties for corporate wrongdoing, though ample penalties already existed. The law further mandated stricter "internal controls" so that corporations could better manage risk. With regard to financial firms, the idea of tighter internal controls helped maintain the illusion that executives could design and adhere to such controls absent well-defined regulatory limits on borrowing. It was the same thinking that had propelled regulators and elected officials to refrain from regulating new financial instruments and setting uniform capital standards on banks' investments.

Enron's failure, in one aspect, pointed up the benefits of financial creativity. The failure was good for the still-tiny credit-default-swap market. This young market had shined in what seemed like a big test. First, credit derivatives had provided investors with important data. By demanding higher premiums to protect against an Enron default, providers of credit-default protection in the swap market signaled that Enron was a big risk long before the credit-rating agencies, tasked with monitoring the quality of Enron's debt, did.[46] Second, when Enron defaulted, institutions that had bought credit-default protection through these derivatives did not lose money. As Greenspan said of credit derivatives in a September 2002 speech to British financiers, with Enron's experience in mind, "so far, so good."[47]

But the economy needed this innovative new market to operate within reasonable limits on borrowing and requirements for disclosure. The government did not provide such rules. In their absence, the financial world used credit derivatives' success in the Enron case as more evidence that it was possible to use financial innovation to engineer away debt's inherent risk. Of course, the financial world couldn't engineer away risk but only distribute it in ever more complex fashion *within* the same universe, magnifying it along the way with opacity and uncertainty, as with Long-Term Capital Management. Enron had done the same thing within Enron, and succeeded—for a time.

CHAPTER 7

SAFE AS HOUSES

A lot of these loans are dangerous. If you have any dip in values, people can just say the heck with it because they don't have any of their own money in the house.... What can I do? My job is to help people realize the American dream.
—Allen Jackson, manager, Bristol Home Loan, Bellflower, California, June 2004[1]

This is a dream come true.
—Kenneth Thompson, Wachovia CEO, upon purchase of adjustable-rate mortgage giant Golden West Financial Corporation, May 8, 2006[2]

ENRON'S 2001 FAILURE WAS THE LAST WARNING sign. Regulations were thoroughly insufficient to protect the economy from the unbridled financial forces that had gathered over the past two decades. The federal government had prevented markets from disciplining the core financial industry since its 1984 rescue of Continental Illinois' uninsured lenders. That rescue, and subsequent rescues, broke down the mechanism—controlled failures of financial firms—through which market forces separated losers from winners. Between Continental's rescue and Enron's failure, banks had relinquished their position as the relatively stable nexus between savers and borrowers, becoming storehouses and merchants of speculative credit.

Derivatives and securitization, the vehicles for banks' speculative new business model, had melted away all clear limits on lending and borrowing. The credit that securitization and derivatives created—short-term profits made from long-term securities—proved vulnerable to unexpected events, as mini-meltdowns in the securitization markets in 1986 and 1994 had shown. Finally, the unregulated derivatives world escaped even rudimentary disclosure requirements. Nobody knew where the risk lay.

By the early 2000s, the only significant policy that the government had left with which to protect the economy from excessive financial speculation was its control of the money supply through interest rates. But monetary policy remained blunt and imperfect, as it was in the twenties and always will be. The government still needed other tools to insulate the economy from its own monetary-policy mistakes. Starting in the early 2000s, the Federal Reserve made what seems, in hindsight, a disastrous monetary-policy error that provided the conditions for uncontrolled financial excesses. After the tech bubble burst in 2000 and after the terrorist attacks of September 11, 2001—which added an emotional wild card in impelling policymakers to revive the economy quickly and show that the terrorists hadn't won—the Fed lowered interest rates. By 2003, it had cut interest rates to just 1 percent—the lowest level in six decades. It kept them there for an entire year. Then it raised rates slowly—too slowly—between 2004 and 2006.

The result was a flood of cheap money, helping to expand a giant credit bubble. Just as in the twenties, global imbalances exacerbated the Fed's mistake. This time, the problem was uneven distribution not of gold but of dollars. China, rapidly becoming an export powerhouse, was on its way toward amassing over $1 trillion in dollar reserves as it sold goods to Americans. It recycled those dollars right back into America, purchasing Treasury bonds, which allowed the American government to borrow cheaply. China's Treasury purchases kept mortgage costs down for Americans, too, as mortgage rates derive from Treasury bond rates. China directly funded American mortgages, too, purchasing securities guaranteed by Fannie Mae and Freddie Mac.

Thirty years earlier, the flood of cheap money might have caused higher inflation in the cost of everyday goods and services. Instead, enabled by the dangerous erosion of regulations on debt, the easy money helped create a historic credit mania. The failure of financiers, investors, and regulators to see the risk that infused the financial world helped them turn one of the safest conceivable commitments for both lenders and borrowers—the purchase of a home—into a malign peril for the economy.

Throughout modern history, buying a home was neither a spectacular investment opportunity nor a flirtation with big losses. As Yale economist Robert Shiller found, after a sharp spike following World War II, house prices in the United States stayed fairly flat, relative to inflation, between the 1950s and the late 1990s. Occasionally, a short boom would feed on itself, but it would quickly go bust before it could do much more than local damage. Houses were good investments only in that they were an effective hedge against inflation.

Housing was not prone to speculative bubbles in part because of reasonable limits on borrowing. Well into the nineties, bankers generally required home buyers to present a down payment of 20 percent of the house purchase price, conforming to conservative standards laid out by Fannie and Freddie. This cash requirement, similar to margin rules for stock purchases, was a brake on debt-fueled speculation. If house prices started to rise precipitously, people eventually would not have enough cash to put up 20 percent of the higher price, thus muting demand.

Once regulations fell away, housing became a perfect host for a speculative-credit bubble, for two reasons. First, the government strongly supported homeownership. In 1997, the Clinton administration and the Republican Congress expanded this nearly century-old policy by enacting a tax policy that allowed people to reap gains from home sales tax-free, as long as the profits were under $500,000. (An equivalent gain in the stock market carried a harsh tax burden.) This favoritism was just the latest of many ways in which the government stoked housing demand, from tax deductions for mortgage interest to mandates on banks' lending to minority and low-income buyers.[3] Second, after the tech bubble burst, the middle class became distrustful of the stock market. The purchase of a home, by contrast, seemed safe.

Starting in the mid-nineties, the illusion that the financial industry had quantified and quarantined all risk found an all-too-willing repository in housing. Wall Street, through its securitization model, thought that it could engineer whatever slim risk remained. For example, on mortgages that didn't qualify for a Fannie or Freddie guarantee, financiers would determine that the loss risk was higher for a pool of 1,000 homeowners with poor credit than it was for a pool of homeowners with good credit. But Wall Street, as discussed in Chapter 4, was now adept at making AAA-rated securities out of any class of loan, no matter how risky. Financiers simply had to find more investors for the junior tranches of the pool, with those investors agreeing to take all the losses if, say, defaults and resales of foreclosed houses caused the entire pool of loans to lose 30 percent of its value. Because these "junior" investors bore disproportionate risk, the senior investors, who bought the AAA tranches, believed they had nothing to worry about. The mortgage securities, even when backed by loans to first-time home borrowers with bad credit, still seemed as safe as Treasury bonds because losses from subprime-mortgage defaults often would have to reach twice their historical levels before losses would reach the AAA investors.[4]

Even as Wall Street engineered riskier loans into AAA-rated securities, they gave themselves less room for error. Wall Street took pooled mortgage securities that the bankers had already tranched, and tranched these securities a second time. Senior investors' protection now rested on yet another layer of assumptions.

The designers, sellers, and buyers of the securities felt comfortable with these assumptions, though, because they had nearly two decades' worth of default data on all manner of loans to back them up. The securities' salesmen could have given the same assurance that the publicity man of the New York Stock Exchange had given, in the mid-1920s, about brokers' loans: "It is a fair statement that the increasing popularity enjoyed by security col-

lateral loans is due to the growing recognition that no safer investment exists. There is not a single instance of a loss suffered by
lenders within the memory of those engaged in the handling of
this type of loan."[5]

Mortgage securities enjoyed other levels of protection provided by Wall Street engineering. AIG, which boasted its own
AAA rating throughout most of the 2000s, eventually sold half a
trillion dollars' worth of its credit-default protection through the
unregulated derivatives markets. Putting little or no money down
as reserves, AIG promised investors in AAA-rated mortgage-
backed securities that if the magnitude of defaults ever exceeded
the securities' buffer levels—an unthinkable event—AIG would
make good on the losses.

Mortgage lending seemed so riskless for most investors
that financiers increasingly cast away the protection that Fannie
and Freddie offered. In 1996, before the housing boom began,
Wall Street sold $441 billion in securities insured by Fannie and
Freddie. By contrast, it sold only $52 billion in mortgage securities
without such a guarantee, just 12 percent of the share guaranteed
by Fannie and Freddie. By 2004, mortgages not guaranteed by
Fannie or Freddie were gaining. That year, Wall Street sold $1.4
trillion in Fannie and Freddie securities and $532 billion in mort-
gages not guaranteed by the two behemoths—38 percent of the
guaranteed securities. By 2006, the peak of the housing bubble,
mortgage securities without a guarantee from either housing
giant had nearly closed the gap, with $917 billion in such secu-
rities issued, compared with $1.2 trillion in Fannie and Freddie
securities. Also by 2006, securities backed by home-equity loans,
which didn't carry a guarantee, had grown tenfold in a decade, to
$581 billion.[6] Investors' demand for securitized loans had grown
so insatiable that marquee financial firms started buying the fly-
by-night mortgage brokers that dealt with the bad-credit end of
the market, to assure themselves of steady supply.

Fannie and Freddie, too, contributed to the lowering of credit
standards. In the mid-nineties, Fannie and Freddie started buying
and guaranteeing loans that escaped their previously tight requirements. In 1994, for example, Fannie, in response to congres-

sional pressure, modified its rules to give banks "more flexibility in lending to people who already owe a considerable amount of money or who cannot afford a down payment equal to 20 percent of the price of a home," with a long-term goal of "broadening the economic and ethnic diversity of homeowners," the *New York Times* reported. Freddie made a similar move.[7] They had to fulfill their market-distorting mission, aggressively supported by the Clinton and then the Bush administration, of encouraging homeownership, particularly among the poor and minorities. But so many qualified people, including lower-middle-class people, already owned their own homes that Fannie and Freddie needed to lower standards to keep the numbers rising.

In addition to political concerns, Fannie and Freddie, answerable to private shareholders, had to keep up with the times and maintain their market share. Otherwise, their reason for existence—to support the broader mortgage markets—would disintegrate, harming investors. As they became more aggressive, the market still outpaced them. "Until the past couple of years, Fannie Mae and Freddie Mac either bought or guaranteed most U.S. mortgage loans," the *Wall Street Journal* reported in late 2005. "More recently, though, Fannie and Freddie have lost market share. . . . [T]hey haven't been major buyers of the increasingly popular interest-only loans and other mortgages that let borrowers defer principal payments. Freddie executives say they are gearing up to buy more such mortgages but promise to do so prudently."[8]

Fannie and Freddie once worked with the banks to reinforce high standards; now, they worked to reinforce low standards. Before financiers convinced themselves that they had dispatched all risk, Fannie and Freddie had created a huge, safe market that the two firms dominated. The agencies' standards for mortgage underwriters, who wanted the Fannie and Freddie guarantee, made mortgage securities safer. Indeed, Fannie's and Freddie's very existence in the mortgage market helped to create those decades' worth of data that lulled investors into thinking that *all* mortgage lending was safe.

But this dominance had a pernicious effect. Because quasi-government dominance in the mortgage market constrained profits in an important area of the financial world, Wall Street had to become more creative to earn higher profits in the mortgage-lending business. And when Fannie and Freddie embraced ever more aggressive underwriting standards in pursuit of the government goal of expanding homeownership, it was a signal to Wall Street and to investors that it was fine to keep doing the same in pursuit of their own profit motive. Fannie's and Freddie's activity reinforced financiers' confidence that they had engineered away risk.

As easy mortgage credit flourished, house prices skyrocketed. By 2006, the average person who purchased a single-family house in any one of twenty sprawling metropolitan and suburban areas in 2000 had doubled his money. These home-price increases exceeded growth in personal income, which determines people's ability to pay the debt holding up their house values. As each year passed, the speculative cycle spun faster. Easy credit, initially enabled by low interest rates, pushed up house prices; rising prices made credit even easier, because the collateral backing the debt—the house—could only rise. Or so the thinking went.

Perceiving only safety, financial firms lowered their standards still further. Gone were even 10 percent down payments. Buyers, toward the end of the bubble, could simultaneously take out a mortgage and a "piggyback" home-equity loan to borrow *more* than their houses were worth—effectively a negative down payment—because financiers assumed that the house value would rise quickly after the purchase. Gone was the requirement that borrowers be able to pay their loans out of their income. Instead, Wall Street assumed that borrowers would refinance their mortgages frequently, taking new cash out of the ever-rising home value to keep up with the house payments.

Even if the borrowers could not keep up, it didn't matter. They could sell their unaffordable houses at higher prices, repaying their loans. Even a foreclosure would not result in a loss for the holder of the mortgage-backed security, because administrators would sell the house into a rising market. Gone, too, was the old thirty-year, fixed-rate mortgage; instead, mortgages often came with a low initial "teaser rate," with payments so low over the first two years that they covered only interest costs—sometimes only part of the interest costs—and didn't go toward paying back any of the actual loan. Wall Street posited again that the borrower would refinance—often paying a big fee to the investors in his current mortgage—before the rate jumped up to an unaffordable level.

By the mid-2000s, the mortgage world had turned itself upside down. In 2006, only 45 percent of approved mortgages were of the conventional variety. Subprime mortgages for people with poor or no credit, along with something called "Alt-A" for borrowers with good credit but poor income records or who wanted far more house than they could reasonably afford, accounted for fully 40 percent of the total. Subprime mortgages had more than doubled in five years, from 9 percent of the market in 2001 to 20 percent in 2006.[9]

As the bubble expanded, mortgage fraud flourished on both sides. Mortgage lenders did not scrupulously disclose the real risks behind exotically structured mortgages to unsophisticated buyers—some whose English was poor. Mortgage borrowers lied about their income and assets. A nation based on the rule of law cannot tolerate rampant fraud. But just as in the 1920s, the government could not have reined in the housing market through criminal prosecutions. As house prices inexorably increased, underwriters and the investors who bought their securities did not care if borrowers were lying to them, and borrowers did not care if lenders lied. A manic bubble needed only warm bodies.

Regulations to constrain speculative credit undeniably would have prevented this mania. Regulators could have recognized the bubble for what it was, as two decades earlier Fed chairman Paul Volcker had seen through the junk-bond mania. They could have prohibited average investors from borrowing with no money or little money down to buy a house, just as Volcker had prohibited hostile-takeover companies from borrowing without putting up cash to complete their purchases.

Even a requirement for a 10 percent cash down payment would have prevented the housing bubble from expanding so dangerously. Though borrowing would still have been cheap in an easy-money environment made possible by lax Fed monetary policy, working-class and middle-class buyers would have had to overcome the hurdle of saving $20,000 for a $200,000 house. Marginal buyers at all price levels—the poor person who couldn't afford a house at all, the middle-class person who couldn't afford a rich person's house, and the rich person who couldn't afford two houses—would have found themselves shut out. Fraudsters would not have risked their own cash on their transparent lies.

Regulators could have used their ample credibility and discretion, too, to prohibit average people from finding their way into too-complex investments, something that regulators actively forbid in other investment markets. People without mid-six-figure incomes and seven-figure savings aren't allowed to invest in hedge funds, since regulators have determined that the average person doesn't have enough information to assess the funds' true risks. Exotic mortgages were sophisticated investments, too. An adjustable-rate mortgage, for example, because its rate increases if global interest rates increase, is an unhedged bet on the direction of interest rates. Regulators did not treat these mortgages as what they were: sophisticated, wildly risky, speculations.

Disclosure rules, too, would have constrained risk-taking. Since the Depression, stockbrokers and corporations have been prohibited from making "can't-lose" pitches to potential investors. They must carefully explain the potential for real loss. But real-estate brokers—even today—operate under no such restriction. Agents telling unsophisticated investors that they couldn't lose money on a house were just as common as exotic mortgages.

Regulators didn't allow themselves to realize that housing had become yet another speculative investment, requiring the same protections that governed other speculative investments, including the stock market. Action would have levied a serious cost on the economy. Wall Street was making tremendous profits; the financial sector's profits as a percentage of the nation's income more than doubled in each of the last two decades leading up to the global financial meltdown. Just as important, Americans had grown accustomed to borrowing from their homes so that they could spend more money, feeding economic growth. In 2005, Americans borrowed $200 billion against the value of their houses for the purposes of direct spending, up 80 percent from three years earlier.[10] Policymakers and regulators did not want to interfere with profits or seeming prosperity.

Political advocates exacerbated complacency. Democrats won the support of a social-justice industry built up around expanding homeownership for minorities. However, the housing bubble persisted and grew because it had a middle-class constituency, a constituency that expanded as lax requirements allowed people to purchase their first homes at ever-earlier ages.[11] Democrats and Republicans alike wanted to do nothing to slow down the house-price growth that was making the middle class feel rich and savvy. Further, if the magic of markets could help poor minorities with no savings and scant incomes buy homes, that was a good thing, almost everyone agreed.

Wall Street didn't chafe at pressure to lend to unqualified borrowers; far from it. The industry had found political cover for a growing, lucrative, and seemingly riskless business that otherwise might have seemed unsavory. In 1977, when Washington first mandated mortgage lending to the poor through the Community Reinvestment Act, banks considered the mandate akin to an annoying tax; now, a similar business was a profit font. In 2004, Angelo Mozilo, CEO of Countrywide Financial, which marketed exotic mortgages to often-unqualified borrowers, won the Person of the Year award bestowed by the National Housing Conference, an affordable-housing advocacy group.

Reining in the right to own a home seemed un-American on both sides of the aisle. In 1999, then-president Bill Clinton invoked the legacy of Rev. Martin Luther King, Jr., in touting a new agreement with a financial firm to offer "home mortgages . . . to help 78,000 minority and low- and moderate-income families unlock the door to homeownership."[12] Two years later, in 2001, Senator Phil Gramm said, "I look at subprime lending and

I see the American dream in action."[13] President Bush focused domestic policy on an "ownership society" and regularly heralded rising homeownership rates. Fannie and Freddie used their considerable power both to bribe and to intimidate politicians and the media; but their unique power to do so came from their carefully preserved apple-pie image as every homeowner's friend.

Herd psychology tended the bubble, too. It was difficult to suggest that the emperor had no clothes. As late as 2007, after the housing boom had peaked, conventional wisdom still held that the boom in housing was helping the nation to enjoy a "Goldilocks" economy, with the Dow Jones Industrial Average stock index on its way to 14,000 and everything right with the world. Anyone who suggested otherwise was considered ignorant of economic reality.

In August 2006, Europe Pacific Capital president Peter Schiff, an economist, went on the business-news channel CNBC to point out what was already becoming obvious. "The basic problem . . . is we have too much consumption and borrowing . . . and what's going to happen is the American consumer . . . is going to stop consuming . . . , especially when he sees his home equity evaporate," Schiff observed. Schiff's fellow guest, Art Laffer, chairman of Laffer Associates and a former Reagan economic adviser, was dismissive, arguing that "the United States economy has never been in better shape. . . . Monetary policy is spectacular. . . . I think Peter's just totally off base, and . . . I just don't know where he's getting his stuff." Said Schiff in response, "All that's increased is paper value . . . of real estate. . . . All that phony wealth is going to evaporate, and all that's going to be left is all the debt that we've accumulated." Laffer concluded by repeating that Schiff was "just way off base. There is nothing out there that tells us this."

A few months later, in February 2007, Schiff had a similar experience on another CNBC show. After the economist observed that "the housing market is just beginning to unravel," the incredulous anchor, Mark Haines, asked him, "How do you put together all this gloom and doom? What *data* tells you this, Peter?" Schiff answered, incredulous himself, "Aren't you looking at the news reports? Aren't you looking at the glut of houses on the market with no buyers?" Haines's confident rejoinder was that collapses such as the one experienced in the stock market in 2000 were "usually once-in-a-lifetime events, and you're suggesting that in very short order . . . we're gonna have another one?"[14] It wasn't that people couldn't predict what was going to happen. They couldn't grasp what was happening.

With nearly all skepticism evaporated, debt mania extended beyond homes. The financial world had applied the same theory of riskless lending to almost every conceivable real-estate asset, from commercial office towers to shopping centers. By 2006, the mortgage-securities market had grown to nearly $8.5 trillion in outstanding debt in the market, while the securities market backed by loans other than mortgages, such as car or credit-card loans, had grown to $2.1 trillion.[15] These figures, together, had more than doubled in just six years. From 2000 to 2006, debt as a percentage of the nation's economy rose by nearly 30 percent. It represented more than 350 percent of the nation's annual production, nearly double its twenties-era highs. Borrowing within the financial industry itself had risen sixfold since the eighties.[16] Debt growth resembled a straight line up. To protect the investors in the securities that underpinned much of this debt from losses, the global credit-default derivatives market had grown from nearly nothing five years previously to $29 trillion by the end of 2006. It had nearly doubled in just one year.[17]

Easy money created its own profits outside of the traditional real-estate sector. In 2006, an Australian bank and a Spanish bank together paid $3.6 billion to buy a toll road from the state of Indiana, borrowing more than that amount for the purchase. The interest costs on this debt exceeded the profit from the road. But the banks believed that they would refinance the road in a few years, taking the cash from the road's rising value to keep up with the debt. The banks further assumed that because the financial world was becoming less risky, they would have to pay less in interest to borrow for the road in the future. The banks weren't in the road business but in the easy-credit business. The road's valuation made no mathematical sense, in terms of expected revenues being greater than expected costs, absent a credit bubble that distorted reality.

Without an external force, the financial markets proved unable to stop themselves. The external force with the least damage to the economy would have been clear regulatory limits on speculative risk-taking. Seventy years previously, the Great Depression had demonstrated how severely the economy suffers when, without such limits, obliviously manic speculation has to wait for the only other external force that can stop it: the sudden evaporation of the confidence that created the mania in the first place.

By the mid-2000s, far more than it had in the twenties, most of the long-term debt that buoyed the markets and the economy rested on the ceaseless maintenance of short-term confidence. By 2006, securitized debt had grown from next to nothing less than two decades previously to nearly half of all household and business debt outstanding.[18] Wall Street had found buyers for these debt-backed securities often by telling investors that they could instantly price, buy, and sell them, like common stocks on an exchange.

But instantly traded stock securities are much more vulnerable to short-term confidence swings than long-term bank loans are, as the junk-bond boom had proved. Further, the pricing and trading for debt-backed securities was never as transparent as financiers made it out to be, nor was the market ever as deep as financiers claimed. The financial institutions themselves were doing much of the buying and selling, as they had once done in the junk-bond market. Often, two well-acquainted mid-level traders at rival firms determined the price of a mortgage-backed security, making that valuation vulnerable to systemic misjudgment and fraud. By contrast, with equity securities, a market of millions of anonymous buyers and sellers determines prices. Wall Street had turned the long-term credit markets into a short-term trading market with only a pretense of the real liquidity and valuation that robust trading markets need.

Short-term confidence and easy credit depended on multiple layers of increasingly fragile assumptions. But the suppositions behind even the simplest structured-finance concoctions—like those early mortgage securities, circa 1986 and 1994—had proved vulnerable to unexpected events. This time around, bankers and ratings analysts figured that default levels would look like they did in the past. Further, in the event of defaults, they thought that recovery rates—the amount of money that banks' loan administrators could recoup by selling a house or another asset—would also look the way they did in the past. Financiers and purchasers of mortgage-backed securities failed to consider the risk that house prices would fall precipitously across the nation—because prices never had fallen across the nation before. Financiers had confidence that people with teaser-rate mortgages could always refinance the loans before the teaser rates jumped up. And they thought that a mistake in any of their variables wouldn't affect the other variables—never considering, for example, that a decrease in house prices would increase default rates and at the same time lower the value of resold homes. For their part, investors blindly trusted that Wall Street knew what it was doing in quantifying and efficiently distributing all this risk. Each layer of theory and each layer of trust allowed investors to pile on another layer of seemingly safe debt.

The biggest assumption that so many people made was that even as financial companies transformed themselves and transformed credit, they hadn't in the process changed borrowers' behavior. They didn't think that many borrowers would find themselves with a new, perfectly rational economic incentive to walk away from their homes if house prices declined, because they had no equity in those homes to lose. Financiers' models about how people would behave toward their houses based on how they had always behaved—sacrificing almost everything else just to keep up with their mortgage—were now obsolete. After the financial system turned purchasing a house into a speculative venture, Americans started to treat it as one—and Americans always have enjoyed the right to walk away from a bad investment.

The economy had little room for error if the fragile assumptions underpinning all this debt failed. First, financial firms held much of that debt on their own books, both for short-term trading purposes and because they often kept lower-rated tranches of mortgage-backed securities in order to sell the higher-rated tranches off. To magnify profits from those holdings, financial firms borrowed. By 2006, financial firms' ratio of borrowing to actual capital was more than two-thirds above its modern long-term average. If financial firms took even moderate losses on the securitized loans that they had to value each quarter to report their profits from the gain or loss in these securities, they would need more capital. In such a case, they would not have the money to create more securitized debt, cutting credit to the economy. Financial firms' increasing dependence on short-term debt to fund their operations, rather than on FDIC-guaranteed bank deposits or long-term bonds, compounded this problem. If financial firms took losses on their instantly priced debt securities, their own short-term uninsured depositors, as well as purchasers of their short-term debt through the money markets, could vanish.

Second, global investors were a big source of demand for America's securitized credit. By selling securitized mortgage debt to overseas investors, including European and Asian banks, financiers—and regulators—thought that they had transferred the risk so thoroughly that losses among a few of these widely dispersed investors wouldn't diminish their own investors' appetite for more debt. As the *Wall Street Journal* reported in 2005, "when the American housing boom winds down, some of the first howls of pain are likely to be heard in Europe and Asia."[19] But these remote investors did not know—and had never wanted to know—that their perfectly safe mortgage-backed debt was subject to gradations of risk as the markets and the economy changed. Investors had bought AAA-rated securities for one reason: to assure airtight AAA safety. If that debt turned out not to be so safe, it wouldn't be worth less. It would be worthless to these buyers, who had bought it for this express purpose.

Third, many of these same institutional investors had returned the debt's risks straight to Wall Street via the credit-default swaps they purchased from companies like AIG. Because of this market's opacity, people groped to understand where this risk lay as the housing bubble started to deflate, in early 2006. As the *Journal* warned then, "the market for financial deals called credit derivatives . . . has grown so fast that it has overwhelmed the . . . infrastructure. . . . [A] minor hiccup might become a financial calamity with repercussions for the whole economy."[20]

Lastly, regulators, even as they created the conditions in which unbridled optimism could feed on itself, ensured that at some point, unbridled pessimism would grow of its own momentum, too. In 2007, the SEC decided to do away with the uptick rule—that Depression-era restriction on selling a stock "short" if the price was already falling, thus exacerbating the stock's fall. The rule forced short-sellers to wait until the price of a particular security improved before they could make their trade, keeping them from pushing the value of a stock down to zero. Now, this external force pushing back against fear was gone.

If confidence vanished, the government would face a test of its ability to save the financial world from itself and to save the broader economy from that financial world—just as it had in the Great Depression, a situation that rational regulations had successfully prevented since.

Politicians and regulators could not have understood all the implications of these changes over two and a half decades and could not have done everything possible to reduce the risks to the economy that these changes posed. But they seemed to miss every bit of it, doing nothing whatsoever to reassert the decades-old principles that had gently guided and protected free markets for so long.

CHAPTER 8

CREDIT CRUNCH, ECONOMIC CALAMITY

When the music stops, in terms of liquidity, things will be complicated. But as long as the music is playing, you've got to get up and dance. We're still dancing.... The depth of the pools of liquidity is so much larger than it used to be that a disruptive event now needs to be much more disruptive than it used to be.
                      —Charles Prince, Citigroup chief, July 8, 2007[1]

—Citigroup is threatened with insolvency.
—Who is threatening Citigroup with insolvency?
—They are threatening *themselves* with insolvency.
         —overheard, Manhattan bankers' dinner party, October 2008

O N SEPTEMBER 16, 2008, THE NATION'S OLDEST money-market fund, the Reserve Primary fund, "broke the buck," or lost value for its investors. It was a new development for the credit-crunch-turned-credit-crisis. Though the financial world had grown numb from blow after blow—from the bailout of Bear Stearns's creditors in March to Lehman Brothers' bankruptcy a day before—this loss "is really, really bad," Don Phillips, a founder of the fund-analyst firm Morningstar, stated. "You talk about Lehman and Merrill"—the venerable investment bank then on the brink of failure—"having been stellar institutions, but breaking the buck is sacred territory."[2]

A money-market fund seemed indistinguishable, in investors' eyes, from an FDIC-guaranteed savings account. Investors used money-market funds to park cash for a low return before sending that money on to pay bills or make other investments. Money-market managers, in turn, invested the funds in the safest securities around, including short-term bonds issued by big financial firms. Over forty years, these funds had come to serve the same vital function that banks had once performed for borrowers as well as lenders, growing to 30 percent of the size of commercial-bank lending. High-quality borrowers—including universities, corporations, small businesses, states, and cities— could borrow at reasonable rates from these funds for their day-to-day needs.

No money-market fund had broken the buck in nearly a decade and a half, and investors saw the previous instance, in 1994, as an isolated occurrence. Back then, California's Orange County had bankrupted itself with derivatives trades, hurting the value of its debt in which money-market funds had invested.

Now, though, a vicious panic hit money-market funds. By contrast with 1994, investors worried that Reserve's announcement was only the beginning. Reserve lost value because it had invested in Lehman Brothers' debt. Investors wondered how many other funds had done the same and how many other financial institutions could fail, triggering more losses across other funds. The funds enjoyed no protections from fear because their depositors had no FDIC guarantees; such guarantees hadn't seemed important until recently. Terrified investors pulled $200 billion out of this $3.3 trillion market. The run on the funds instantly became a crisis for the economy, with companies, municipalities, and other entities unable to borrow.

To stanch this drain of money and credit, Washington took a page from its thirties-era playbook. By midweek, the Treasury Department guaranteed all money-market funds for at least a year upon request, ensuring that investors would not lose any money.

The Treasury Department was able to act so quickly because a 1934 law authorized it to "deal in . . . instruments of credit and securities" to promote financial stability.[3]

For many investors, the failure of a supposedly safe money-market fund was the final realization that the financial sector had failed at its main job under its modern business model: identifying and distributing risk. The government no longer had any regulatory buffers between core credit markets and the mass-scale panic that such a realization set off. By the end of 2008, the only thing protecting the American economy from the vaporization of the financial industry was the printing presses of the U.S. Mint.

More than a year earlier, in early 2007, the fragile theories underpinning the financial industry's tower of debt had begun to disintegrate. As the housing boom sputtered to a halt, people realized that asset values wouldn't rise forever, supporting ever-higher amounts of debt. A March report showed that the number of subprime borrowers over ninety days late on their mortgages had spiked 20 percent from the year before. At the nation's biggest mortgage lender, Countrywide, 19 percent of recently approved subprime mortgages were delinquent. In April, another major mortgage lender, New Century Financial, declared bankruptcy.

Another assumption—that homeowners could always stay ahead of rising rates on adjustable-rate mortgages by refinancing—soon collapsed, too. Subprime borrowers had trouble refinancing mortgages, as the volume of new mortgage-backed securities fell below the previous year's levels for the first time in half a decade. Borrowers unable to refinance and take cash out of the rising value of their houses wound up stuck with unaffordable mortgages.

Analysts struggled to understand how this turmoil would affect the financial industry. "Does the flow of mortgages to the securitization machine slow? That's what I'm most worried about," one analyst said, fretting that investment banks' profits could suffer if the driver of those profits—mortgages—dried up.[4] "Potential risks to the big [investment] banks are relatively modest," another said, figuring that mortgage losses could cost Lehman Brothers only 3.2 percent of earnings and Bear Stearns just 4.1 percent.

The financial industry and Washington, though nervous, generally believed that losses would be "contained." That became the season's popular new word, borrowed from Federal Reserve chairman Ben Bernanke's reassuring congressional testimony in March. But the market kept giving off odd signals. The credit-default market, by demanding sharply higher payments from the investors who wanted to buy protection against the possibility that Bear Stearns would default on its debt, telegraphed that the chance of a default had increased 40 percent from winter to mid-spring.

By June 2007, with the mortgage market's foundational premises discredited, observers had honed in on the higher-order suppositions that the financial industry had made in fashioning debt securities out of those mortgages and all manner of other debt. Investors had trusted financiers to structure securities so carefully as to insulate the investors in the securities from losses. Now, the ratings agencies were reviewing and downgrading their mortgage-securities ratings as losses started to creep up. While their early actions mainly affected lower-rated securities, investors who had put their money in AAA-rated securities grew nervous, too, at this hasty revision of expectations.

Another weakness of mortgage-backed securities, too, became apparent. Because financiers had sliced and diced the underlying mortgages and spread them across the world, it was difficult—almost impossible—for the administrators that handled payments collection and other tasks on behalf of the investors to get such a disparate group to agree to cut a borrower's mortgage to a more affordable level or to allow the borrower to delay payment, common approaches that old-fashioned banks take to lessen losses.

Wall Street firms struggled to contain the damage. Bear Stearns had to pump $3.2 billion into two of its own hedge funds that owned such securities to keep them afloat. The bailout gave "it and its prestigious mortgage business a black eye," the *New York Times* observed. But Bear Stearns had no choice, as short-term lenders to the funds had fled, and the firm didn't want to sell the funds' assets into a declining market. "[M]any on Wall Street speculated how the firm could let the funds get in such a precarious position," with tremendous leverage backing securities that suddenly seemed inscrutable.[5]

Similarly, AIG spent $2.5 billion bailing out two funds that it held off its books. Prominent European banks, too, tried to stem emerging problems in their own hedge funds, many heavily invested in the same mortgage debt. Nervous investors watched mortgage-default rates climb quickly toward those levels that protected the "senior," AAA-rated securities. It was no longer unthinkable that 30 percent or more of recent subprime-mortgage borrowers might default—in fact, by mid-2007, the loss rate on lower-quality mortgage securities issued in 2006 and earlier that year broke through the 20 percent barrier. As the summer wore on, ratings-agency downgrades began to reach the very safest portion of the market: AAA-rated securities. While ratings agencies and bankers tried to convince investors that most of the highest-quality securities downgraded still offered "very strong prospects for full repayment of principal," the investors wanted no part of this new uncertainty.[6] People started to read the reports that the ratings agencies released to explain their methodology—and found that they didn't understand any of it.

Nor was it unthinkable any more that the once-staid bond insurers such as MBIA and Ambac would lose their own AAA ratings, since they had to make good on guarantees that suddenly looked more expensive. If MBIA and Ambac lost their own ratings, the hundreds of billions of dollars in mortgage-backed securities that the insurers guaranteed would lose their AAA ratings, too. In late 2007, news emerged that the big banks were pondering pumping cash into the insurers so that they didn't falter, which would force the banks to take even more losses on the securities guaranteed by credit derivatives sold by the giants.

But the problem with this idea, observers grasped, is that if the banks had to bail out their own protectors, they hadn't really transferred any risk to those protectors, just as they hadn't really transferred risk to AIG through similar credit-default swaps and just as they hadn't really structured away risk through their complex securitization structures. Uneasily, people remembered the bond insurers' old pitch: that only a financial Armageddon could endanger their AAA ratings.

The conviction that short-term lenders would ceaselessly provide the funding for the nation's long-term mortgages and other credit weakened, too. Previously, global lenders had provided credit by lending to financial firms, through short-term money markets and uninsured deposits, and also by lending to the special funds that the financial firms had set up off their books to warehouse mortgage-backed and other securities. By August 2007, though, short-term lenders to the financial world's off-the-books funds had vanished, following the desertion of lenders to Bear Stearns's hedge funds. Short-term lenders finally understood how tenuous some of the models driving the securitizations were. They also balked at buying other debt-backed securities. Long-term credit dried up almost overnight; it became impossible to get all but the most conservative of mortgages.[7]

Short-term investors fled because the last great tenet of the credit markets—the idea that all long-term debt could be easily priced and traded on a short-term basis, almost as instantly as cash—was disintegrating. Instantaneously priced and traded securities need transparent markets. And suddenly, the financial world was telling its remaining lenders to ignore what the markets were saying. AIG, for example, insisted in summer 2007 that the market's grim new assessment of its exposure to unregulated derivatives contracts—which would require big payouts if the mortgage markets continued to plummet—was wrong. AIG insisted that "the bulk of [the] mortgage and residential loans" that it had guaranteed "aren't at risk" and that the problem was that "there isn't a market for the insurance contracts."[8] AIG's statements were meant to alleviate investors' fears, but in asking investors to ignore markets, they only stoked alarm.

In October 2007, the *Wall Street Journal* ran a story showing that the breakdown of each of the assumptions holding up the economy's credit was so profound that it could shake the nation's biggest money-center bank: Citigroup. The U.S. Treasury, the paper reported, had recently hosted representatives of the nation's three biggest banks—Citigroup, Bank of America, and JPMorgan

Chase—to formulate a plan for one particular aspect of what was becoming a crisis. The problem was in structured investment vehicles—the funds that Citigroup and other financial firms had created off their own books to attract hundreds of billions of dollars in short-term financing for mortgage-backed securities and other debt. As short-term lenders fled these funds, those securities, hemorrhaging in value, had become long-term loans that nobody wanted. Somebody now had to pay for them.

The government's fear was the same as it had been two decades earlier with Continental Illinois and Long-Term Capital Management, but amplified: a catastrophic market meltdown, as the illusion of liquidity disappeared across all manner of financial investments and financial firms. Without a source of funding for the mortgage-backed securities held off their books as investor fear mounted, Citigroup and other institutions would have to sell tens of billions of dollars' worth of these securities and other assets at fire-sale prices. Mass-scale distressed selling would force down the prices of similar assets around the world, starting a cycle of more forced sales and more write-downs of similar securities, weakening other financial institutions. "The ultimate fear: if banks need to write down more assets or are forced to take assets onto their books, that could set off a broader credit crunch and hurt the economy," the *Journal* reported.[9] The systemic risk to the economy that the unregulated financial world posed, once considered hypothetical, was now becoming real. To avoid cataclysmic sell-offs, the Treasury and top bankers realized that someone would have to rescue the orphaned securities, as the big banks had done with Long-Term Capital Management's holdings.

The three big banks and the Treasury, then, tried to unscramble the securitization egg. They planned a *new*, bank-controlled investment fund, a "Super Structured Investment Vehicle," or Super-SIV, that would purchase "as much as $100 billion in [these] shaky mortgage securities and other investments." This time, the fund wouldn't be backed by short-term lenders' faith in structured finance but in something far simpler: "[B]ecause the [fund] would be backed by the big banks themselves, it's expected this would reassure investors," the *Journal* reported.[10] Further, the banks wouldn't rely on markets to set the prices at which the fund purchased the orphaned securities. The banks instead would huddle together and figure out reasonable prices among themselves, buying the securities and putting them in quarantine—away from the markets that the banks now wanted to disregard.

But just as you can't put a scrambled egg back into its shell, the banks couldn't "de-securitize" their scrambled investments. It was too late. Some investors had already come to their own conclusion that the market was working and that the mortgage-backed securities truly had plummeted in value. That conclusion would mean, of course, that the banks' structural assumptions behind the securities were wrong. Alternatively, some investors concluded that the market *wasn't* working, meaning that they'd lost confidence in the core tenet behind these securities and the institutions that traded and marketed them: that these securities could always be priced and traded in a market deep and broad enough to assure that sellers could always find buyers, similar to the stock market. Such markets don't mysteriously cease to function one day, as now seemed to be the case with the securitization market.

The rescue attempt, which ultimately failed, raised more disquieting questions than it answered. Looking at trillions of dollars of securitized debt, investors wondered if $100 billion would be enough. They also wondered whether the bailout was an attempt by the government to help Citigroup avoid using its own capital to rescue its off-the-books funds. Citigroup didn't technically guarantee the funds, as Enron often had done with similar funds. But as Citicorp's Wriston had observed a quarter of a century earlier, investors wouldn't make such a distinction in a crisis.

A smaller but growing number of investors began to understand that the worst-case scenario wasn't that Citigroup would have to bail out these funds but that it wouldn't be able to. Investors saw how little room for error the financial industry had built in to its seemingly airtight models. A catastrophic error in those calculations, as it became apparent, would overwhelm many financial firms' thin capital bases, and losses in subprime securities alone were starting to make such an outcome seem well within the realm of possibility.

Other commercial and investment banks around the world had hundreds of billions of dollars in similarly structured debt, on their books as well as off. Banks were becoming stranded, holding securitized assets that they often had planned to sell quickly in order to fund even more securitized assets in what now looked like a house-of-cards business model. Chillingly, banks started refusing to lend to one another, as each institution, slowly realizing its disastrous errors, saw that its competitors had made the same mistakes. Nine years previously, investors remembered, Citi was one of the banks that helped save the economy from Long-Term Capital Management's bank-enabled missteps. But because the government had done nothing about too-big-to-fail financial firms, the problem had grown so large that it was now unclear whether Citi and other banking giants were the rescuers or in need of rescue.

As the government's efforts failed to quell the panic, bankers and government officials relearned what a previous generation of bankers had discovered when they tried to prop up stock prices after the 1929 crash. A few determined men cannot hold back a market seeking a new price in a world where everything that everyone knew has turned out to be wrong.

No amount of human intervention could stop the brutal market correction once financial institutions started reporting earnings in autumn 2007. Just as in the Depression, nobody could agree on what anything was worth. Financial firms, just as they had back then, had compounded the problem by taking all of tomorrow's profits today. This time, they had done so by converting many of those long-term loans into securities to profit from instant sales and trading rather than waiting to earn interest from borrowers over decades. In the bubble, the securities' values had reflected unrealistically optimistic expectations of the future. Now, possibly, they reflected unrealistically pessimistic expectations. But nobody knew.

In announcing unprecedented declines in asset values, bank executives used a baffling excuse: securities, they now said, were "hard to value." When Morgan Stanley announced that a loss from one clump of securities had risen from $3.7 billion to $7.8 billion because of "inadequate risk-monitoring procedures," investors seemed confused more than anything. "How could this happen? How could one desk lose $8 billion?" William Tanona, a Goldman Sachs analyst, asked Morgan Stanley CEO John Mack in December.[11] Depression-era stock-exchange chief Richard Whitney's words rang true once again: "These days, you do not know whether anything is worth anything."

Securities pricing seemed random. Investors watched as Wachovia, a major commercial bank, marked one complex debt security, itself backed by other debt securities, at $600,000, then cut the price to $297,000 to $138,000 to $30,000. It later sold the security for $60,000. Merrill Lynch shocked investors when it sold some mortgage-related securities to a hedge fund for 22 cents on the dollar. Executives at other investment banks, including Lehman, insisted that their opaque securities were worth much more than any outsider would pay. Fed chairman Ben Bernanke said of complex financial structures that he wished he "knew what the damn things are worth." Wall Street watched as its major competency, in investors' eyes, deteriorated along with the market: that is, its ability to structure perfectly priceable, nearly riskless debt and ceaselessly to attract short-term financing and leverage based on that ability.

By 2008, faith in that ability had utterly vanished. Worse, since financiers had built debt towers based on extrapolations of value that, as in the case of Samuel Insull in the thirties and Enron seventy years later, extended decades into the future—and had thus taken all of tomorrow's profits today, by wringing short-term gains out of securitized debt and unregulated derivatives—they now had to give those profits back. In February, AIG admitted that it had found "material weakness" in the valuation of its hundreds of billions of dollars in credit-default swaps, meaning that previous values and profits were wrong.

AIG insisted that it could withstand such losses because it had $16 billion to $21 billion in "excess capital." But more investors were starting to do the math. They calculated that if AIG had made a 10 percent error on all the protection it wrote on mortgage-backed and other securities through these unregulated derivatives markets, it would owe as much as $50 billion—enough to overwhelm that "excess capital." AIG insisted further that it had the ability to "hold devalued investments to recovery," making their current market values irrelevant. But investors realized, belatedly but surely, that AIG, under the unregulated derivatives contracts that it freely signed while putting no money down, would have to pay tens of billions in cash out to counterparties instantly if the mortgages continued to deteriorate.[12]

As bond insurers MBIA and Ambac faltered, too, because of the AIG-like guarantees that they had made on mortgage securities, investors and regulators realized with dread just how interconnected markets were. MBIA and Ambac had offered default protection on risky mortgage securities, but they had also offered guarantees on hundreds of billions of dollars' worth of old-fashioned municipal-bond debt. If the insurers lost their AAA ratings because of their mortgage ventures (as they eventually would), all that municipal debt would lose its AAA ratings, too, throwing a much safer market into turmoil. Financiers hadn't structured away risk, the markets realized all at once. Instead, they had allowed risk to stealthily infect parts of the financial world, such as the municipal-bond markets, that previously had been straightforward and safe.

Investors also noticed how thoroughly another Depression-era principle upon which proper valuation depended had eroded: disclosure. "Since the invention of the ticker tape 140 years ago," the *Wall Street Journal* reported, "America has been able to boast of having the world's most transparent financial markets. . . . These days, after a decade of frantic growth in mortgage-backed securities and other complex investments traded off exchanges, that clarity is gone. Large parts of American financial markets have become a hall of mirrors."[13]

Investors examining the contents of these fancy financial structures found that the debt underneath was inscrutable. Such impossible securities were worth what the financial world said they were worth—until the world stopped believing. Then, they seemed less than worthless—they seemed "toxic," the new term used by the government, the financial industry, and the press. And because the SEC had lifted the uptick rule, that gentle restriction that dampened short-selling in a plummeting market, the previous year, market participants could show exactly what they thought of financial companies by driving their stock prices straight down to the single digits, exacerbating the panic.

It was inevitable that the government would become the risk-taker of last resort. The regulatory principle of protecting money and credit supplies from panic hadn't grown less critical since the thirties. From the thirties through the eighties, deposit guarantees had protected the core of the financial system from immediate, uncontrolled panic. Reasonable limits on the debt creation enabled by derivatives and securitization would have muted the boom, lessening the bust, too. All such protections were gone.

Now, too, these securitization markets, vulnerable to a market stampede, were integral parts of the economy. Of the $25 trillion in debt that American homeowners, consumers, and corporations owed by the end of 2008, a full $10 trillion came from securitization.[14] As the confidence that supported these markets disappeared, it took with it nearly a third of the private credit markets, and far more efficiently than when thirties-era Americans had lined up to withdraw their money from banks. What William Ogden had said about Continental Illinois' lesson two decades previously was truer now: "A modern run on a bank doesn't show up in lines at the teller windows."

The nation was right back where it had been before FDR declared his 1933 bank holiday—making it up as it went along. In March 2008, Bear Stearns's short-term lenders fled, even as its chief, Alan Schwartz, appeared on television to insist that "we don't see any pressure on our liquidity, let alone a liquidity crisis."[15] As rumors of trouble spread, other firms, terrified that Bear's assets weren't worth what it claimed, stopped trading with Bear seemingly as quickly and carelessly as they had traded with it in the previous weeks. If its lenders continued to flee, Bear Stearns, like Enron seven years earlier, would run out of cash.

The government's worries at this point should sound familiar. If Bear entered bankruptcy, its remaining short-term funders could yank their collateral all at once and sell their assets. The price of mortgage-backed securities and all other manner of debt would fall even more precipitously, and finding new buyers for new debt would become an even more hopeless task. Bear was also a major participant in the unregulated derivatives market, with only its credit backing its ability to make good on such trades. If the firm failed, its unregulated derivatives agreements would fail, too. Such failure would rip through the financial system, as investors around the world unwound derivatives agreements with other fragile-seeming partners all at once. Worse, if the investing world lost confidence in Bear, it might lose confidence in Lehman Brothers, Morgan Stanley, and so on down the line—all the way to Goldman Sachs.

To halt this cascade of fear, the government offered Bear's lenders and other creditors, including its derivatives-trading counterparties, a rough approximation of FDIC deposit insurance, expanding what it had done with Continental Illinois more than two decades earlier. Beneficiaries in both cases were sophisticated global investors and had lent money to each firm knowing that they had no such explicit insurance and thus stood the risk of real losses. The Federal Reserve swept in to guarantee nearly $30 billion in Bear's most complex mortgage-related assets, so that the far more secure JPMorgan Chase would be comfortable enough to buy the company, protecting all creditors permanently, including Bear's derivatives-trading partners.

The Fed hoped that this government-protected sale would mollify institutional investors and traders with regard to risks at other institutions. Regulators, in stemming a bank run, aren't acting to rescue a particular bank, after all, but to help all other banks and thus stabilize the economy's money and credit supplies. To assuage such fears further by lessening the risk that the investment banks would run out of money, the Fed also declared that investment banks, like Lehman, could borrow directly from it, just as commercial banks could, something it hadn't allowed since 1932.

After Bear came the deluge. The effort to quell the panic didn't work because the fear and the demand for government protection were rational. Elected officials, regulators, and bankers finally realized the extent of the systemic risks that the financial industry had created, aided by the government's distortion of market signals for a quarter of a century. In August 2008, the White House, after receiving congressional authority, nationalized Fannie Mae and Freddie Mac. Global investors had fled the two firms' securities, realizing that losses of just a few percent in the two mortgage behemoths' $5.3 trillion mortgage portfolios would render them insolvent and unable to make good on their guarantees. They saw, further, that such losses were becoming a reality, as even "prime" mortgage borrowers had used the credit bubble to take on debt that they seemed unlikely to repay, and as the resale value of foreclosed homes plummeted. Investors no longer were content with the government's implicit support of Fannie and Freddie; they wanted explicit support. The government had no choice because the private mortgage markets—demand for securities that didn't carry a Fannie or Freddie guarantee—had disappeared.

In September 2008, after two and a half decades of saving bad financial institutions and their funders, the government experimented with an alternative approach. On September 15, Lehman Brothers, with no bailout forthcoming, declared bankruptcy. Chaos ripped through financial markets. Hours after Lehman failed, short-term lenders deserted AIG, too. Panicked by the market disarray set off by their Lehman approach and realizing that AIG's sudden failure would cause the financial infrastructure the world over simply to shut itself down quickly to protect itself from more losses, as in a power outage that happens in an instant yet takes time to fix, the Treasury and the Federal Reserve organized the first of four bailouts for the insurer, with the government taking 80 percent ownership. Without such a bailout, "there will be no economy on Monday," Fed chairman Bernanke reportedly said.

Consistency was absent. A week later, the government allowed the FDIC to take over a big commercial bank, Washington Mutual, and sell it quickly to JPMorgan Chase, with uninsured depositors protected but bondholders and other uninsured lenders taking losses. These hopelessly mixed signals only pointed up, again, how badly the market needed a consistent, orderly way to allow big financial firms to fail without endangering the rest of the economy. The ad-hoc Bear rescue hadn't worked; the ad-hoc Lehman failure didn't work, either.

The remaining pillars of investment banking fell in a heap. The same week, tottering Merrill Lynch, which the financial community once casually believed safer than the much scrappier Lehman or Bear, found refuge in the arms of Bank of America. Morgan Stanley and Goldman Sachs converted themselves into commercial bank holding companies so that they could enjoy permanent, rather than temporary, borrowing privileges at the Federal Reserve. The SEC, too, tried to offer financial companies some sanctuary. Because it had abandoned its uptick rule, it no longer had a reasonable regulation in place to temper the fear hitting financial stocks, so it used blunt force instead, temporarily banning investors from selling the stocks short.

The markets, though, would not be deterred in their efforts to root out losses and uncertainty. In November 2008, the financial world insisted that the government protect it from the possibility of a Citigroup insolvency—the meltdown of America's flagship financial institution. As the banking giant's stock price fell 90 percent from its 2006 heights, the government devoted $300 billion in guarantees of particular assets as well as cash to the company so that it would not lose its uninsured lenders, later taking 34 percent ownership in the bank. The government later offered the same protection to Bank of America. The FDIC, too, allowed financial institutions, including investment banks and the financial arms of companies like General Electric, to issue bonds that would be backed by the agency's guarantee for three years, finally erasing, at least temporarily, the formal distinction between insured mom-and-pop depositors and uninsured, sophisticated global lenders. The government tried to shore up the banks through the back door, too, offering financial support to institutions willing to refinance unaffordable mortgages so that fewer homeowners would default, lessening bank losses.

Throughout the crisis, the vestiges of the regulatory system worked. Contrast the government's extraordinary actions regarding Bear Stearns, Citigroup, and AIG with its calm response to another financial implosion. In July 2008, President Bush reassured a nation rattled by the sight of Californians lining up to withdraw money from the failing commercial bank IndyMac. "If you have a deposit in a commercial bank in America, your deposit is insured by the federal government up to $100,000," he said. Echoing FDR so many decades earlier, he continued: "My hope is that people take a deep breath and realize that their deposits are protected by our government." Depositors at other banks, reassured by this government guarantee, did not flee their own FDIC-backed accounts. For the vast majority of the credit system, the FDIC wasn't there.

By autumn 2008, Americans understood how quickly an uncontrolled financial shock could become a broad-based economic shock. The nation lost more than half a million jobs that November, the worst monthly hemorrhaging in over three decades. The grim news showed how swiftly a Depression-level demand drop can occur. Almost every class of employer, from domestic and foreign automakers to global steel producers to diamond retailers, announced double-digit-percentage sales declines. Production freezes and layoffs accompanied the death of demand. Storage lots at California's biggest port filled with thousands of foreign-made cars because the dealers' lots were too crowded to hold any more.[16] A sinking economy further weakened investors' confidence in structured debt not related to mortgages, as previous estimates of loan-loss rates on securitized loans—encompassing everything from credit cards to auto loans—now seemed unrealistic. By year's end, the financial system's participants were so terrified of lending without government guarantees that interest rates on short-term Treasury debt turned negative. Investors paid the government to keep their money safe.

Having failed to stop the global run on the unregulated credit market, the government looked back to its actions in the last economy-wide credit crisis—the Great Depression—and determined to do the opposite this time. In 2002, Ben Bernanke, then a member of the Fed's board of governors, spoke at a party honoring Milton Friedman's ninetieth birthday. Bernanke noted that he had first read *A Monetary History*, Friedman and Anna Jacobson Schwartz's classic text on Depression-era monetary policy, as a graduate student at MIT, learning how the government had dithered through the early thirties as banks failed and credit dried up.[17] Bernanke promised: "I would like to say to Milton and Anna, regarding the Great Depression: You're right. We did it. We're very sorry. But thanks to you, we won't do it again."

Bernanke kept his pledge six years later, first using tried-and-true methods to jump-start lending. The Fed slashed the interest rate at which it lends to banks to near zero for the first time ever, so that those banks, in turn, could borrow and lend more. Though it carried the grave risk of runaway inflation, it wasn't an unorthodox step. The effort did not work, though, as financial institutions simply used their cheap money to buy Treasury bonds, giving it right back to the government.

The Treasury and the Fed now turned to the "radical innovations" that Friedman and Schwartz, back in the thirties, had confidently said wouldn't be needed to "cut short the tragic process of monetary deflation and banking collapse" and "ease the banking difficulties."[18] In October 2008, Congress, panicked by the prospect of economic calamity, authorized the Troubled Asset Relief Program, the soon-to-be-infamous TARP. TARP gave the Treasury Department discretion to spend $700 billion buying toxic assets from financial institutions, freeing them to make new loans. When the promise of the TARP failed to thaw credit markets, Treasury secretary Henry Paulson changed course, pumping $250 billion of the money directly into banks in exchange for non-voting stakes. The Treasury even forced some healthy banks to take TARP money in an attempt to keep markets from figuring out which banks were truly desperate. Paulson hoped that this tactic would liberate capital for new lending.

The government didn't confine its furious credit-creation efforts to the banks. Realizing that banks couldn't take over the entire credit-making function that the securitization markets once performed, the Fed and the Treasury implemented a second radical innovation. Over the last months of the Bush administration and the first months of the Obama administration, the government devoted over $1 trillion in guarantees and cheap financing in an attempt to entice investors back to the securitization markets— not only to buy old, bad loans from banks to get them lending again but to create new loans directly.

The Fed and the Treasury hoped to create a synthetic, government-guaranteed version of the intricate infrastructure that had been the private securitization markets, by offering to take the risk in these markets to protect private investors. The Fed further started using its own resources to buy up new mortgage securities guaranteed by Fannie and Freddie at a price that would make mortgage interest rates fall to record lows, thereby encouraging home purchases.

Often, these actions only demonstrated Washington's limitations. As they did in the Great Depression, banks hoarded much of their new government capital against future losses. This behavior wasn't irrational, as many government officials seemed to think, echoing Hoover-era complaints about "parasite" banks. The banks just weren't sure how many existing borrowers—from credit-card holders to big corporations—were going to default, and they were also unsure whether there was more federal money on tap if borrowers kept defaulting in large numbers. Banks also hoarded capital because their private investors—the few left— wanted them to.

Moreover, borrowers weren't as interested in taking out loans, cutting demand for credit even as the supply dried up. Consumer debt, including mortgage debt, had more than doubled between 1999 and 2007, largely based on unsustainable increases in home and other asset prices.[19] With house prices plummeting, consumers who had depended on constant refinancings to take cash out of their homes could do so no longer. As for businesses, while they hadn't swelled their own debt by quite so much during those years, consumer borrowing had often driven their growth. Customers used money, often borrowed from their homes, to purchase goods and services ranging from home renovations to flat-screen televisions to plastic surgery.

The problem wasn't merely financial or technical. It was a problem of human capital. Banks had forgotten how to be banks— that is, how to assess the long-term capacity of people and institutions to repay debt based on judgments about income, character, and future economic growth. Even if the banks regained their institutional memory quickly, which was unlikely, nobody had any real idea, after a decade of almost unimaginable credit distortion, of how much credit the economy needed or could reasonably support.

Confidence mattered, too. Just as in the Great Depression, the world's financial elite saw their convictions crumble. "Those of us who have looked to the self-interest of lending institutions to protect shareholders' equity, myself included, are in a state of shocked disbelief," a chastened Alan Greenspan told a House committee in October 2008. When pressed further about whether his "ideology" had "pushed you to make decisions that you wish you had not made," Greenspan said candidly, "Yes, I've found a flaw. I don't know how significant or permanent it is. But I've been very distressed by that fact."[20]

Greenspan's words echoed those of National City Bank's Charles Mitchell seventy-five years earlier. When pressed by Ferdinand Pecora about the mistakes that bankers had made leading up to the Depression, Mitchell admitted that "there are so many factors over which the men in finance have no control. . . . We are human, we are filled with error, and it does not matter how good our intention may be, we are going to make mistakes."[21] Such shattered faith among the elite in themselves and their world is not the stuff of a quick return to "normal."

Despite the government's best efforts, household debt— encompassing everything from mortgages to credit cards— declined in the autumn of 2008, after having expanded month on month since 1952, when the Fed first started keeping consistent records. "Major sectors of the US economy are experiencing a debt deflation that is causing a massive destruction of wealth, thereby curtailing jobs, income and spending," analysts at Hoisington Investment Management noted in December.[22]

The popular narrative after the financial system's collapse held that capitalism had failed. Citigroup, an emblem of American finance with branches from Buenos Aires to Paris, seemed a potent emblem of this defeat. But capitalism didn't fail; companies did—after having adopted the idea, en masse, that any loan, bond, or other bank asset could be sliced up and turned into an instantly liquid, priceable, and tradeable security, with all its risk quantified and distributed scientifically to parties willing and able to bear it.

Citi's fate, in fact, testified to the enduring power of markets. By the end of 2008, Citigroup and other banks, in concert with the government, had tried for more than a year to hide the real losses that were starting to seep through the industry's balance sheets and toward the government's books. Their efforts at concealment had begun in October 2007 with the failed idea of the Super-SIV of sequestering bad assets in the special fund jointly owned by the three big banks.

Despite all the efforts of government and corporate leaders, the markets showed that something was very rotten at companies like Bear Stearns, Lehman Brothers, Merrill Lynch—and, finally, Citigroup. While financial executives and government officials kept insisting that all was under control, the markets became more convinced that the opposite was true, forcing firm after firm to capitulate to reality. The government was the last such entity to do so. Throughout 2008, Treasury secretary Paulson and others still seemed to think that by handing out TARP capital to a big-enough group of banks, it could hide which of the biggest surviving firms were actually desperate for the money. The market saw through the smoke screen, forcing the Citigroup bailout.

In truth, markets had been trying to work since 1984, with Continental Illinois, desperately sending signals that the modern financial system was shot through with untenable risks that required a renewal of long-held regulatory principles. But government bailouts thwarted real market information at every turn. Washington allowed failure only when it didn't threaten systemic risk, as in the case of Enron, and did not learn the subtler lessons that such failure provided.

If the government had permitted failure in 1984, in Continental's case, the immediate consequences would have been dire, perhaps too dire. As uninsured depositors and other short-term lenders fled the banking system, other banks could have followed Continental into insolvency. Surviving financial firms would have tightened lending, bringing the risk of a deep recession, just two years after a debilitating downturn had lifted. And if it turned out that Continental really was too big to fail without taking down the entire financial system with it—a question whose answer is unknowable now—the government would have had to step in with its explicit, blanket guarantees of every element of that system nearly two and a half decades before it eventually did so in 2008. Political consequences, in either case, would have been serious. President Reagan might have had a different legacy, as intense pain would have hit financial and job markets. But a disorderly failure and a financial meltdown would have taught the nation something it would learn, anyway, in 2008: its financial system was becoming unsustainable. Back then, the nation would have learned this lesson before debt reached untenable levels.

It would have been possible for the government to avert disorderly failure in Continental Illinois' case via its ad-hoc rescue, and still prevent the rescue from becoming a precedent. Regulators and elected officials could have presented the episode to the financial industry and the public as harsh evidence that the old regulations to wind down bad banks in an orderly fashion had stopped working. Washington could have imposed credible new regulations that would prevent future systemic failure while letting uninsured depositors and other unprotected lenders to banks take warranted losses. Such enforcement of market discipline— requiring a new type of FDIC-style conservatorship or corporate bankruptcy through which large or complex financial firms could fail—might have prevented Long-Term Capital Management from ever happening fourteen years later.

When the Long-Term Capital Management debacle did happen, the government compounded the problem instead of solving it. Again, the panicked reaction in the immediacy of the moment was natural. But elected officials and regulators continued to provide no way for financial firms to fail in an orderly fashion, with uninsured lenders taking losses. Moreover, policymakers also failed to see that new financial instruments, especially unregulated derivatives, badly needed regulation to protect the broader economy in the event that they failed.

Credible action after 1998 to prevent yet another too-big-to-fail event probably would have altered history—financial, economic, and political. Lenders' acute understanding of the risks that they bore when trusting financial institutions with their money—absent government guarantees against losses—would have slowed the rate of credit creation, meaning a less painful correction starting in 2007. Regulation of the financial instruments that made credit seem riskless would have slowed credit growth, too, perhaps to a more sustainable level.

The world's biggest financial and political powers couldn't hide the truth forever. In each of its precedent-setting bailouts—Continental Illinois and Long-Term Capital Management—the government's goal was to avoid a wholesale breakdown of the entire financial system. But two and a half decades after the Reagan administration began the too-big-to-fail policy, the entire financial system failed anyway—when, in September 2008, even the money-market funds, the safest of all conceivable investments that lacked an explicit government guarantee, required such support.

The markets finally forced the government's hand, exposing the whole state-subsidized, too-big-to-fail financial sector as impossible. Without adequate regulation of financial instruments and without adequate market discipline of financial firms, the nation got the opposite of free markets: wholesale socialization of the financial industry to prevent a replay of the 1930s.

CHAPTER 9

DESTROYING THE SYSTEM IN ORDER TO SAVE IT

Like any other system designed by man, capitalism is not perfect.... But it is by far the most efficient and just way of structuring an economy. At its most basic level, capitalism offers people the freedom to choose where they work and what they do, the opportunity to buy or sell products they want, and the dignity that comes with profiting from their talent and hard work.
—President George W. Bush, November 2008[1]

You don't need banks and bondholders to make cars.
—unnamed Obama administration official, April 2009[2]

I N NOVEMBER 2008, PRESIDENT BUSH STOOD BEFORE an audience at New York's Federal Hall to explain his administration's extraordinary actions. Running through a long list of eight months' worth of financial shocks, the president said, "We are faced with the prospect of a global meltdown. And so we've responded with bold measures. I'm a market-oriented guy, but not when I'm faced with the prospect of a global meltdown."[3]

President Bush's immediate reaction to the financial crisis was understandable, no less than his predecessors' panicked reactions to Continental Illinois in 1984 and to Long-Term Capital Management in 1998. In fact, the president's words echoed those of the Reagan official who had said, during the Continental bailout, that though he cherished free-market principles, letting the bank fail was "thinking the unthinkable." President Bush would not stand by and watch as the entire global economy—in his twice-repeated words—"melted down." He had to do something—anything—and his administration tried anything and everything in its last five months in office to restore some semblance of order to the financial system.

Everything that the administration did—from Treasury secretary Henry Paulson's about-face on what to do with the $700 billion in TARP funds to the inconsistency of the White House's saving AIG while letting Lehman die—warrants criticism. But the truth is that there were no good options for the Bush administration, circa 2008. The time to recognize the potential for catastrophe and avert it had already passed, along with every missed warning sign over more than two decades.

By 2008, it was too late. The disintegration of an unsustainable financial system, born in part from government distortion, pushed the economy to the brink of a modern global depression. "There is no playbook for responding to turmoil we have never faced," a visibly exhausted Paulson explained in November 2008. "We adjusted our strategy to reflect the facts of a severe market crisis, always keeping focused on our goal: to stabilize a financial system that is integral to the everyday lives of all Americans.... [T]his financial crisis is unpredictable and difficult to counteract."[4]

Could free markets have sorted out the mess without extraordinary government action? Yes, but only by destroying the remains of the financial system and possibly putting tens of millions of people out of work. Despite virulent public opposition to the Bush bailouts, society would not have tolerated the price that a sudden free-market correction of decades of financial excess would have exacted. The consequences of standing by while the markets did their work, correcting their own and the government's mistakes, would have been disastrous.

The administration's response may have staved off depression, though that outcome is not assured. But the government has severely damaged four elements upon which free markets and the future well-being of the nation depend: prices, disclosure, failure, and fairness. Lawmakers and regulators have harmed the faith of global investors and regular citizens alike in American free markets—a faith essential to growth and progress. President Obama has made the problems worse.

Consider the immediate tangle that the Bush administration's fixes left behind. A big cause of the financial and economic crisis was distorted prices, as easy money pushed up the price of everything from McMansions to masterpiece paintings. When a distortive bubble bursts, people have to figure out what stuff is actually worth without all that debt holding it up. Meanwhile, purchases and sales come to a halt, because nobody can agree on a price for anything. Government action has warped the essential process of what's called "price discovery."

In the nation's last major banking debacle, the savings-and-loan crisis of the late eighties and early nineties, price discovery acted as a healthy, revitalizing force. In November 2008, the late William Seidman, who handled the savings-and-loan aftermath as head of the FDIC and the federal Resolution Trust Corporation, reminisced about how it worked. At first, he noted, "there was no real market" for the $600 billion in assets that the government inherited from failed banks. "We decided we had to create a market. We said, we're going to start selling these properties at whatever price we could get." As for the reaction from the private owners of similar assets, "You can imagine the reception: 'You're driving the market down,' " Seidman remembered. "Congress asked us to keep the assets for five years.... I said if I'm sitting here just waiting to sell my assets ... the price isn't going to go up."[5]

In summer 2008, Merrill Lynch's sale of some mortgage-related assets for 22 cents on the dollar was a key step toward such price discovery. This sale gave traumatized, uncertain markets a valuable commodity: information about what a real third party thought the toxic securities were worth. But the government stopped these deals cold when it put forward its TARP plan, approved in October 2008. Because the government had no consistent way to let big financial firms fail without endangering the economy, part of its strategy in late 2008 was to use taxpayer funds to obscure the plummeting asset prices that were causing the firms' insolvency. The TARP set out to pay higher-than-warranted prices for toxic mortgage-related and other securities to keep afloat the financial institutions that held them. When this idea proved politically and practically untenable, the Treasury used the money instead to pump capital directly into banks, as seen in the previous chapter.

Federal agencies have propped up asset values in other ways, with the FDIC guaranteeing assets held by banks like Citigroup and with the Federal Reserve expanding its own investment books to purchase mortgage-related and other securities. In November 2008, the Federal Reserve, through a new entity set up for this purpose, paid $50 billion to purchase mortgage-backed and other asset-related securities from AIG. Because that price—a little less than half of the securities' initial value—appeared random, it proved useless to markets struggling to adjust to a new reality. The Obama administration has also offered cheap financing to government-approved financial firms willing to buy bad assets from banks.

All these measures gave weak financial firms an incentive to hang on to their bad debt in the hopes of getting a higher price than the private investors would pay. Tom Marano, CEO of the mortgage company Rescap, then on the brink of insolvency, is a case in point. "I get calls from people wanting to buy nonperforming [mortgage] loans all the time," Marano said in November 2008, "but the problem is that they want 20 to 25 percent returns" on assets that include delinquent loans, after taking a discount for mortgages already deep in default.[6] That is, buyers wanted to buy the loans at prices low enough to ensure that, when they eventually sold them again, the returns would be hefty. No thanks,

Marano told them: he'd wait for the government to buy on better terms.

Private investors had excellent reasons for their low bids. Even after accounting for mortgages already in default, potential buyers knew that there was a good chance that a substantial portion of the other homeowners would default, too. The collateral behind their mortgages—house values—was falling. With their equity vanishing, homeowners had little left to lose by walking away. Further, potential buyers now understood that these mortgage securities were structured precariously and that they weren't the instantaneously tradeable, cashlike investments that sellers once described. Investors needed new compensation for all these risks.

At the same time, these potential buyers themselves had less money to invest. During the boom, hedge funds and other investors could borrow vast amounts and, in doing so, turn the small returns that supposedly safe mortgage-backed securities offered into enormous returns on their slim capital. After the bust, that strategy no longer worked. Borrowing to purchase securities was much more expensive, and the securities were far more volatile than investors had once thought, making such borrowing a dangerous proposition. The market wasn't wrong; reality had changed.

Washington, with its guarantees of securities' value for their current holders and its promise of cheap financing for new buyers, made finding appropriate pricing much more difficult. The process of determining a new price in a changed environment always starts at the bottom. The speculators who are the first to jump in need plenty of room to make a profit on the risk that they're willing to take when nobody else will. When asset managers are successful, they ultimately sell for a profit the loans they bought at low prices. These first, early resales at higher prices encourage more investors to purchase similar assets, raising the prices still higher at future sales.

In the mortgage-securities market, initial low prices for distressed assets were important for an additional reason. Low prices would enable the securities' purchasers to address a core problem affecting the economy: too many foreclosures. The lower the price an investor paid for a mortgage-backed security, the more room he had to work with the security's administrator, with other investors, and with underlying mortgage borrowers to slash the homeowners' debt to more sustainable levels. Distorted prices could continue to haunt the economy as it recovers from the credit debacle, with asset values artificially maintained by the government's continuing to send the wrong signals. The Federal Reserve, in its extraordinary efforts to keep mortgage rates down, could assure that Americans continue to spend too much of their money on costly housing, rather than investing it in more productive assets such as growing companies. With Washington adding more noise to market signals, entrepreneurs will have a harder time pulling the economy away from stagnation.

Washington impedes recovery and future financial and economic health by muddying another element integral to free capital markets: disclosure. A lack of good information helped create the credit crisis, with investors and regulators often having no idea of the risks that unregulated derivatives posed, and good information is crucial to cleaning up the mess and moving on.

In October 2007, Washington tried to let Citigroup, Bank of America, and JPMorgan Chase hide away a nominal $100 billion in mortgage-backed securities in their proposed Super-SIV, giving the banks the authority to value the securities at much higher prices than the market would have indicated. This effort only delayed capitulation to reality. Five months later, when the government kept Bear Stearns out of bankruptcy from a fear of the possible consequences for the rest of the economy, one effect was that armies of bankruptcy lawyers never got to pore over each and every one of Bear's assets and liabilities in order to make the company's true financial condition public.

In mid-2008, the Federal Reserve further obfuscated matters by refusing to disclose the mortgage-backed securities that it had taken over from struggling financial institutions as collateral for loans, forcing a Bloomberg News lawsuit. It was important for markets to know whether the Fed was lending generously against subprime mortgages issued in 2005 and 2006, toward the end of the bubble, thus allowing financial firms to avoid selling those assets at a big loss. In late 2008 and early 2009, the Fed and the Treasury were reluctant to reveal which financial institutions had relied on AIG to provide tens of billions of dollars in credit-default protection and thus had benefited disproportionately from bail-outs of the insurer. When the government capitulated, it turned out that investment banks such as Goldman Sachs had exposed themselves to one company's ability to pay up. The facts were more evidence that Goldman had behaved as imprudently as its brethren or, just as bad, that Goldman had always assumed that AIG, too, was too big to fail.

By the end of 2008, the government was wielding such immense and arbitrary power through its role as savior of big financial firms that the risk of an abuse of this power was palpable. In early 2009, questions emerged about whether the Federal Reserve and the Treasury had pressured Bank of America CEO Kenneth Lewis into suppressing the extent of Merrill Lynch's losses—and the amount of government aid that Bank of America would need to cover those losses—so that his firm could complete its merger with Merrill.[7] Former Treasury secretary Henry Paulson told Lewis in December 2008 that abandoning the merger would "show a colossal lack of judgment and would jeopardize Bank of America, Merrill Lynch and the financial system." Paulson went further, according to his testimony before Congress eight months later, explaining to Lewis that "under such circumstances, the Federal Reserve could exercise its authority to remove management and the board of Bank of America."[8] Fed chairman Ben Bernanke has told Congress that he "expressed concern" that the bank's reneging on the merger "would entail significant risks, not only for the financial system as a whole but also for Bank of America itself."[9]

"Concern," when expressed by the person in charge of whether your company lives or dies, weighs heavily. A free-market system depends on the predictable and consistent application of transparent principles, not on powerful individuals' self-control in reining in their own all-too-human impulses. When reasonable observers can worry that the government is leaning on financial firms to hide crucial information with the goal of consummating a bad deal, trust in markets sustains damage.

The Bush administration's ad-hoc decisions to keep failed giant companies alive created a new business specimen: "zombie" financial institutions. Are these living companies or dead ones? By blurring the distinction between robust and discredited business models in the financial industry, the government introduced potentially investment-killing uncertainty into the economy and undercut viable competitors.

Federal overseers have never made it clear whether companies like AIG and Citigroup, each a recipient of multiple, multi-hundred-billion-dollar bailouts, should live or die. AIG took nearly $180 billion in taxpayer money after its failed credit-default derivatives pushed it into insolvency starting in September 2008, with the government taking an 80 percent ownership stake in return. In a rational world, AIG would be bankrupt—yet in May 2009, Congressman Edolphus Towns instructed company executives to "have in place a solid plan for the future."[10] Less than two months later, AIG persuaded the Federal Reserve to convert some of the loans the Fed had made into stock, meaning that AIG doesn't have to repay the funds.[11] Similarly, after providing Citigroup with $300 billion in November 2008, Washington did not reveal whether the goal was for Citi to sell off its assets to better-managed institutions or to hobble along into the future and hope that everyone would forget its unfortunate episode. By mid-2009, Citigroup was increasing executive salaries, pushing healthier firms to consider doing the same to avoid losing employees to the government-subsidized competition.[12]

A vibrant free-market economy needs a clear dividing line between viability and failure, so that bad companies and bad ideas don't crowd out good ones. When a company fails, a successful firm can purchase its good assets, improving economic efficiency by releasing them from incompetent management and putting them back to work. Failed firms' workers (even those who made the mistakes that led to the failure) can find more useful outlets for their labor. Government money has instead created a risk that failed institutions will survive into the future, sucking capital and talent from the vital parts of the economy, even if these zombie firms lie dormant for a while. Firing the top management of bailed-out companies, as the government directed at AIG, doesn't lessen this risk. The failure is institutional, not personal. Investors—shareholders and bondholders—must understand that no bailout is waiting for them at the end of the rainbow if the companies in which they've trusted founder.

The government, in propping up big, failed banks, and even encouraging them to buy other banks to become stronger, also weakens the resilience of the financial industry itself. In any industry, when a giant totters, it creates an opportunity for a smaller company to rise and mount a challenge—whether it's Microsoft after IBM faltered or Google after Microsoft stumbled. Without artificial government support for the gigantic legacy banks, healthy, smaller banks could become the next kings. But government-coddled financial giants, as they stifle smaller competitors, may cede real innovation overseas, to nations that allow the failure that comes with competition.

The great danger is that the White House and Congress will now turn the zombie companies into instruments of government policy. When President Obama said in early 2009 that top executives at banks and other companies receiving "extraordinary" new federal bailout cash would have to cap their own cash compensation at $500,000 annually, some conservatives approved. The logic seems forceful: When the government controls an industry, why shouldn't it have some say over how that industry manages its affairs? Having put their hands out for extraordinary assistance, Citigroup, AIG, and others had justifiably lost some latitude over how they use their resources.

In the wake of the bailouts, a company like Citigroup had no idea whom it was supposed to please: Its few remaining shareholders and private creditors? Its customers? Or the government that kept it in business? For instance, the government wanted Citi and other banks to increase mortgage and credit-card lending, but private creditors and shareholders, worried about how high the unemployment rate—and loan defaults—would go, thought such credit expansion a bad idea. To whom should Citi have deferred?

Such pressure is particularly dangerous because, through the back door of its power over the financial industry, the government could control much of private industry. Washington is now able to exert tremendous control over the allocation of capital among businesses and individuals, which is the financial sector's job. Soon after forcing even relatively healthy banks like JPMorgan Chase to take TARP money, Congress decreed that TARP recipients had to restrict their hiring of foreign workers. Could government funders further insist that bailed-out banks, in their lending, favor companies that keep jobs in America, rather than outsourcing some of them overseas? Such hidden power is far more insidious than the government's overt control of General Motors and Chrysler, since the inevitable whispering among financial executives and their patron congressmen and the results of those whispers will be harder to track.

In lurching from bailout to bailout with no consistent, replicable rules, Washington has weakened another foundation of free markets: the law's respect for a well-defined capital structure. A company's capital structure works roughly as follows. Its shareholders take the most risk that it might fail, in return for a theoretically unlimited return, since stock prices have no ceiling. When a company goes under, shareholders usually lose everything. As for the lenders (as opposed to the stockholders), the first in line for losses are the junior bondholders, who earn a higher interest rate on their debt in return for taking on this risk. By contrast, the senior bondholders and senior bank lenders get repaid first and hence earn a lower interest rate in return for the relatively low risk they shoulder.

Early in 2008, the government threw out these rules. In its Bear Stearns bailout and its Fannie Mae, Freddie Mac, and AIG nationalizations, the government did force shareholders to take their deserved losses. But all lenders—whether junior or senior—benefited from new government protection (as Continental's lenders had two decades previously); lenders did not lose a penny.

The strategy of protecting lenders—and protecting them regardless of place in line in the capital structure—is bound to encourage them to take ever more risk in lending to "too-big-to-fail" financial institutions.

The government's strategy will distort market signals long after the credit crisis is over. When a company is in distress, the first sign of trouble is often in the higher rates that it must pay to lure buyers for its riskier junior debt. But if junior lenders to big financial firms can expect the same protection that senior lenders enjoy, so much for that crucial market warning of heightened risk.

What the Bush administration began, the Obama administration has blown up to giant scale, using its power over big, bailed-out banks to bully smaller financial firms and shred the capital structure further to the detriment of fair free markets. The Chrysler bankruptcy is a prime case in point. After Chrysler could no longer pay its debts in late 2008 and early 2009, the Bush and Obama administrations provided financing so that it could continue to operate. After Washington bailed out Wall Street, it was inevitable that it would bail out Detroit. Politically, both Republicans and Democrats thought, how could officials protect fat-cat bankers while letting blue-collar workers languish?

The Obama administration used its money and power to subvert the normal order of losses in the bankruptcy, protecting junior lenders and other junior creditors—namely, the auto workers' union—at the expense of senior lenders. In April 2009, the government pressured senior lenders to agree to a deal under which they gave up much of their claim on Chrysler's assets in favor of a union health-care claim whose benefits otherwise likely wouldn't have been paid.

The lenders agreeing to these concessions had taken bailout billions months earlier. "For the [big] banks, defying the administration was never a serious option," the *New York Times* observed.[13] The big senior lenders that had taken government money had enough voting power to push the agreement through, despite smaller senior lenders' vociferous protests. Said George Schultze, a manager of a smaller hedge fund, "We lent money to Chrysler under a contract that gave us the first lien on its assets. There was no agreement that union members or other unsecured creditors could jump ahead of us in claims. This is about contract and bankruptcy law, and upholding agreements."[14]

Even a representative of a big bank felt uneasy. "The government had one eye on the social element and one eye on not abrogating contracts, but can you reconcile these two goals?" the banker anonymously asked in the *Financial Times*.[15] The government said that it imposed its conditions as a key financier of Chrysler's bankruptcy, not as a political player, and that the big lenders who agreed to the plan did so for financial, not political, purposes. But even if this tale were true, nobody would believe it; just as with Bank of America and the Federal Reserve, government power is too vast to ignore.

Most troubling for a nation that wants to remain one of the world's financial capitals was President Obama's castigation of Chrysler's smaller lenders. "While many stakeholders made sacrifices, some did not," the president said, fingering "a small group of speculators" for blame. "I don't stand with them," he said. "I stand with Chrysler's employees, management, and suppliers."[16] But without "speculators," there can be no markets—and no "employees, management, and suppliers" of new companies.

America attracts the world's investors because its consistent system of laws—including the bankruptcy process—and its requirements for full disclosure of information have created a reasonably level playing field. "Americans remember Washington as a far more paternalistic place in 1979," when Chrysler was first bailed out, *Financial Times* columnists concluded after the Chrysler deal, "but respect for private contracts ... was higher" back then, too.[17] If the world comes to hold such a worry about U.S. dedication to the rule of law, American businesses and consumers alike will pay higher interest rates as lenders demand extra compensation for shouldering this new political risk. America will struggle hard to remain preeminent in the global capital markets, for the world would no longer look to it as the safest place on earth to invest its wealth.

The highest price that America might pay for subverting market principles to save failing financial firms over more than two decades became clear in early 2009: a poisonous mob mentality seeping into the American spirit as citizens perceived that big government was letting big business escape the consequences of failure while many ordinary people suffered losses.

The immediate catalyst was the March 2009 news that a government-owned AIG would pay out nearly $200 million to its workers in "retention bonuses." This controversy would not have arisen if elected officials and regulators had learned the lessons of Continental Illinois and Long-Term Capital Management, and made sure that no private company was too big or complex to fail. In an orderly liquidation—the optimal outcome for a failed company, as AIG was—an impartial judge and an impartial administrator would have taken on all the tasks that the government and AIG itself handled so erratically. The court would have decided which employees from AIG's exploded "financial products unit," which created the mortgage derivatives that blew up the company, should be encouraged to stick around to help the new administrators sort out the mess. With the court's permission, the administrator would have determined how much to pay such employees, as had happened in the Enron case seven years earlier.

Such an impartial accounting of AIG's assets and liabilities would have defused the bonus controversy that provoked outrage. Instead, because it had lost faith that the government would allow failed executives to take financial losses or failed companies to die, the citizenry tried, bluntly, to do the job itself. It was an ugly spectacle. AIG instructed its workers not to put their personal safety at risk by going out wearing anything with the corporate insignia. Executives paid security guards to stand outside their mansions and protect them from angry trespassers. Congress was content to stir up the anger, deflecting its responsibility for the financial crisis toward AIG's useful caricatures of corporate America.

As rage mounted, many AIG employees gave back their bonuses. But they made their decisions out of fear. Bankruptcy, by contrast, enables a consistent, transparent treatment of contracts, even in an environment of anger.

In its arbitrary, unpredictable efforts, Washington risked sacrificing the public's confidence that the government can act fairly in serving as a referee and regulator of free markets, not an active chooser of winners and losers. Such lost confidence would be catastrophic not just for the nation but for the world. While the U.S. is hardly the only nation providing massive taxpayer money to prop up financial institutions and other industries, it is the world's free-market leader. When America favors some companies and industries over others, it makes it seem more respectable for other countries to do the same. Already, bailouts around the world have created a sort of financial nationalism, with banks cutting back their lending to foreign borrowers because their government rescuers would rather see them lend at home.[18]

If America does not draw back from government intervention and the introduction of Third World–style political risk into markets and instead return to consistency and respect for law and process, free markets the world over could shrivel.

Washington may be tempted to fix the problem that it has created by selling off its remaining stakes in banks such as Citi, collecting the money lent to firms such as AIG, and declaring that everything is back to normal. Doubtless, the government should extricate itself from its direct private-sector investments. But such action by itself would create a dangerous illusion. Washington must do the tougher work of reasserting the core principles by which the government regulated the financial world from the Depression until the 1980s. Otherwise, its reaction to this crisis will prove to be an even stronger precedent than its previous legacy of panicked bailouts. An industry that has proved adept over the decades at using its too-big-to-fail subsidy to exploit other gaps will efficiently exploit this precedent, too, exacting an even higher price from the citizenry.

CHAPTER 10

FREE MARKETS: OUR CHOICE

I am proposing that the Federal Reserve be granted new authority—and accountability—for regulating bank holding companies and other large firms that pose a risk to the entire economy in the event of failure.... If you can pose a great risk, that means you have a great responsibility.
—President Barack Obama, White House, June 17, 2009[1]

Too-big-to-fail should be tossed into the dustbin.
—FDIC chairman Sheila Bair, speech to the Economic Club of New York, April 27, 2009

A DYNAMIC ECONOMY WILL ALWAYS HAVE BOOMS and busts. But the story of the past twenty-five years is that Washington has created a financial system that cannot withstand the destructive part of creative destruction—necessary for free markets—without destroying the economy. We've grown so accustomed to government-subsidized failure in finance that we feel we have no choice. In accepting subsidized failure, we harm America's trust in free markets, we harm the world's trust in American markets, and we harm the financial innovation that advances the economy rather than smothers it.

The good news is that we know how to fix it. As 2007 and 2008 unfolded, conventional wisdom held that the financial crisis was a "black swan," a term popularized by Nassim Nicholas Taleb to denote a "highly improbable" event that nobody could have anticipated because nobody had ever seen it before. People who'd only seen white swans, Taleb pointed out, couldn't imagine that black swans existed before their discovery.[2]

Given the slow erosion of almost all reasonable limits on the financial system by 2007, the black-swan event would have been the absence of a historic financial crisis. Washington's too-big-to-fail policy had insulated financial firms from market discipline, distorting financial markets for a quarter of a century. Meanwhile, every regulation protecting the economy's money and credit supplies from twenties-style speculative forces had become inadequate, allowing financial firms a unique opportunity to create great wealth while creating great risk.

We already know what the regulatory and market solutions are. Elegant principles—many of them created in the 1930s—protect financial markets from themselves and keep them free. Elegant regulations also protect financial markets from government distortion and protect the global economy from speculative excesses.

We know that regulations work because regulations did work; they just weren't enough. Seventy-five years after its creation, the FDIC worked as thirties-era lawmakers had envisioned. Insured depositors at Citigroup entrusted Citi with their money even as headlines screamed that the bank was insolvent. The FDIC was an effective solution to systemic risk, but it couldn't stem a modern financial panic because so much of the financial world had moved beyond banking.

Some of the Depression-era Securities and Exchange Commission's regulations succeeded, too. Regulations to keep clients' money safe at investment banks worked well. When a firm like Lehman goes bankrupt, its creditors—lenders, trading partners, and the like—must get in line and fight for what's left over. But its clients—people and companies who simply warehouse their money and securities at the firm—aren't creditors. They're supposed to get their funds back fairly quickly. The Securities and

Exchange Commission protected such assets by forbidding investment firms from using their account holders' securities and cash
as collateral for other company or client borrowing—that is, the
firms can't use your stocks and bonds to speculate or to help other
account holders speculate.

In protecting investment customers, American regulations
worked better than Britain's. In the U.S., administrators transferred customers' accounts to other brokerage firms quickly and
efficiently. In London, which competes with New York as a global
financial center, assets remained frozen for months, and figuring
out who owned what and where proved vastly more complicated.
The biggest customers were not pleased. "Hedge funds have been
quietly shifting billions of dollars of assets out of London to the
US, claiming that the US legal system provides greater protection," reported the *Financial Times*.[3]

Disclosure worked, too—but, as with the FDIC, only to a
point, because credit derivatives, for one, escaped disclosure rules.
Citigroup's 168-page 2005 annual report, issued before the crisis
started, was easy for a literate investor armed with Google to read
in a few days. In the report, Citigroup disclosed some of the risks
that had become apparent by 2007—admitting, for instance, that
it could be liable for the performance of $55 billion in securities
that it managed off its books.

AIG and Bear Stearns released annual reports that made clear
how byzantine their financial businesses had become and that
they were taking on ever more risks in obscure areas of the markets. Mortgage securities, too, offered their own multi-hundred-
page reports. Their lack of clarity was itself valuable information.
For every hundred people who invested blindly in the worst mortgage-backed securities, a few—like short-sellers David Einhorn
and James Chanos—read the fine print, didn't like what they saw,
shorted financial stocks, and discussed their findings. This disclosure helped markets slowly understand that something was
rotten.

Even at the height of the crisis, in September 2008, disclosure offered comfort. After Lehman Brothers failed, the financial
world paralyzed itself over fear of which institutions had written

credit-default swaps based on the value of Lehman's own debt, requiring them to pay up as the debt became nearly worthless. Had traders and bankers signed billions of dollars' worth of contracts that tracked the value of Lehman's debt—or hundreds of billions? The Depository Trust and Clearing Corporation had an idea of the figure, in large part because the Fed, two years previously, had made its effort to get financial firms at least to record the contracts they held with other firms, and the DTCC handled that job.

In September 2008, the DTCC released the information that it had collected on Lehman credit-default swaps over the past two years, saying that the figure outstanding was only $6 billion, not $400 billion, as rumored, slightly calming the market. In the end, the exposure turned out to be $5.2 billion.[4] Markets had a valuable piece of information, but this voluntary, inconsistent disclosure was not enough.

The first step to restoring the robust financial markets that can support global capitalism is to reassert the market's ability to discipline itself without endangering the economy. Through its too-big-to-fail policy, expanded over the quarter of a century after Continental Illinois, Washington's leaders, from Presidents Reagan to Clinton, unwittingly supported financial recklessness even as markets warned against it. The predictable result was more recklessness.

Bad companies, including big, bad financial companies, must be allowed to fail, so that their bad ideas can have a chance of dying with them. This principle is the cornerstone of assuring healthy financial markets. Unless Washington credibly repudiates its too-big-to-fail policy, any other worthy regulations it enacts won't matter. The lack of market discipline that the doctrine promotes will guarantee that big financial firms continue to have the cheap money and the motive to find their way around such rules.

Failed financial firms must not collapse chaotically; they must be liquidated through a formal, consistent system, by which investors take their losses according to their predetermined place in line in the capital structure. The White House, Congress, and regulators must do what they should have done two decades ago: create an FDIC-style conservatorship for too-big-to-fail financial institutions. Ideas abound as to the mechanics. University of Texas business-law professor Jay Westbrook, for example, has suggested a new type of bankruptcy for large or complex financial institutions. Such extraordinary-case bankruptcies would keep some lenders to financial firms from seizing their collateral immediately (or even quickly) and selling it, reducing the possibility that sales of billions of dollars in securities instantaneously would destabilize the financial system.[5] Lenders would once again have to worry that their money is at risk when in the hands of a big or complex financial institution. Markets then could do their work. Smaller, less complex financial institutions would no longer be at such a disadvantage in competing for funding and clients.

In another elaboration of the conservatorship idea, economists R. Glenn Hubbard, Hal Scott, and Luigi Zingales have proposed an elegant FDIC-managed system that would begin by splitting failed financial firms in two. One new entity would take over the assets that caused the firm's problems. This "bad bank" would also bring the failed firm's lenders with it, and the lenders would take losses based on an estimate of the collapsed value of the assets. The other new entity, no longer weighed down by the bad assets, could meet the original firm's remaining obligations and raise new funds. It could then free itself from government administration, as in any corporate exit from bankruptcy. Lenders to the original failed firm, now lenders to the bad bank, would receive stock in the restructured firm, sharing in its future profits, just as lenders to an ordinary bankrupt firm can.[6]

A modified bankruptcy for financial firms would not represent nationalization, any more than ordinary bankruptcy or FDIC receivership does. Though the government could provide financing to assure the institution's continued operation temporarily to maintain stability, it would have the clear intent of liquidating the failed firm within a predetermined time period (perhaps one year), even if it had to sell assets at fire-sale prices and inflict big losses on lenders. Financial institutions should not have to compete with a bank whose boss works at the White House.

Credibility is crucial. Lenders to big firms must believe that the government will allow the system to work. Witness how quickly banks were able to issue debt in early 2009 to bondholders, even sometimes without the guarantee offered by the FDIC under the emergency program that was launched the previous autumn. The banks—and the government—heralded this success as evidence that investors were regaining confidence in the financial sector. It was not. Investors were confident that the government would continue its bailout policy if the need arose. Consistency is vital, too. Investors must be able reasonably to predict how the system will work from case to case. Otherwise, they'll be tempted to lend to companies that seem to present special cases—starting the whole problem all over again.

Too-big-to-fail has been around for so long that as Washington started debating how to reregulate finance in 2009, thoughtful people said that they consider the regime an unavoidable part of the financial landscape. "The authorities cannot make a credible promise that they would be prepared to put all affected institutions through bankruptcy in a systemic crisis," *Financial Times* columnist Martin Wolf wrote in July. "This would be a recipe for still-greater panics. 'Too big and interconnected to fail' is a reality."[7]

If the nation thinks that it has no choice but to protect lenders to financial firms from market forces, it should treat the industry as an arm of government, with carefully regulated salaries and the like. But surely, before Washington permanently nationalizes finance, so important to the economy, it at least should try the other approach first. The nation hasn't done so in a quarter of a century—directly leading to the type of systemic crisis that Wolf describes, a crisis that perversely seems to justify the current policy.

Washington can credibly enforce a not-too-big-to-fail policy for financial firms only if it strengthens financial markets so that they can withstand such failure. As recently as 1995, Barings could go bankrupt without crippling the economy. But in the years between Continental Illinois and AIG, presidents, congressmen, and regulators let financiers quietly and gradually introduce such scale and scope of brittle risk that a similar failure could bring the most sophisticated, most robust markets in the world crashing down. The White House and Congress can strengthen markets by applying core regulatory principles to new markets and instruments, current and future, that represent the same systemic risk to the economy that the old ones do. The principles are just as they were in the thirties: limiting speculative borrowing, circumscribing reckless exposure, and requiring disclosure.

The unregulated credit-default-swap market is a prime example of current fragility. Within less than a decade, the financial institutions that traded in credit derivatives grew the market from nothing to $29 trillion. No government regulations limited borrowing, or required investors and speculators to limit exposure or even to disclose activity. Exploiting these loopholes, AIG, with negligible money down, made $500 billion in promises that it couldn't keep—and nobody knew to whom the promises were made.

The Obama administration's May 2009 proposal that Congress reverse its 2000 decision and give regulators the authority to oversee all derivatives was a correct—if obvious and belated—step. The proposal would require all standard derivatives, including swaps, to trade on central clearinghouses, cutting systemic risk. First, clearinghouses would impose regulators' margin requirements to limit borrowing. Second, as described in Chapter 5, clearinghouses reduce financial firms' exposure to other financial firms, cutting the risk that markets would seize up in the wake of a failure of a big derivatives participant, as AIG was before the current crisis and the Long-Term Capital Management hedge fund was in 1998. In each case, uninsured lenders to banks and investment firms had no idea which institutions would be left with billions, or tens of billions, of dollars in losses after the failure of its derivatives counterparty. In 1998, regulators feared that lenders' withdrawal amid the uncertainty would hurt credit availability for the economy or, worse, cause other financial firms to fail, a fear that became a reality a decade later. Going a step further, the administration would encourage, though not require, derivatives traders to conduct their business on exchanges. While all exchanges use clearinghouses to reduce their own and the markets' exposure to financial instruments and firms, all clearinghouses do not use exchanges. One difference between the two is that clearinghouses can keep some trading information from the public, while exchanges give all market participants equal access to trading information.

Though the proposals would allow customized uncommon derivatives to continue to trade off exchanges and clearinghouses, regulators would require that dealers in such bespoke derivatives impose higher margin requirements than clearinghouses would require for standard instruments. These higher capital requirements would encourage bankers and traders to move their activities to the clearinghouses and exchanges except in cases where the extra value that the custom derivative adds is compelling enough to justify the added cost.[8]

The proposal struck a blow for disclosure, requiring that clearinghouses as well as dealers in customized products report their activities so that regulators can watch for manipulation or other irregularities. For example, a judge and fellow lenders should know whether a big lender to a company like General Motors has bought credit protection through a derivatives contract to hedge the risk behind its debt. Such protection would change the lender's incentives to cooperate in reducing losses stemming from GM's bankruptcy, as the lender would know that its derivatives counterparty, not it, would bear such losses.

While regulating speculative borrowing in financial instruments is necessary to rein in the excesses of optimism in a boom, another regulation can aptly rein in the excesses of pessimism in a bust. Here, too, we know exactly what to do. For over seven decades, the SEC forbade investors who thought the price of a stock was going to fall to short that stock unless that stock had first traded upward from its previous trade. This "uptick rule," implemented in the Depression, made sense, because with short-sellers having to wait until the price improved to make their trades, it kept them from pushing the value of a stock to zero.

But the SEC jettisoned the uptick requirement in 2007. The panic selling of bank stocks in 2008 showed that the uptick rule was a needed check against blind panic, and needs reinstatement. In this area, as in many others, an existing rule needs better enforcement. The SEC requires that short-sellers actually borrow the stock that they want to short from other investors who own the stock, so that short-sellers cannot sell more stock short than exists in the market, artificially distorting the price. During the boom, the SEC became lax, helping the run on financial-company stocks.

In regulating financial institutions, as well as financial instruments, Washington's goal should be to strengthen the system so that it can better withstand failure. It can accomplish this goal by setting clear limits within which innovation can flower. Regulating financial institutions today is a different task from what it was seven decades ago because the financial industry has changed. But the core principle of insulating money and credit and the financial system itself from speculative excesses still holds.

A return to Glass-Steagall—the Depression-era regulation that separated banking from the securities-investment business—is not the solution. The financial world has changed too much. In the twenties, banks kept long-term loans on their books; the problem was that they had used the customer deposits that supported such loans to entangle themselves in securities, too. It was easy to separate the two functions because they were two separate businesses.

Today, there is no longer a clear line between long-term bank loans and debt securities. Investors largely create credit directly by purchasing securities, rather than indirectly by putting money in banks. The people who manage trillions of dollars of the world's capital through pension funds, mutual funds, and the like have grown accustomed to investing in tradeable securities, not long-term loans.

Both market and regulatory forces could push financial firms and markets to embrace traditional lending models. But permanently reverting to a credit system in which most people and corporations get their financing through bank loans rather than through the securities market is not likely, nor would it likely be beneficial. To see why, look to Europe. Just as America has learned about the acute risk of depending on credit created through poorly regulated securities markets, Europe is trying to wean itself off its far more clubby, old-fashioned method of bank lending, in which borrowers must go to their traditional bank for a long-term loan.

That system has encouraged cronyism and opacity. Companies that want to borrow money do not, as bond issuers do, have to release information publicly to broad markets but only privately to bankers. Younger companies also struggle to raise financing from conservative bankers, as American firms did before the junk-bond markets existed. As public European bond markets grow to supplant this private market, "companies used to discussing their finances behind closed doors are now having to adjust to doing so in the open," a positive development, the *Financial Times* reported in May 2009.[9] European finance is becoming more like America's, even as America sees new risks in its model.

The goal of regulators should be to protect the modern money and credit stores from short-term overexuberance and hysteria. The place to start is with capital requirements. Such requirements require financial firms to limit borrowing against their investments to protect them from unsustainable losses on these investments. Commercial banks, savings and loans, and the like have long operated under far tighter constraints than investment banks, which never relied on insured customer deposits. Hedge funds escape capital requirements altogether.

Regulators should impose standard rules governing capital— and thus borrowing—across financial institutions, recognizing not only that the banking and securities worlds have blurred but that unregulated hedge funds and inadequately regulated insurance firms can style themselves as credit creators, as Long-Term Capital Management and AIG did. Regulators should ensure that uniform capital requirements cover firms' off-the-books ventures.

Robust capital standards should be uniform not only across institutions but across the assets—loans and other investments—that the capital supports. Regulators must correct the mistake of requiring firms to hold less capital against assets that bankers and their regulators perceived to be less risky, such as certain AAA-rated securities in the boom.

Cutting capital in line with perceived risk created a systemic danger—one that helped ensure that financial firms would fall like dominoes. Financial firms structured and traded in similar securities because structuring a security similar to the thousands that had gone before it was the most straightforward route to a rating of AAA. Because nobody saw any risk, nobody needed much protection—and the entire system primed itself for a melt-down when the risks emerged.

With uniform capital requirements across asset classes, financial firms wouldn't have a regulatory incentive to jump all at once into one asset class or type of security favored by regulators and bond raters. Instead of gaming the system by engineering certain securities so that they garner AAA ratings, financial firms would earn profits by demanding higher interest rates on investments that they perceived to be riskier and lower interest rates on those that they saw as less risky against the same amount of capital. Bankers and traders will innovate on merit rather than to avoid regulation.

Uniform capital regulations also would cut ratings agencies out of an official role. Reliance on ratings agencies contravenes market principles. The ratings-agency world is small and homo-geneous, populated by a few thousand people with similar edu-cations filling in similar boxes of financial-ratio calculations and going out for drinks with one another afterward. Further, each rat-ings agency operates by consensus. The agencies have no system for rewarding a person who speaks out against the conventional wisdom, writing a report contrary to his colleagues' opinion. The incentive—indeed, the requirement—is to cooperate as a team, coming up with a unanimous verdict on every security. Teams find safety in convention—catastrophic if the team is trapped in a bubble. Eliminating raters' official role would also reduce remaining bond-insurance firms' business of "renting out" their own AAA ratings to investors in financial securities. In guaranteeing the securities' performance for a fee, the insurers cut the investors' capital needs. This phenomenon distorted markets and led to the downfall of bond insurer MBIA and others. Markets, through interest rates, should determine the risk of a security.

As twenty-five years of history have shown, financial firms that rely on fickle short-term lenders and uninsured depositors rather than on long-term lenders or FDIC-insured depositors face a sharp risk. Firms that use such volatile sources of money to create or purchase tradeable securities that are vulnerable to panic pricing face a double jeopardy. Encouraging financial institutions to fund more of their investments with longer-term lending would buy more time to wait out a panic.

Banks have always made long-term loans to borrowers with short-term financing from lenders, exposing themselves and the economy to a confidence drop. But when financial firms started to trap so much of the nation's credit in tradeable securities, they made credit far more vulnerable. Financial firms must report the market value of most of their tradeable securities each quarter, so that investors can measure the firms' real business—namely, making profits from trading. Even before the firms report, investors can know the immediate value of other, similar securities, and by proxy guess the value of banks' securities as well as long-term loans not packaged into securities. Market panic instantly reflects itself in falling securities prices, which in turn intensify investors' panic. This vicious circle is a modern bank run: a global sell-off of credit.

Regulators can lessen, though not eliminate, this risk by requiring financial firms to hold capital proportionate to their reliance on short-term, uninsured lenders, thus encouraging them to attract long-term funding that allows them to hang on to their assets in a fire-sale pricing environment. This idea springs from Alan Greenspan—in 1984, before his days as Federal Reserve chairman. As Greenspan said in an economists' roundtable after the Continental Illinois rescue, the capital cushion that banks must hold against losses should depend "on the type of liabilities it has. For example, a bank which has nothing but certificates of deposit that mature in ten years can do with a lot less capital than one which has borrowed overnight money."[10]

Regulators can better protect the financial system—and thus the economy—from the peaks and troughs of optimism and pessimism by taking other creative approaches to financial firms' funding sources. Former St. Louis Federal Reserve president William Poole suggests that all banks issue junior debt—the last debt in line for repayment in bankruptcy—in the amount of 10 percent of their borrowing. Such debt would carry a mandatory ten-year maturity term, meaning that the lenders could not flee in a panic. The rule would require that each bank issue the debt on a rolling basis, so that 10 percent of such debt would come due every year, necessitating the bank to find new investors for that 10 percent. Such a requirement, imposed on all financial institutions, would introduce a valuable market signal, as investors could make known their assessment of individual banks, insurers, and investment houses through the interest rates demanded to hold such debt.

Regulators can use capital requirements to protect the financial system in another way. They should follow Spain's example, requiring financial firms to set aside extra money during boom times to cushion against the losses they expect over an entire economic cycle. In America, by contrast, accounting rules, to prevent financial firms from using gimmickry to smooth out reported earnings, prohibit them from setting aside extra loss reserves except when a big loss is likely—when, for example, executives see credit-card losses rising and believe that they will accelerate. By 2007, American banks had set aside reserves adequate only for the low losses they had seen at the peak of a credit bubble, when borrowers could easily refinance debt to avoid defaults. A year later, thanks to this enforced short-term horizon, the banks had to increase their reserves dramatically to cover a sudden increase in defaults and losses, just when they could least afford to hoard capital.

If regulators required American financial firms to base reserves on average losses, they could build up a store of capital reserves during the good times upon which they could draw during the bad times. This extra capital cushion would help protect them from having to sell good assets at low prices to cover losses. Such regulations aren't fail-safe; financial firms and regulators can underestimate expected losses over an entire economic cycle. Spanish banks have taken tremendous losses on property loans. But in not basing loss reserves on a cycle's peak or trough, Spain helped insulate its banks and its financial system from the short-term panic that destroyed other nations' financial systems in 2008. Investors knew that Spain's banks had surplus capital, and thus some room for error.[11]

The government could use capital requirements to address another cause of the credit crisis: Wall Streeters, like everyone else, will take more risks with someone else's money. Bankers and traders work under a compensation system that offered unlimited potential for gains but limited loss exposure. When investment banks were private partnerships, each partner's capital—and net worth—depended on his firm's performance. Today's publicly traded firms, by contrast, pay employees annual bonuses with no open-ended liability. As James Glassman and William Nolan have written, Brown Brothers Harriman, which did not convert from a partnership, has remained a "solid institution" partly because it has maintained a "quite manageable" borrowing ratio of $11 borrowed to each $1 in hand.[12] Because employees of publicly traded firms have a natural impulse to take more risk, regulators should require these firms to hold higher capital. Publicly traded firms would have a new check on recklessness, while partnerships would have a chance to compete fairly.

Capital requirements that vary according to a firm's funding sources could partly address the problem of money-market funds, a problem with no easy solution. In 2008, after Lehman Brothers' collapse, the Treasury Department stepped in and offered a government guarantee for such funds, as discussed in Chapter 8. Yet investors in money markets were supposed to understand that the funds carry slightly greater risk than do FDIC-insured savings accounts, in return for a higher interest rate. Regulators could require the funds to hold more capital to protect against the risk that their short-term investors could flee.

Such a solution doesn't completely address the reality that investors believe it unlikely that the government would ever let such a fund fail in the future, though. In fact, it's quite possible that the government should accept this reality, with an FDIC or similar guarantee of all small money-market accounts akin to deposit insurance. Otherwise, money markets will be the weakest point of the government's new not-too-big-to-fail policy—and it may be better to invite them into the tent of explicit protection than allow for uncertainty that will weaken all-important credibility.

To protect ordinary Americans from financial exotica like adjustable-rate mortgages and the like, Washington does not need a Consumer Financial Protection Agency, as President Obama has proposed, to micromanage financial products in an attempt to protect the public. Here, too, Washington should allow creativity and competition to blossom within clear limits on borrowing and exposure.

As elsewhere, it's a matter of applying core principles across markets. Just as people can't borrow 100 percent of the price of a stock, they should not be permitted to borrow 100 percent of the price of a house—or any other investment. Similarly, though regulations prohibit middle-class Americans from investing in hedge funds and other financial instruments because of the perceived risk involved, nothing stopped them from taking out adjustable-rate mortgages. Existing SEC regulations prevent stockbrokers from telling potential customers that they "can't lose" on an investment—but real-estate brokers continue to make such promises.

In particular, when it comes to average people's retirement savings, regulators should push back against a generally healthy force: Americans' natural optimism, which often causes them to put all their eggs into one basket. Though investors should be free to speculate on the next big thing, they shouldn't be allowed to do so in retirement accounts like 401(k)s and IRAs, which enjoy favorable tax treatment. The government should revive a failed Enron-era proposal banning employees from investing more than 10 percent of in-house retirement savings in their employer's stock. Congress should also prohibit the owner of any independent 401(k) or IRA from investing more than 15 percent of retirement assets in one company, or 20 percent in one industry. (Investors could still do so elsewhere, of course.) And Congress should continue to prevent people from using their 401(k) accounts to invest in their homes. Instead, Congress should encourage people to save and invest money elsewhere, through better tax policy.

Within these broad guidelines, regulators should encourage competition in consumer investments. Currently, it's legal for an employer to tell its workers that they have no choice but to invest in one family of mutual funds in the corporate 401(k). It's also legal for states to mandate that families direct savings for their children's college educations to a particular asset manager to benefit from tax breaks. Such restrictions reduce choice and invite corruption—and Washington should scrap them.

In the credit collapse's aftermath, politicians want to rearrange organization charts, just as they did after 9/11. It's soothing to think that faceless institutional structures failed, rather than admit that people of authority and experience failed over and over again to apply commonsense principles to changing markets.

President Obama, in June 2009, dusted off a proposal first made in the Bush administration to create a "systemic risk regulator" or a "prudential risk regulator," akin to a Department of Homeland Security for financial markets. The Treasury, supported by a council of other regulators, would monitor financial markets to protect the economy from systemic meltdown, while the Fed would monitor important financial institutions. Proponents of this new regulatory role see it closing a gap, since currently nobody is responsible for the entire financial system. The Federal Reserve guards against inflation and unemployment and helps regulate banks and financial products; the SEC oversees disclosure and polices fraud for most financial markets; and the

Commodity Futures Trading Commission does the same for regulated derivatives.

But an omniscient regulator would not have prevented the crisis. The Fed has acted as a de-facto systemic risk regulator for decades, and it has ample discretion to do so. Sometimes it has used that power wisely and sometimes not. In 1985, Fed chairman Paul Volcker showed how adeptly the Fed could act, when, worried about overexuberant borrowing for corporate takeovers, he acted under Depression-era powers to limit borrowing for stocks. By contrast, throughout the nineties, the Fed used the same discretion to thwart derivatives regulation. The Fed, as the steward of bank holding companies, had the power, too, to rein in banks' off-the-books ventures, but deemed them safe enough to persist and grow.[13] If the Fed had identified an area of the financial world in distressing need of regulation, its clout with Congress was such that Congress would have granted it the requisite authority.

Regulators' biggest failure was in not using their discretion to apply hard-and-fast rules to an evolving marketplace as a nimble financial industry naturally found ways around constraints. In the derivatives market and elsewhere, Washington confused what kind of financial risk-taking warranted clear, uniform limits and what kind warranted discretionary attention and surveillance. Clear limits on some financial risk-taking are necessary for one overarching reason: sometimes, nobody sees any risk at all.

Creating a systemic risk regulator would be a continuation of that regulatory confusion. Just as bad, a systemic risk regulator would work against Washington's credibility in ending too-big-to-fail. Investors would be lulled into false confidence that the government is looking out for them just as it looks out for insured bank depositors. But a systemic regulator would be no more effective than the former USSR's central planners were in seeing and knowing all. Just as markets seeking profits are better planners than central bureaucrats, markets protecting themselves from a *credible* threat of failure would be more effective regulators than a central office that stifles that threat.

The staffers drawing up Washington's plans also have counseled regulatory consolidation on a domestic level to reduce redundancy and on a global level to avoid a new race to the bottom. Though some consolidation may be appropriate, appointing a monolithic regulator—particularly a global one—is a bad idea.

Many independent regulators bring their competing ideas about risk and reality to the task of evaluating markets, while one regulator could make a catastrophic, systemic mistake that goes unchecked for years, holding the entire world hostage either to low growth or to the potential for financial catastrophe. Indeed, the credit crisis became inevitable partly because over twenty-five years, national regulators implemented global guidelines, agreeing to use the international Basel capital standards that encouraged banks to set their loss reserves based on subjective risk assessments.

Nations should compete on regulation as they compete on tax rates. Further, domestic regulators can use their discretion to rein in firms that seem to do too much regulatory shopping. A national regulator that thought that a financial firm was taking too much risk in London would have one key point of leverage: its control over the company's right to operate in American markets.

With financial instruments and firms subject to market discipline and fair-playing-field regulation, financial innovation could thrive once again, with success and failure alike benefiting the industry and the nation's competitiveness.

Both securitization and credit derivatives are financial innovations that can benefit the economy, just as the junk-bond market eventually grew past its meltdown nearly two decades ago and continues to finance growth. Securitization is an elegant solution to financing credit: the concept of pooling loans and slicing them into securities in which investors take different levels of risk is sound, and it did protect investors in AAA-rated securities in the credit crisis, as investors in lower-rated tranches took their overwhelming losses first. Credit derivatives, too, offer value. In early 2008, the credit-default-swap market predicted that Bear Stearns was at risk of going under before regulators or analysts did. Seven years previously, credit derivatives pointed to Enron's bankruptcy first.

The problem was that without the full market discipline of failure under a regime of reasonable regulation, financiers and investors took innovations to absurd extremes. Succumbing to a potent bubble psychology, they thought that their formulas for estimating and engineering risk gave them an ability to quantify all uncertainty and structure away all danger.

Regulated properly, the securitization and credit-derivatives markets would have had a much harder time destroying themselves. Uniform capital requirements for financial institutions' assets would have discouraged firms from acting as if AAA-rated mortgage-backed securities were risk-free, rather than merely less risky. Down-payment requirements for home buyers would have barred many unqualified borrowers or speculative property flippers, whose shaky loans infected so many mortgage-backed securities. Margin requirements for credit derivatives to cushion the firm and its trading partners from the effect of possible losses would have discouraged AIG from lulling the world into thinking that hundreds of billions of dollars in securities collectively posed no danger.

The reasonable application of existing regulatory principles to new markets is superior to the inevitable alternatives: doing nothing and letting the current system fester, or resorting to outright bans that kill innovation or micromanagement that injures it. With borrowing limits and disclosure rules governing the next generation of financial instruments, regulators wouldn't have to approve products on a case-by-case basis. Instead, they could be comfortable that such instruments, even if they went sour, wouldn't pose an unacceptable risk to the broader economy. Such a framework for creativity would benefit firms that make money creating and trading derivatives.

Uniform capital requirements also encourage the next generation of risk-takers. With everyone operating within consistent parameters, powerful banks and their friends on Capitol Hill couldn't game the existing system at the expense of smaller firms.

Conservative firms' executives wouldn't feel as much pressure to compete with reckless rivals in a race to the bottom.

Markets have already begun to adjust healthily to a changing reality, showing flexibility and regeneration even in their weakened state. In the credit-default-swap market, financial institutions began to move transactions onto clearinghouses a year before the White House announced its proposal. By late April 2009, surviving hedge funds temporarily breathed easier, as they no longer had to compete against so many big banks doing their own in-house trading on the cheap, since the big banks had pulled back significantly.[14] The same month, the former chief of a small Brazilian investment bank, Pactual, repurchased his firm from Swiss banking giant UBS for the same price he had sold it for several years earlier, saying that he would return the bank to a partnership model because "a partnership was better suited to making financial bets than a large bureaucratic institution."[15]

Healthy markets can address other tough issues more subtly than blunt government forces can. As citizens have voiced outrage over the bonuses that bankers and traders reaped retroactively on the taxpayers' dime, politicians have voiced support for executive-pay "reform." But private firms should pay their executives and other employees whatever they wish.

If allowed to work, market forces can rein in executive pay. Over the past quarter-century, financial firms would not have had the cheap money to take their reckless risks and pay their executives outlandishly if lenders had not thought that the firms were too big to fail. When the government puts in place a credible, orderly method for big financial firms to fail, lenders to those firms will act prudently.

The broader economy can adeptly adjust to a world in which market discipline once again governs finance. Between the early eighties and 2006, the financial industry's profits doubled twice as a share of national income.[16] The financial industry's recent dominance of the economy would be fine if market forces had created it, but the industry found nourishment in the government subsidy of failure that started with Continental Illinois. Finance has consumed capital and talent that might have gone elsewhere, including to technology and engineering firms, because it did not have to compete fairly. Firms in other industries ramped up pay to compete with Wall Street bonuses subsidized by too-big-to-fail. But in the past year, smart young people have been forced to look for jobs off the Street. Likewise, Americans have started to decrease the unsustainable consumer borrowing that a government-subsidized industry long encouraged.

The biggest peril that the economy and the nation face is that Washington won't muster the political willpower to do its job and to keep doing it as Wall Street creates new ways to escape limits on risk-taking. Solid regulations, even if enacted quickly and well, would take some time to adjust to, as happened in the thirties—and they would slow the economy in the short term. It's not clear that the current administration will let people take pain now in return for long-term prosperity, as Ronald Reagan did when he allowed Volcker to hike interest rates in the early eighties to break inflation.

Every politician in the world has a rational immediate motive not to change anything. The American financial industry helped create the modern global economy, with American consumption supporting the world's manufacturing capacity. But finance was unrestrained by either market discipline or appropriate regulation. Over the past two and a half decades, it exposed that global economy to such enormous imbalance and risk that by late 2008 and early 2009, the world's Western leaders were compelled to provide trillions of dollars in rescue money not just to the financial system but, through stimulus spending, to the economy itself. The financial world and the government together, though, may try to pretend that nothing ever happened, with financial firms using the cheap money available under the too-big-to-fail regime trying to wring out one last cycle and postpone the mathematically inevitable adjustment: Americans borrowing less and buying less, and much of the rest of the world doing the opposite.

Parts of the financial industry are all too willing to try to continue business as usual. "It's too early to say 'never again,' " said Jay Dhru, head of S&P's financial-institutions ratings group, at a late-2008 conference. In early 2009, banks, ensconced in their government cocoon, were still lending freely to hedge funds. After demanding no cash up front for unregulated derivatives trades in 2006, they demanded a 1 to 2 percent margin—hardly an improvement. By July 2009, Goldman Sachs and Barclays Capital, which bought Lehman Brothers' American operations, were tinkering with new securitization permutations, "inventing schemes to reduce the capital cost of the risky assets on banks' balance sheets," the *Financial Times* observed.[17] The same month, Goldman Sachs reported record quarterly profits of $3.4 billion. Goldman could continue to take opaque risks using money from lenders that know that the investment house is too big to fail.[18]

Washington may also be tempted to go on as before for the same reason it did in the wake of its Continental Illinois and Long-Term Capital Management bailouts. Back then, government regulators and financial executives came to believe: if we can fix this, we can fix anything. If the economy allows Lehman's collapse and the visceral fear that it created to recede into history, elected officials and regulators may feel a similar sense of accomplishment that they rescued the economy from a new depression—not that they won a temporary reprieve that, without real reform, only increases future danger.

The next time the markets try to correct our unsustainable financial system, as they brutally have tried in this crisis, Washington may not be able to pull us back from the brink of depression, even if it does so this time. With trillions devoted to bad financial institutions and to economic stimulus to lessen the effects of the financial disaster, the U.S. flirts with further deterioration of its physical infrastructure, making it harder for private companies to grow. We also risk inflation and the desertion of the dollar even as Social Security and Medicare lay claims on growth.

A financial industry in need of even bigger bailouts after yet another cycle could take down with it the ability of the U.S. government to issue bonds affordably. In such a case, we'd have to revive our economy after having lost the world's confidence and hampered our economy's ability to recover and prosper.

The public can help avert such a dismal outcome. Despite elite concerns of a public backlash against capitalism, it has been the public, not Wall Street or Washington, that has supported capitalism all along. Financiers were disconcertingly quick to run straight into the government's arms, while the public has stuck up for markets and fought against taxpayer subsidy of failure. The hope for free markets is "political constraint," says former St. Louis Fed president William Poole.

The public intuitively grasps unfairness when it sees it. In poll after poll, citizens have opposed bailout after bailout, not just for the banks but for their own neighbors. This opposition is not a reflection of heartless and mindless populism. Ordinary people understand that bailouts have perversely punished individuals and companies that acted responsibly, creating an incentive to act irresponsibly in the future. They can perceive the difference between a government that acts as an honest, transparent referee of competitors and one that acts as a guarantor of perceived favorites.

Washington must realize that rationally regulating Wall Street doesn't impede capitalism. As history and recent events demonstrate, such regulation is a necessary condition for capitalism's survival.

BIBLIOGRAPHY

Ahamed, Liaquat. *Lords of Finance: The Bankers Who Broke the World* (New York: Penguin, 2009).

Bainbridge, Stephen M. *The Complete Guide to Sarbanes-Oxley: Understanding How Sarbanes-Oxley Affects Your Business* (Avon, Mass.: Adams Business, 2007).

Bernanke, Ben S. *Essays on the Great Depression* (Princeton, N.J.: Princeton University Press, 2004).

Ellis, Charles D. *The Partnership: The Making of Goldman Sachs* (New York: Penguin, 2008).

The First Fifty Years: A History of the FDIC 1933–1983 (Washington, D.C.: FDIC, 1984).

Fraser, Steve. *Wall Street: America's Dream Palace* (New Haven, Conn.: Yale University Press, 2008).

Friedman, Milton, and Anna Jacobson Schwartz. *The Great Contraction, 1929–1933,* new ed. (Princeton, N.J.: Princeton University Press, 2008).

Graham, Benjamin, and David Dodd. *Security Analysis* (New York: McGraw Hill, 1940).

Greenspan, Alan. *The Age of Turbulence: Adventures in a New World* (New York: Penguin, 2007).

Harris, Ethan S. *Ben Bernanke's Fed: The Federal Reserve After Alan Greenspan* (Boston: Harvard Business Press, 2008).

Kaufman, Henry. *On Money and Markets: A Wall Street Memoir* (New York: McGraw-Hill, 2000).

Lowenstein, Roger. *When Genius Failed: The Rise and Fall of Long-Term Capital Management* (New York: Random House, 2001).

Masters, Brooke A. *Spoiling for a Fight: The Rise of Eliot Spitzer* (New York: Henry Holt, 2006).

McLean, Bethany, and Peter Elkin. *Smartest Guys in the Room: The Amazing Rise and Scandalous Fall of Enron* (New York: Portfolio, 2003).

Morris, Charles R. *The Trillion Dollar Meltdown: Easy Money, High Rollers, and the Great Credit Crash* (New York: PublicAffairs, 2008).

Phillips, Kevin. *Bad Money: Reckless Finance, Failed Politics, and the Global Crisis of American Capitalism* (New York: Viking, 2008).

Samuelson, Robert J. *The Great Inflation and Its Aftermath: The Past and Future of American Affluence* (New York: Random House, 2008).

Shlaes, Amity. *The Forgotten Man: A New History of the Great Depression* (New York: HarperCollins, 2007).

Sutherland, Edwin H. *White Collar Crime: The Uncut Version*, new ed. (New Haven, Conn.: Yale University Press, 1983).

Taleb, Nassim Nicholas. *The Black Swan: The Impact of the Highly Improbable* (New York: Random House, 2007).

Volcker, Paul A., and Toyoo Gyohten. *Changing Fortunes: The World's Money and the Threat to American Leadership* (New York: Times Books, 1992).

Wasik, John F. *The Merchant of Power: Sam Insull, Thomas Edison, and the Creation of the Modern Metropolis* (New York: Palgrave/ MacMillan, 2006).

ACKNOWLEDGMENTS

I thank my *City Journal* editors and colleagues Brian Anderson, Paul Beston, Steven Malanga, and Ben Plotinsky, and my Manhattan Institute colleagues Howard Husock and E. J. McMahon. I thank the Manhattan Institute, its president, Larry Mone, and its invaluable staffers Lindsay Young Craig, Vanessa Mendoza, and Clarice Smith. I thank Roger Kimball, Lauren Miklos, and Heather Ohle at Encounter Books for their patience and Janice Meyerson Scheindlin for her manuscript treatment.

Myron Magnet merits exceptional appreciation.

I thank my former employer, Thomson Reuters, and my former Thomson colleagues, Rod Morrison and Alison Healey.

I thank the New York Public Library for its invaluable research resources.

Finally, I thank my husband, Matthew Civello, my parents, Mary Gelinas and John Gelinas, my grandmother, Mary Moussette, my brother, Sean Gelinas, and my sister, Melissa Prudente.

NOTES

PREFACE

1 Wendy Gramm, "In Defense of Derivatives," *Wall Street Journal*, September 8, 1993.
2 "Financial Regulatory Reform: A New Foundation," United States Department of the Treasury, June 2009.

INTRODUCTION

1. "Last Court Hurdle Cleared by Insull," *New York Times*, June 15, 1935.
2. Governor Franklin D. Roosevelt, speech to the Commonwealth Club, San Francisco, September 23, 1932.
3. Alexei Barrionuevo, "Two Chiefs Are Convicted in Fraud and Conspiracy Trial," *New York Times*, May 26, 2006.
4. "Last Court Hurdle Cleared by Insull."
5. Douglas Martin, "Albert Gordon, Who Rebuilt Kidder Peabody, Dies at 107," *New York Times*, May 2, 2009.
6. Mart Laar, "Freedom Is Still the Best Policy," *Wall Street Journal*, February 13, 2009.
7. "Discounting the Future," *Wall Street Journal*, July 19, 1928.

CHAPTER 1

1. "Discounting the Future," *Wall Street Journal*, July 19, 1928.
2. "Call Loans Safest Bank Investment," *Wall Street Journal*, June 22, 1926.
3. "Money Market Ease Accentuated," *Wall Street Journal*, April 8, 1926.
4. "Broad Street Gossip," *Wall Street Journal*, February 15, 1929.
5. New York Stock Exchange.
6. "Simmons' Views on Speculation," *Wall Street Journal*, May 25, 1929.

7. Hoisington Investment Management Co., "Quarterly Review and Outlook," fourth-quarter 2008. (While debt reached three times GDP in the 1930s, this increase was due to the precipitous fall in GDP itself, not a new increase in debt.)

8. "Gambling and Speculation," *Wall Street Journal*, May 15, 1928.

9. "Senate Revelations 5:1," *Time*, October 30, 1933.

10. John F. Wasik, *The Merchant of Power: Sam Insull, Thomas Edison, and the Creation of the Modern Metropolis* (New York: Palgrave/MacMillan, 2006), p. 167.

11. Ibid., pp. 234–35.

12. "Reserve Policy Still Unformed," *Wall Street Journal*, October 15, 1929.

13. "Owen Defends Brokers' Loans," *Wall Street Journal*, April 5, 1929.

14. Joseph P. Kennedy, SEC chairman, speech to the National Press Club, Washington, D.C., July 25, 1934.

15. "The Money Situation and Brokers' Loans," *Wall Street Journal*, June 26, 1928.

16. Liaquat Ahamed, *Lords of Finance: The Bankers Who Broke the World* (New York: Penguin, 2009).

17. "Loss of Credit Control," *Wall Street Journal*, September 10, 1928.

18. "Sec. Mellon Decries Stock Frauds," *Wall Street Journal*, May 10, 1926.

19. "Raids Planned in Fraud Drive," *Wall Street Journal*, October 19, 1929.

20. "Stock Frauds Drive Effective," *Wall Street Journal*, September 11, 1929.

21. "Stock Fraud Losses," *Wall Street Journal*, September 18, 1925.

22. "55 Are Indicted in Stock Scandal," *New York Times*, June 26, 1927; "20 Jersey Firms Quit," *New York Times*, November 16, 1927; "Selling 'Blue Sky,' " *New York Times*, August 2, 1928.

23. "Simmons Emphasizes Security Scrutiny," *Wall Street Journal*, April 10, 1925.

24. "Security Swindler a Growing Menace," *Wall Street Journal*, September 21, 1927.

25. As quoted in Albert J. Hettinger, Jr., "Director's Comment," included in Milton Friedman and Anna Jacobson Schwartz, *The Great Contraction, 1929–1933*, new ed. (Princeton, N.J.: Princeton University Press, 2008), p. 212.

26. Ahamed, *Lords of Finance*, p. 362.

27. Wasik, *The Merchant of Power*, p. 232.

28. "Whitney Says Pool Faced Heavy Loss," *New York Times*, June 3, 1933.

29. "Eight Carolina Banks Fail as Boom Ends," *New York Times*, November 21, 1930.

30. "981 Banks Fail in 11 Months, Record for the United States," *New York Times*, December 24, 1930.

31. "Say Nation's Banks Are on Sound Basis," *New York Times*, November 25, 1930.

32. *The First Fifty Years: A History of the FDIC 1933–1983* (FDIC, 1984), p. 36.

33. "Bank Sales Tactics in Stocks Revealed," *New York Times*, December 20, 1930.

34. "Now It Is Told," *Time*, June 5, 1933.

35. Ahamed, *Lords of Finance*, p. 448.

36. "Along the Highways of Finance," *New York Times*, March 18, 1934.

37. Milton Friedman and Anna Jacobson Schwartz, *A Monetary History of the United States, 1867–1960* (Princeton, N.J.: Princeton University Press, 1971), p. 8.

38. Idem, *The Great Contraction*, p. 8. "The Great Contraction" was originally a chapter in *A Monetary History*. See n. 33 above for the stand-alone edition of *The Great Contraction*.

39. Ibid., p. 217.

40. "Notable Story of the Past Financial Year," *New York Times*, December 31, 1930.

41. "Bank Parley Holds It Can't End Crisis," *New York Times*, May 21, 1931.

42. "Investigating the Panic of 1929," *New York Times*, December 6, 1931.

43. "Reconstruction Corporation: Its Aims and Plan of Work," *New York Times*, January 17, 1932.

44. "Pomerene Assails 'Parasite Banks,'" *New York Times*, November 18, 1932.

45. "Banks' Funds Fail to Expand Credit," *New York Times*, April 29, 1934.
46. "Banks Fail to Find Sound Borrowers," *New York Times*, May 6, 1934.
47. "The Man Who Will Question Morgan," *New York Times*, May 21, 1933.
48. Steve Fraser, *Wall Street: America's Dream Palace* (New Haven, Conn.: Yale University Press, 2008), p. 48.
49. "A Dole to the Wealthy," letter, *New York Times*, April 16, 1932.

CHAPTER 2

1. "Young for One Bank Authority," *Wall Street Journal*, February 5, 1931.
2. James M. Landis, speech to the Investment Bankers Association of America, December 4, 1936, http://www.sec.gov/news/speech/1936/120436landis.pdf.
3. Transcript of banking-crisis speech, March 12, 1933, FDIC archives.
4. William L. Silber, "Why Did FDR's Bank Holiday Succeed?," Federal Reserve Bank of New York, *Economic Policy Review* 15, no. 1 (July 2009): 19.
5. Transcript of banking-crisis speech, March 12, 1933, FDIC archives.
6. "Aldrich Criticizes Bank Act 'Fallacy,' " *New York Times*, December 7, 1933.
7. "Sisson Denounces Glass Banking Act," *New York Times*, June 23, 1933.
8. "Declares Banking Is Being Cleansed," *New York Times*, October 24, 1934.
9. Timothy L. O'Brien, "Shaping a Colossus," *New York Times*, April 8, 1998.
10. "Text of Report on Regulation of Security Exchanges," *Wall Street Journal*, January 30, 1934.
11. "Dawes Concedes Bank Abused Laws in Insull Loan," *New York Times*, February 17, 1933.
12. "Dillon's Pyramid," *Time*, October 16, 1933.
13. "Senate Revelations 5:4," *Time*, November 20, 1933.
14. "Senator Wheeler Assails Mitchell," *New York Times*, February 23, 1933.

15. "Wall St. Worried by Light Trading," *New York Times*, June 6, 1937.
16. Commissioner Garland S. Ferguson, Jr., Federal Trade Commission, on Securities Act of 1933, Washington, D.C., September 12, 1933, via radio.
17. Baldwin B. Bane, speech to Affiliated Better Business Bureau, New York, September 12, 1933.
18. "Wall Street Is Watching Its New Boss," *New York Times*, October 24, 1937.
19. Paul P. Gourrich, speech to the American Statistical Association, New York, December 30, 1935.
20. Benjamin Graham and David Dodd, *Security Analysis* (New York: McGraw Hill, 1940).
21. Thomas F. Woodlock, "Credit Control," *Wall Street Journal*, February 3, 1931.
22. Baldwin B. Bane, speech to National Association of Securities Commissioners, Milwaukee, September 19, 1933.
23. Kennedy, speech to the National Press Club, July 25, 1934.
24. "Securities Act Called a Damper," *New York Times*, October 16, 1933.
25. "Along the Highways of Finance," *New York Times*, October 8, 1933.
26. "Whitney Sees Curb as Nationalization," *New York Times*, March 1, 1934.
27. Richard W. Hale, letter to the editor, *New York Times*, August 23, 1934.
28. "The Congress Bank Bill," *Time*, March 20, 1933.
29. Thomas Philippon, "The Evolution of the US Financial Industry from 1860 to 2007: Theory and Evidence," working paper, New York University, November 2008.

CHAPTER 3

1. Walter Wriston, testimony before Senate Banking Committee, Washington, D.C., October 29, 1981; as quoted in "Business and the Law: Wriston 'View' of Banking Bill," *New York Times*, September 18, 1984.
2. "The High-Stakes Scramble to Rescue Continental Bank," *New York Times*, May 21, 1984.

3. John Andrew, Daniel Hertzberg, and Tim Carrington, "Confidence Game: Large Banks Are Hit by New Set of Rumors," *Wall Street Journal*, May 25, 1984.

4. Jeff Bailey and Tim Carrington, "Run Continues on Continental Illinois Deposits, " *Wall Street Journal*, July 2, 1984.

5. Kenneth B. Noble, "Wider Washington Role," *New York Times*, July 27, 1984.

6. William M. Isaac, "Bank Nationalization Isn't the Answer," *Wall Street Journal*, February 24, 2009.

7. G. Christian Hill, "Losses from Penn Square Bank's Failure Total $1.22 Billion and Are Still Growing," *Wall Street Journal*, April 12, 1984.

8. Ibid.

9. Jeff Bailey, John Helyar, and Daniel Hertzberg, "Troubled Bank: Continental Illinois, Its Safety Net in Place, Ponders Next Hurdle," *Wall Street Journal*, May 16, 1984.

10. Lee Berton, "Early Warnings: Long Before the 'Run' at Continental Illinois, Bank Hinted of Its Ills," *Wall Street Journal*, July 12, 1984.

11. William Blaylock et al., "Banking Takes a Beating," *Time*, December 3, 1984.

12. Tim Carrington, "U.S. Won't Let 11 Biggest Banks in National Fail," *Wall Street Journal*, September 20, 1984.

13. Leonard Silk, "Pressure to Change Banking Builds after a Near Disaster," *New York Times*, July 29, 1984.

14. Noble, "Wider Washington Role."

15. Jeff Bailey, John Helyar, and Tim Carrington, "Anatomy of Failure: Continental Illinois: How Bad Judgments and Big Egos Did It In," *Wall Street Journal*, July 30, 1984.

16. Tim Carrington, "Faced with a Continental Illinois Failure, U.S. Decided Bailout Was Worth the Price," *Wall Street Journal*, July 26, 1984.

17. "Reagan Calls Rescue of Bank No Bailout," *New York Times*, July 29, 1984.

18. Carrington, "Faced With a Continental Illinois Failure."

19. Idem, "U.S. Won't Let 11 Biggest Banks in Nation Fail."

20. Thomas H. Olson, "Does the U.S. Need Superbanks?," *New York Times*, June 28, 1987.

21. "Fallout from Continental's Collapse," *New York Times*, August 5, 1984.
22. Sylvia Nasar, "The Risks and the Benefits of Letting Sick Banks Die," *New York Times*, February 20, 1991.
23. "After the Fall: Banks Act to Minimize Risk in Their Dealings with Large Brethren," *Wall Street Journal*, October 15, 1984.
24. Ron Chernow, "Political Cowardice, Financial Panic," *Wall Street Journal*, January 9, 1991.
25. Steve Lohr, "When a Big Bank Went Under, U.S. Presence Stemmed the Panic," *New York Times*, February 18, 1991.
26. R. Alton Gilbert, "Requiem for Regulation Q: What It Did and Why It Passed Away," Federal Reserve Bank of St. Louis *Review* 68, no. 2 (February 1986): 22–37.
27. Charles E. Schumer, "Banks Aren't for Gambling," *New York Times*, June 7, 1984.
28. Idem, "Restore Banking Confidence," *Wall Street Journal*, August 28, 1985.
29. Bernard Baumohl, "Are Banks Obsolete?," *Time*, June 28, 1993.
30. Jacob M. Schlesinger, "The Deregulators: Did Washington Help Set Stage for Current Business Turmoil?," *Wall Street Journal*, October 17, 2002.
31. Saul Hansell, "Bank Is Set to Buy a Brokerage Firm," *New York Times*, April 7, 1997.
32. Linda Sandler, "Investment Banking Proves a Tough Field for Commercial Banks—They Lack Ties to Investors, Can't Hold Top Talent, but Have Size, Money," *Wall Street Journal*, September 19, 1984.
33. "We're Solvent, Citicorp Says," *New York Times*, July 8, 1992.
34. Data from Brad Hintz, Sanford C. Bernstein and Co., via Nicole Gelinas, "Gotham Needs Wall Street; Does Wall Street Need Gotham?," *City Journal* (Winter 2006).
35. Robert D. Hershey, Jr., "Greenspan Opposes Rescue of Failing Securities Firms," *New York Times*, March 2, 1990.
36. Saul Hansell, "Europe's Turmoil Aids U.S. Banks," *New York Times*, August 4, 1993.
37. "Banks Rely More on Trading, but Say Little About It—Companies Deny Taking Risky Bets, but Wall Street Wants More Data," *Wall Street Journal*, July 30, 1993.

38. Saul Hansell, "A Bad Bet for P&G," *New York Times*, April 14, 1994.
39. James Sterngold, "Can Salomon Brothers Learn to Love Junk Bonds?," *New York Times*, November 16, 1986.
40. Leonard Silk, "The Argument over the Banks," *New York Times*, February 8, 1991.
41. Stephen Labaton, "Congress Passes Wide-Ranging Bill Easing Bank Laws," *New York Times*, November 5, 1999.
42. Author's calculations based on Federal Reserve data.
43. Philippon, "The Evolution of the US Financial Industry from 1860 to 2007."
44. William Greider, *Secrets of the Temple* (New York: Simon & Schuster, 1989), via *An Examination of the Banking Crises of the 1980s and Early 1990s*, FDIC history, 1:246.
45. Michael Lewis, "The End," *Portfolio* (December 2008).

CHAPTER 4

1. Lowell Bryan, "The Selling of America's Loans," *Wall Street Journal*, October 20, 1986.
2. Laura Jereski, "Mortgage Derivatives Show Signs of Life," *Wall Street Journal*, October 3, 1994.
3. James Sterngold, "Rate Squeeze Snares Dealers," *New York Times*, August 4, 1986.
4. Charles R. Morris, *The Trillion Dollar Meltdown: Easy Money, High Rollers, and the Great Credit Crash* (New York: PublicAffairs, 2008), p. 39.
5. Sterngold, "Rate Squeeze Snares Dealers."
6. Michael R. Sesit, Ann Monroe, and Peter Truell, "Prosperity and Peril in the Brave New Market," *Wall Street Journal*, September 29, 1986.
7. Laura Jereski, "Mortgage Derivatives Claim Victims Big and Small," *Wall Street Journal*, April 20, 1994.
8. Michael Siconolfi, "Kidder Says Review Approves the Way It Values Its Mortgage-Backed Bonds," *Wall Street Journal*, May 13, 1994.
9. Jereski, "Mortgage Derivatives Show Signs of Life."
10. Saul Hansell, "Investment Funds Are Liquidated," *New York Times*, April 1, 1994.
11. "Crunch? Fall of the House of Drexel," editorial, *Wall Street Journal*, March 19, 1990.

12. Christopher Lehmann-Haupt, "Books of the Times: Conquering the Financial World with Junk Bonds," *New York Times*, June 16, 1988.

13. Felix Rohatyn, "Junk Bonds and Other Securities Swill," *Wall Street Journal*, April 18, 1985.

14. Robert D. Hershey, Jr., "Fed Adopts 'Junk Bond' Curbs," *New York Times*, January 9, 1986.

15. Michael Siconolfi, "Debt Load: Junk-Bond Funds Fall in Investors' Esteem as Their Values Skid," *Wall Street Journal*, March 21, 1990.

16. Ibid.

17. Diana B. Henriques, "Wall Street: Debunking the Junk 'Bomb' Theory," *New York Times*, March 22, 1992.

18. Fred R. Bleakley, "Bad Hangover," *Wall Street Journal*, October 9, 1990.

19. "Economic Scene: Buyout Fever: The Patient Lives," *New York Times*, December 13, 1989.

20. Michael Siconolfi et al., "The End of Drexel—Rise and Fall: Wall Street Era Ends as Drexel Burnham Decides to Liquidate," *Wall Street Journal*, February 14, 1990.

21. James Grant, "Of Michael Milken and MCorp," *Wall Street Journal*, April 12, 1989.

22. Glenn Costello and Grant Bailey, "Update on U.S. Subprime and Alt-A: Performance and Rating Reviews," Fitch Ratings, March 20, 2008.

23. Michael Quint, "Market Place: 'Securitization' Finds New Uses," *New York Times*, August 12, 1988.

24. "Global Finance and Investment," *Wall Street Journal*, September 29, 1986.

25. Susan Pulliam, "State Regulators Scrutinize Insurers Using New Method to Shed Risky Assets," *Wall Street Journal*, May 11, 1992.

26. David B. Hilder, Craig Forman, and Marcus W. Brauchli, "Big Banks Are Cooling to 'Hot Money,'" *Wall Street Journal*, April 9, 1991.

27. Peter Passell, "Banking's Reins: Too Tight and Too Loose," *New York Times*, December 17, 1990.

28. Fred R. Bleakley, " 'Hot New Game' in Financing," *New York Times*, June 4, 1985.

29. "Global Finance and Investment," *Wall Street Journal*, September 29, 1986.
30. John Rather, "Economy Is Seen as Slightly Stronger," *New York Times*, January 14, 1996.
31. Dennis Hevesi, "Giving Credit Where Credit Was Denied," *New York Times*, June 8, 1997.
32. Nathaniel C. Nash, "Agreement on Banks' Capital Set," *New York Times*, July 12, 1988.
33. Joshua Cooper Ramo et al., "The Big Bank Theory," *Time*, April 27, 1998.
34. Gillian Tett, "Genesis of the Debt Disaster," *Financial Times*, May 1, 2009.
35. Martin Wolf, "The Cautious Approach to Fixing Banks Will Not Work," *Financial Times*, June 30, 2009.
36. Kevin G. Salwen, "SEC Is Seeking Updated Rules for Accounting," *Wall Street Journal*, January 8, 1992.
37. Lee Berton, "FASB Votes to Make Banks and Insurers Value Certain Bonds at Current Prices," *Wall Street Journal*, April 14, 1993.
38. Walter Wriston, "Mark to Market Wild Accountants' Crazy Idea," *Wall Street Journal*, June 11, 1992.
39. Louis Uchitelle, "Calling Bank Supervision Archaic, Greenspan Seeks Major Change," *New York Times*, February 10, 1991.
40. Hershey, "Greenspan Opposes Rescue of Failing Securities Firms."
41. Albert Karr, "Bank Regulators Expected to Drop Plan Pegged to Market Value of Securities," *Wall Street Journal*, November 9, 1994.
42. Stephen Labaton, "Agreement Reached on Overhaul of U.S. Financial System," *New York Times*, October 23, 1999.
43. Securities Industry and Financial Markets Association data, Federal Reserve data.
44. Baumohl, "Are Banks Obsolete?."

CHAPTER 5

1. Charles Sanford, speech at the Federal Reserve Bank of Kansas City's symposium "Changing Capital Markets: Implications for Monetary Policy," Jackson Hole, Wyo., 1993.

2. Leslie Wayne, "Orange County's Bankruptcy: The Temptations; The Search for Municipal 'Cowboys,' " *New York Times*, December 8, 1994.

3. Carol Loomis, "The Risk That Won't Go Away," *Fortune*, March 7, 1994.

4. "Managing the Whiz Kids," editorial, *New York Times*, April 26, 1994.

5. Saul Hansell, "A U.S. Look for Lessons in Barings," *New York Times*, March 6, 1995.

6. John M. Broder, "Chicago Exchanges Seek to Loosen Yoke of Regulation," *New York Times*, June 4, 1997.

7. "Dangerous Derivatives," editorial, *Wall Street Journal*, March 14, 1997.

8. Saul Hansell, "Derivatives as the Fall Guy: Excuses, Excuses," *New York Times*, October 2, 1994.

9. Ramo et al., "The Big Bank Theory."

10. Timothy L. O'Brien, "A Chief Executive Comes Up Short," *New York Times*, December 1, 1998.

11. Gramm, "In Defense of Derivatives."

12. Alan Greenspan, speech to Kansas City Federal Reserve Board, Kansas City, Mo., 1993.

13. Kenneth H. Bacon, "U.S. Announces Some Guidelines for Derivatives—Banks Will Be Required to Adopt Risk Policy Promising No Surprises," *Wall Street Journal*, September 28, 1993.

14. Floyd Norris, "Orange County Crisis Jolts Bond Market," *New York Times*, December 8, 1994.

15. Peter S. Goodman, "Taking Hard New Look at Greenspan Legacy," *New York Times*, October 9, 2008.

16. Steven Lipin, "Risk Management Has Proved Crucial in a Year When Strategies Proved Wrong," *Wall Street Journal*, September 29, 1994.

17. Jeffrey Taylor, "Securities Firms Agree to Set Controls on Derivatives," *Wall Street Journal*, March 9, 1995.

18. Diana B. Henriques, "Reforms and Risks," *New York Times*, October 23, 1995.

19. Ibid.

20. Brooksley Born, testimony before the House Committee on Banking and Financial Services, Washington, D.C., October 1, 1998.
21. Bank for International Settlements data, May 16, 2001.
22. Tett, "Genesis of the Debt Disaster."
23. Paul M. Sherer, "Chase Digs in Its Heels, but Ally J. P. Morgan Embraces 'Fair Value,' " *Wall Street Journal*, October 11, 2000.
24. Timothy F. Geithner, "Risk Management Challenges in the US Financial System," speech to the Global Association of Risk Professionals, New York, February 28, 2006.
25. Lionel Barber, speech at Yale University, April 21, 2009.

CHAPTER 6

1. Richard W. Stevenson, "The Collapse of Barings: The Overview," *New York Times*, February 28, 1995.
2. Paul Lewis, "Acceptable Failure Not Seen as a Threat to Financial Systems," *New York Times*, February 28, 1995.
3. Richard W. Stevenson, "Markets Shaken as a British Bank Takes a Big Loss," *New York Times*, February 27, 1995.
4. George Melloan, "Leeson's Law," *Wall Street Journal*, March 6, 1995.
5. Gretchen Morgenson, "Seeing a Fund as Too Big to Fail, New York Fed Assists Its Bailout," *New York Times*, September 24, 1998.
6. Diana B. Henriques and Joseph Kahn, "Lessons of a Long Hot Summer," *New York Times*, December 6, 1998.
7. Joseph Kahn and Peter Truell, "Troubled Investment Fund's Bets Now Estimated at $1.25 Trillion," *New York Times*, September 26, 1998.
8. Roger Lowenstein, *When Genius Failed: The Rise and Fall of Long-Term Capital Management* (New York: Random House, 2001), p. 102.
9. Henriques and Kahn, "Lessons of a Long Hot Summer."
10. Stevenson, "Markets Shaken as a British Bank Takes a Big Loss."
11. Born, testimony before the House Committee on Banking and Financial Services, October 1, 1998.
12. Patrick McGeehan, "Lehman Offers a Rare Glimpse of Risk Profile," *Wall Street Journal*, October 6, 1998.

13. Kahn and Truell, "Troubled Investment Fund's Bets Now Estimated at $1.25 Trillion."

14. "Bailout Blues," *Wall Street Journal*, September 25, 1998.

15. Lowenstein, *When Genius Failed*, p. xix.

16. Jacob M. Schlesinger and Paul Beckett, "Capital Crunch," *Wall Street Journal*, October 7, 1998.

17. Lowenstein, *When Genius Failed*, p. 30.

18. Ibid., p. 79.

19. Henriques and Kahn, "Lessons of a Long Hot Summer."

20. "Long-Term Capital Case Isn't Federal Bailout, Rubin Says," *Wall Street Journal*, September 28, 1998.

21. Diana B. Henriques, "The Fear That Made the Fed Step In," *New York Times*, December 6, 1998.

22. Schlesinger and Beckett, "Capital Crunch."

23. Ibid.

24. John Steele Gordon, "History Repeats in Finance Companies Bailouts," *Wall Street Journal*, October 7, 1998.

25. "Decade of Moral Hazard," *Wall Street Journal*, September 25, 1998.

26. "Fearful Investors Seek Protection for Derivatives," *Wall Street Journal*, September 28, 1998.

27. Laura Goldberg, "Taking a Long View, Enron Works to Shore Up Confidence," *Houston Chronicle*, August 28, 2001.

28. "Ex-Enron Chief Defiant in Senate Panel Grilling," *Houston Chronicle*, February 27, 2002.

29. Loren Steffy, "Enron's Philosophy of Lies Is What's on Trial Here," *Houston Chronicle*, February 1, 2006.

30. Floyd Norris and Kurt Eichenwald, "Enron's Many Strands: The Accounting," *New York Times*, January 30, 2002.

31. Bethany McLean and Peter Elkin, *Smartest Guys in the Room: The Amazing Rise and Scandalous Fall of Enron* (New York: Portfolio, 2003), p. 158.

32. Ibid., pp. 191–92.

33. Ibid., p. 136.

34. Ibid., p. 133.

35. Mary Flood, "Skilling's Demeanor Takes a Sober Turn," *Houston Chronicle*, April 14, 2006.

36. Michael Brick, "What Was the Heart of Enron Keeps Shrinking," *New York Times*, April 6, 2002.

37. Anita Raghavan, Michael Schroeder, and Jathon Sapsford, "SEC Examines Ties Between Banks and Enron," *Wall Street Journal*, January 15, 2002.

38. Daniel Altman, "Enron's Many Strands: Marketplace; An Innovative Way to Borrow Started at Enron," *New York Times*, January 29, 2002.

39. Michiel van der Voort, letter to the editor, *Wall Street Journal*, October 1, 2002.

40. Christopher Oster and Ken Brown, "Deciphering the Black Box—Many Accounting Practices, Not Just Enron's, Are Hard to Penetrate—Five Companies: How They Get Their Numbers—AIG: A Complex Industry, A Very Complex Company," *Wall Street Journal*, January 23, 2002.

41. Gretchen Morgenson, "AIG: Whiter Shade of Enron," *New York Times*, April 3, 2005.

42. Jonathan Weil, "Should JP Morgan Set Rules for JP Morgan?" *Wall Street Journal*, October 8, 2002.

43. Diana B. Henriques, "The Brick Stood Up Before. But Now?" *New York Times*, March 10, 2002.

44. Glenn R. Simpson, "Deals That Took Enron Under Had Many Supporters," *Wall Street Journal*, April 10, 2002.

45. Ibid.

46. Henny Sender, "Fall of an Energy Giant," *Wall Street Journal*, December 3, 2001.

47. Schlesinger, "The Deregulators: Did Washington Help Set Stage for Current Business Turmoil?."

CHAPTER 7

1. Edmund L. Andrews, "The Ever More Graspable, and Risky, American Dream," *New York Times*, June 24, 2004.

2. Julie Creswell, "Chief Calls Deal a Dream for Wachovia," *New York Times*, May 9, 2006.

3. Steven Malanga, "Obsessive Housing Disorder," *City Journal* (Spring 2009).

4. "Fitch Affirms $20B & Downgrades $2.4B of U.S. Subprime RMBS: New 2005–2006 Surveillance Criteria," Business Wire, August 2007.

5. "Call Loans Safest Bank Investment," *Wall Street Journal*, June 22, 1926.

6. Securities Industry and Financial Markets Association.

7. Keith Bradsher, "Fannie Mae Seeks to Ease Home Buying," *New York Times*, March 10, 1994.

8. "Mortgage Risk: A Hot Export," *Wall Street Journal*, September 22, 2005.

9. Credit Suisse.

10. Alan Greenspan and James Kennedy, "Sources and Uses of Equity Extracted from Homes," Federal Reserve, March 2007.

11. William H. Lucy and Jeff Herlitz, "Behind the Housing Bubble: Home Ownership Rates by Age," Real Clear Markets, available at http://www.realclearmarkets.com/charts/behind_the_ housing_bubble_home_ownership_rates_by_age-58.html.

12. James Bennett, "At Event on King Day, A Mix of Goals Met and Hoped For," *New York Times*, January 19, 1999.

13. Eric Lipton and Stephen Labaton, "Deregulator Looks Back, Unswayed," *New York Times*, November 17, 2008.

14. Kudlow & Co., August 28, 2006; Squawk on the Street, February 15, 2007; clips via "Peter Schiff Was Right" montage available on youtube.com.

15. Securities Industry and Financial Markets Association data, Federal Reserve data.

16. Martin Wolf, "Japanese Lessons for a World of Balance-Sheet Deflation, *Financial Times*, February 17, 2009.

17. Bank for International Settlements.

18. Securities Industry and Financial Markets Association data, Federal Reserve data.

19. James R. Hagerty and Ruth Simon, "Mortgage Risk: A Hot Export," *Wall Street Journal*, September 22, 2005.

20. David Wessel, "Wall Street Is Cleaning Derivatives Mess," *Wall Street Journal*, February 16, 2006.

CHAPTER 8

1. Michiyo Nakamoto and David Wighton, "Citigroup Chief Stays Bullish on Buy-Outs," *Financial Times*, July 9, 2007.

2. Diya Gullapalli, Shefali Anand, and Daisy Maxey, "Money Fund, Hurt by Debt Tied to Lehman, Breaks the Buck," *Wall Street Journal*, September 17, 2008.

3. "Treasury Announces Guaranty Program for Money Market Funds," Treasury Department press release, September 19, 2008.

4. Jenny Anderson and Vikas Bajaj, "Soothing Words and a Stock Market Rebound," *New York Times*, March 1, 2007.
5. Julie Creswell and Vikas Bajaj, "$3.2 Billion Move by Bear Stearns to Rescue Fund," *New York Times*, June 23, 2007.
6. Glenn Costello and Grant Bailey, "Update on U.S. Subprime and Alt-A: Performance and Rating Reviews," Fitch Ratings, March 20, 2008.
7. Inside Mortgage Finance data.
8. Janet Tavakoli, "In Subprime, AIG Sees Small Risk, Others See More," *Wall Street Journal*, August 13, 2007.
9. Carrie Mollenkamp, Ian McDonald, and Deborah Solomon, "Big Banks Push $100 Billion Plan to Avert Crunch," *Wall Street Journal*, October 13, 2007.
10. Ibid.
11. Landon Thomas, Jr., "$9.4 Billion Write-Down at Morgan Stanley," *New York Times*, December 20, 2007.
12. Liam Pleven, "Maybe You Can Win for Losing," *Wall Street Journal*, February 28, 2008.
13. Susan Pulliam, Randall Smith, and Michael Siconolfi, "U.S. Investors Face an Age of Murky Pricing," *Wall Street Journal*, October 12, 2007.
14. Standard and Poor's.
15. Andrew Ross Sorkin, "What Goes Before a Fall: Optimism," *New York Times*, September 30, 2008.
16. Matt Richtel, "A Sea of Unwanted Imports," *New York Times*, November 18, 2008.
17. Friedman and Schwartz, *A Monetary History of the United States*.
18. Idem, *The Great Contraction*, p. 8.
19. Federal Reserve data.
20. Edmund L. Andrews, "Greenspan Concedes Error on Regulation," *New York Times*, October 24, 2008.
21. "Senator Wheeler Assails Mitchell," *New York Times*, February 23, 1933.
22. Hoisington Investment Management Co., "Quarterly Review and Outlook," fourth-quarter 2008.

CHAPTER 9

1. President George W. Bush, speech to the Manhattan Institute, New York, November 13, 2008.

2. Neil King, Jr., and Jeffrey McCracken, "U.S. Forced Chrysler Creditors to Blink," *Wall Street Journal*, May 11, 2009.
3. Bush, Manhattan Institute speech, November 13, 2008.
4. Henry Paulson, "Fighting the Financial Crisis, One Challenge at a Time," *New York Times*, November 17, 2008.
5. Author's notes, Securities Industry and Financial Markets Association conference, November 2008.
6. Ibid.
7. Zachary Kouwe, "U.S. Role Questioned on Merrill," *New York Times*, April 24, 2009.
8. Henry Paulson, Testimony before the House Committee on Oversight and Government Reform, Washington, D.C., July 16, 2009.
9. Tessa Moran, "Bernanke Says He Did Not Orchestrate BOA, Merrill Deal," Reuters, June 25, 2009.
10. Liam Pleven, "AIG Sees Long Road Back from the Brink," *Wall Street Journal*, May 11, 2009.
11. Francesco Guerrera, "AIG Clinches $25bn Debt Deal," *Financial Times*, June 25, 2009.
12. Mark DeCambre, "Dimon Still Polishing JPM Pay Packages," *New York Post*, June 30, 2009.
13. Zachary Kouwe, "The Lenders Obama Decided to Blame for Chrysler's Fall," *New York Times*, April 30, 2009.
14. Serena Ng and Annelena Lobb, "U.S. Tactics Spark Worries over Lenders' Rights," *Wall Street Journal*, May 1, 2009.
15. Henny Sender and Tom Braithwaite, "Banks Seen to Act as Government Agents in Chrysler Bankruptcy," *Financial Times*, May 7, 2009.
16. President Barack Obama, speech at the White House, April 30, 2009.
17. "Chrysler Rescue," *Financial Times*, April 29, 2009.
18. John Plender, "Banks Head Back to Their Home Markets," *Financial Times*, April 29, 2009.

CHAPTER 10

1. "Remarks by the President on 21st Century Financial Regulatory Reform," East Room, White House, June 17, 2009.
2. Nassim Nicholas Taleb, *The Black Swan: The Impact of the Highly Improbable* (New York: Random House, 2007).

3. James Mackintosh, "Hedge Funds Call for Intervention on Lehman," *Financial Times*, October 15, 2008.
4. Michael Mackenzie, "DTCC Paves Way for All Roads to Lead to Its Warehouse," *Financial Times*, July 1, 2009.
5. Author interview, September 2008.
6. R. Glenn Hubbard, Hal Scott, and Luigi Zingales, "Banks Need Fewer Carrots and More Sticks," *Wall Street Journal*, May 6, 2009.
7. Martin Wolf, "The Cautious Approach to Fixing Banks Will Not Work," *Financial Times*, July 1, 2009.
8. Dawn Kopecki and Alan Bjerga, "Capital Requirements Are Key to Derivatives Laws, Geithner Says," Bloomberg News, July 10, 2009.
9. Anousha Sakoui, "End of the Credit Club," *Financial Times*, May 21, 2009.
10. "Fallout from Continental's Collapse," *New York Times*, August 5, 1984.
11. Thomas Catan and Jonathan House, "Spain's Bank Capital Cushions Offer a Model to Policymakers," *Wall Street Journal*, November 10, 2008.
12. James K. Glassman and William T. Nolan, "Bankers Need More Skin in the Game," *Wall Street Journal*, February 25, 2009.
13. Henry Kaufman, "Transparency and the Fed," *Wall Street Journal*, January 3, 2008.
14. Anuj Gangahar, "Bank Cutbacks Aid Hedge Funds," *Financial Times*, April 22, 2009.
15. Peter Thal Larsen and Jonathan Wheatley, "Market Gaps Make for Opportunities," *Financial Times*, April 22, 2009.
16. Nicole Gelinas, "New York's Next Fiscal Crisis," *City Journal*, Summer 2008.
17. Patrick Jenkins, "Banks Reinvent Securitisation to Cut Capital Costs," *Financial Times*, July 6, 2009.
18. "Goldman Sachs Reports Record Second-Quarter Earnings per Common Share of $4.93," press release, Goldman Sachs, July 14, 2009.

INDEX